Or.

An Epic On Perception, The Panoply Of Human Existence, The Molten Pit Of Experience, The Prism, A Millennial's Rage, Tails From The Great Recession, Eulogy Of The American Dream, An Atheist's Hymnal, Bed Time Stories, Kaleidoscope, A Cry Midst Darkness, Burning An Effigy, To Fuck With Feeling, Walking Empty Streets, Horizon's Edge, The Sorrow Of Joy, Losing Yourself In The Familiar, A Birthday Party, The Swirling Vortex Of Creation, A Seed Once Planted, Dreaming And Lying, A Story I Heard Once, Through The Woods Of Emotion, The Last Time, Mothers And Fathers, The Androgyne, A Progressive Painting, Gripping Water, Time's Cruel Reminder, A Revolution, How To Chase Sparks And Ash, Locking Eyes, Tearing The Veil, Monsters And Warmongers, Clutching The Frame, Crying With Friends, Sisters And Brothers, A New Delight, A Past With Presents, Making A Scene, The Dartboard In The Dark, The Aimless, Running With Smiles, How To Grieve, The One Who Walks Midst Giants, Painting With Pain, The Love Of Loss, Grass And Leaves, A Portrait Of The 21st Century

ISBN-10:1522760644
ISBN-13:978-1522760641

To Mara
Without which
The world would have been darker
And now that you are gone
Life seems that much the harder

CONTENTS

Acknowledgments   i

1   The Custodian   Pg. 9

2   Imagination   Pg. 11

3   Seasonal   Pg. 22

4   Sleeping   Pg. 27

5   Gardening   Pg. 35

6   A Child's Family   Pg. 43

7   Nature's Wealth   Pg. 57

8   Transitioning   Pg. 64

9   Science   Pg. 94

10   Objects   Pg. 100

11   Sickness   Pg. 109

12   Friendship   Pg. 116

13   Barnyard   Pg. 123

14   Love   Pg. 132

15   Contemplation   Pg. 169

16   Passion   Pg. 177

17   Philosophy   Pg. 194

18   Masculinity   Pg. 201

19   Emotions   Pg. 213

20   Daily Life   Pg. 227

21   Heart's Journey   Pg. 245

22   The Forgotten   Pg. 251

23	Trials Of Life	Pg. 270
24	Mainstreet	Pg. 277
25	Letters	Pg. 297
26	Wallstreet	Pg. 308
27	Moral Quandary	Pg. 320
28	Human Climate	Pg. 328
29	Relationships	Pg. 336
30	Politic	Pg. 347
31	Technology	Pg. 376
32	America	Pg. 388
33	Aging	Pg. 418
34	Revolution	Pg. 432
35	Time	Pg. 442
36	War	Pg. 461
37	Mourning	Pg. 486
38	Veterans	Pg. 499
39	The Poet's Library	Pg. 510
40	Death	Pg. 519
41	Author	Pg. 547
42	Mara	Pg. 567
43	The 'New' Atheism	Pg. 575
44	The Janitor	Pg. 633

To everyone who assisted me and was there for me in this process, thank you.

Christian Ramdhanie, Jason Curley, Mary Ann McLaughlin, James William Moeller, Jesse Slankas, Jimmie Scoggins, Rosa Singer

And, finally, without further a due, I thank warmly and with a smile, my ever mysterious cover artist.

Mamabliss

I do not know your name, your alias is all I have, but I am honored to have had you sculpt for me the dreamscape that you did, others told me it could not be done, but you, you accepted, and I, I cannot thank you enough. I'm honored that this picture accompanies my work is the outer shell by which others gaze upon it and are drawn to its inner contents, the exterior which houses the inner beauty. Thank you.

The Custodian

Oh, hi there, just checking in to see if you're comfortable. The stage is getting warmed up right now, you know, in preparation for the vignettes. The orchestra is also getting arranged, and I'm supposed to be down there right now, but I just thought I'd pop in quickly to see if you're comfortable. It's all a bit nerve wracking, but I guess it's always like this, having an audience see your work. I know some of you will hate it, and some of you will like it, while others will be indifferent, but I just would like you to know, I'm honored you're here. Hope you enjoy the show, and, do try to get immersed, lose yourself for just a little while, see you soon.

Kaden Moeller

<u>Imaginary</u>

Kaden Moeller

Inner Beauty

I was born into darkness
And grew up far and estranged
And as I left my blackness
I went to a meadow lane

I watched the children, like myself
They played together gaily
And anxiously, I broke my stealth
I went out to them; happily

But then they all did freeze
Struck solid as a stone
And no matter all my pleas
They would not move a bone

And so I ran off crying
I had just killed my friends
And hunters then came vying
To take my head for them

So now I sit in my deep dark cave
Surrounded by my statues
These frames and figures of the brave
Who came to run me through

Calling me "monster!" and "demon spawn!"
They laid siege to my lonely home
But when they saw me, they were gone
Forever turned to stone

I don't know what to say
I look at them and weep
Their bodies, cold and grey
Frozen, for me to keep

Desire I a touch, of a hand, so warm
As reaching out, do I, in vain
The tears fall as I morn
Clutching these stones in shame

And so, my collection grows
These suitors of my death
And no matter where I flee, I know
My sight, they will regret

I beg "Please stay away from me!"
But come still they to slay
This monster who they see
Will turn them cold and grey

And so I pray for death, it seems
But know it will not come
As bath I in the echoes of my screams
Wishing this loneliness was done

So time did wax and wane
Surrounded by my sorrow
Until another came
And I cried "Oh god no!"
+
I'm lost, and I have wandered
Off of my beaten path
My caravan has left me, now somber
I walk to a cool patch

Feeling the shade caress me
A cool soothing touch
As I sit upon a stone, a breeze
It howls round me, much

Hear I the water droplets
They echo round me too
But as I listen for it
Hear, do I, something new

This howl, it is sorrow
These drops, oh they are tears
I call out, and what follows
Is a great cry of fear

"Away, away! Do not come near
Just leave me alone!
Please listen to this voice you hear
And don't become a stone"

This voice, so sweet and scared
I said "Don't be afraid
I'm only here to rest" I said

"For I have lost my way"

I heard movement, away
And so I walked towards
All the while I heard her say
"Please listen to my words!"

"You do not want to see me!
Please, no closer come
I'm evil and I'm ugly!"
As away, I heard her run

But then, her feet, did stop
And I felt I was close
Her voice, it was distraught
It cracked and quivered most
+
I see him coming nearer
He was still far enough away
As screamed I "Don't come in here!
Stay living, don't turn grey!"

The tears, they started streaming
As he walked up to me
And I saw his eyes were staring
Wide were they, and milky

I broke down in my fear, again was I alone
Collapsing on the floor
Another turned to stone
'What else am I good for?'

But then I hear a voice
And then also some footsteps
I don't believe this noise
I'm too steeped in regret

"Oh miss, are you ok?
I heard you just fall down
I'll help you, but I must say
It's hard to get around"
+
I heard the weeping near my feet
As I knelt down before it
And slowly, reached out my hand, to meet
Where this weeping girl did sit

+
He reached out towards my face
As if for him to feel
He seemed, so out of place
As before me he kneeled
+
My hand did touch the skin
Twas clammy and so strange
Not like the soul within
The one crying in pain

I ran my hands now through her hair
Which seemed the hiss and move
I felt her tremble, as if scared
And this then did behoove

"Oh please don't think me callous
I hope that you don't mind
My hands, they are my eyes, yes
As you can see, I'm blind"
+
I heard his words, and felt his touch
My mind it then went blank
This kindness, it was too much
And nearly did I faint
+
"If you still want me to go
I will need some assistance
Please lead me to the road
And point me to town, perchance?"
+
He wanted now to leave
I then felt great distress
And though now did I grieve
I then made one request

"I'll take you to the street
But please just give me this
Oh you may be discreet
But please give me a kiss"
+
I was confused, but she was sweet
I smiled and then said
"Oh why should I be discreet?"

As I cupped my hand around her head
+
Then over come was I with love
And with great happiness
I leaned into him, and with a shove
He gave a passionate kiss

The serpents, they fell from my head
My skin was smooth and then
As he pulled away, he said
"What has just happened?"
+
My eyes, oh they could see!
I blinked out all the blur
And there standing before me
Was the one that I had heard

Her long and flowing hair
Against her soft smooth skin
Her tears, no longer scared
Showed the happiness within

She jumped up and embraced me
Saying things that were insane
That twas because of she
That so many lived in pain
+
But he, he called it nonsense
And then we left my cave
Oh he, he is my prince
He saved me, though not brave
+
He gave a bit of love to one
Who had desperately needed
To feel compassion from someone
Whose words he hadn't heeded

Oh so hard had she tried
To make sure no one would see her
But now she felt him, as he eyed
The beauty of her figure

And so they wandered down the road
In joy, and blushing laughter
As walking, hands did they hold
And they lived happily ever after

Romeo

At night, you let me sing to you
Our nightly lullaby for two
I suck the air into my throat
And let out a deep operatic croak

My rhythm is quite strong and steady
Memorize you, do I, with my melody
And lull you into tranquil thought
As atop the lily pad I squat

Then from my pad, on which I float
I jump, do I, into the moat
And hit the water with a plop
To signal, I've now chose to stop

Now I swim up to the castle in the water
Near the window of the king's young daughter
And then I rest upon a log
I am no prince, I'm just a frog

Letter From A Vampire

You don't want this
Really, you don't
Do you?
Could you possibly understand?

You'll live forever
You'll perpetually exist!
You'll never die!

Your family
Your friends
Everything you love
Twill pass away
Into the winds of oblivion
Like the leaves of autumn
But you
You will remain

You say you love me

That, it does not matter
So long as we're together

But no
You don't want this

For when everything is gone
All that will be left is me
Me and you

And you will not see the man you love
Rather, the monster who, looms over you
Day by day and night by night
Holds you trapped within his curse
Bound by endless life

And what is there?
What future do you see?
Is it the one I see?
No, it cannot be

The one, where all the stars have burned out
And life, long since extinguished
Is now the nothing we talk of
As we keep company in the dark
Us two, together forever

Is this what you want?
Really?
Do you know?
For the future to be only memory?
You love me?

No!
I will not turn you
For I love you too
And I love you too much to do such a thing
To put you through that
To take from you your special treasure
Though you know it not

Curse me
Leave me
Hate me
But please
Do not join me in this life eternal

Live and love right now
Don't put off to tomorrow
The tragedy of the past
Holds not the time of today

It's the most beautiful gift you have
You mortals are so blessed
For death gives you
A present

Story Of Us

Human history
Is like this
A man had a stick
And he was beating his fellows
Over and over
Again and again

Until
By chance
One of them
In midst if striking he
He spotted something

A glimmer of himself
He saw
In those eyes
A bit of him

And so
He took pity on him
Broke his stick in two
And offered it to him

Then
He joined the man in beating

Until he
And the other
Took pity on another
Each had spotted
They broke their sticks again

And two more joined
Four beaters
But eventually they broke again
Again
Again
And again

Until all they held in their hands
Were splinters
And further beatings hurt their hands
And found they that they had none left
To beat

And they
They looked at those splinters
And opened their hands wide
Letting the wind take them away

What did they need them for?
Why were they fighting?
What happened?

The Last

Another bright blue day
The sun's warmth upon my skin
It seems to want to say
"Do you feel warmth within?"

The breeze around me whispers
As it gives me a hug
"Why have you wandered here?
Are you looking for love?"

The leaves, they rustle round me
Paying sweet complements
"You'd make another happy
With you they'd be content"

The brooks, babble they loudly
The waves among the ripples
"Oh we know why you're lonely
But to say it would be cruel"

Oh these, my friends, are there

Every day for me
But them, I want to share
And let another see

So every day I look
And check round every bend
My heart wants to be took
And held close by a friend

Every hill, a hope
And every field a chance
Each but a desperate grope
For any outstretched hands

But as the sun sinks low
And bids a fond farewell
The moon beams with its glow
And lights the tears that fell

Another night alone
Upon this cold black earth
I feel my spirit groan
"Alone, what am I worth?"

But the moon, it seems to stay
To my soul, now withdrawing
"Despair not of yesterday
A new day will be dawning"

And so, alone now in the night
I wait there, tired and still
To see the new day's morning light
And look over new hills

I cannot give up now
What if one like me
Were looking all around
Because, they too, were lonely

<u>Seasonal</u>

Wind

A flowing stroke of cool time
Calming the stillness with motion
An uncontrolled drifting pattern

Treetop

The wind blows me across the path
Between the trees and through the grass
A sleepy loneliness I feel
A type of strangeness made surreal

As look, do I, upon the trees
And see my fellows in the breeze
Swaying, back and forth, together
Feeling as loved by the weather

I feel so tired and aged now
And envy I their youth somehow
I float a bit, and then I stop
I miss my home on that treetop

Watching

I'm going to watch the changing leaves
These reds and golden browns
To watch them rustle with the breeze
As they come raining down

Oh how I love this time of year
This time of nature's sighing
A time of beautiful deathly drear
This vibrant colored dying

These leaves do sway round in the trees
And with each chilling breath
Fall brown, red, and gold, but never green
As gripped are they by death

Piling high, upon the roots, do
These children of the trees
This sight, it makes their hearts blue
As, one by one, lose they their babies

Watching helplessly, these trees do stand
As dry to death their leaves
This dehydration by death's hand
The trees but watch and grieve

The leaves can but look upwards
Seeing their outstretched arms
Though on the wind, they float towards
Their parents, to their alarm

And so I watch the changing leaves
Oh yes, what pretty colors
A sight I sometimes can't believe
Without knowing this before

Season

The spirit whispers through the breeze
It weaves through orange and golden leaves
And guides them as drop they softly down
To final resting place; the ground

The trees, they shiver at its passing
This spirit, death, is everlasting
Its breath blows over water; still
Freezing it deep with its dark chill

This spirit of the leaves now fallen
This spirit we all know as autumn

The Snowflake

I am hovering way up high
Watching the sun come greet the sky
I am floating through the air
Feeling his rays caress my hair

I am drifting on a cloud
Feeling loved and feeling proud
I am soaring with the wind
His tingling presence on my skin

I am dropping down below
For his gaze but melts me so
I am falling to the earth

Filled with happiness and mirth

Temperate

The winds do blow the mist
It sprinkles through the trees
Who howl and they hiss
With their long and pointy leaves

The mist then beads upon the ends
Of these needles of the pines
Falling down upon their friends
The creepers and the vines

The water, then it pools
And runs off in little streams
Beneath the shade so cool
They keep the forest green

The moss, it grows upon the roots
Of these skyward reaching totems
It cloths them with soft fuzzy boots
And keeps their feet unfrozen

So, as the mist now turns to snow
The waters, now to ice
The trees stand silent in the cold
In gowns of flowing white

Solstice

I bathe in the moon's pail glow
Its rays reflect off ice and snow
The stars they flicker and they twinkle
The trees adorned with icicles

The night is black in space between
With ice covering both lake and stream
This night's air is so refreshing
What a moment, what a blessing

Standing Out

The landscape is a snowy white

Except, one bud beneath the moon
Who, with the morning's light
Opens this blood red bloom

A contrast of a vibrant life
Amidst cold desolation
Like blood carved open from the knife
Staining the white snow's skin

This flower, it but peeks
Round the vast expanse
This strange place that she keeps
A ballroom before the dance

This crimson crusader that she is
Standing out above the rest
Tis almost like a loving kiss
This snow is surly blessed

Oh this scarlet one so bold
Sings forth her song of life
And though this world round be cold
She stands; though snow be rife

And as the time, it trickles on
Others come up to join her
Until every drop of snow be gone
Spring bidding farewell to winter

Oh under now a clearer sky
The rose now sheds its petals
As slowly, this red dye
Turns brown, and then it shrivels

<u>Sleeping</u>

Morning

Dewdrops on leaves
A sleepy breeze
I am tired

Tired

Sleeping isn't fixing it
No matter how much I stare and sit
It seems I need to calm my mind
But takes it much convenient time

Sleep

How blissful to be asleep
How cheerless to be about
One night we'll pray for sleep, and say
"Let us never be without"

What Not To Do

Don't be as the lazy man
Who but turns in his bed
Who like the door upon its hinge
Moves much but goes nowhere
A funny parable this may be
An interesting picture
But why do you insult the door?
It is in no way lazy

The Black

Into the black
The dreamless sleep
Where wake I not
From that rest; deep

While others wake with stories
Me; I wake with none
I don't remember sleeping
No dreams or nightmares come

My eyes are closed
My mind is dark
Tis like I've gone away

Until I wake to morning lark
At dawning of the day

The only way I know I've slept
Is, time has passed away
My eyes open, I feel the rest
Acquired quietly

Though when I dream
Though if at all
It be so odd to me
I do not seem to like it, though
I don't mind what I see

Giving

When all I give to you are dreams
I wonder what they're worth
And ponder what it is you'll glean
As watch you dreams to birth

What to this world am I to bring
When all I give to you are dreams
For dreams leave not a single thing
They're only vapors that's been seen

Oh do you live where you have been?
These places far and wide
When all I give to you are dreams
In them, choose you reside?

Do you accept these gifts from me,
And end my sleeping fantasy?
Alas, oh this can never be
When all I give to you are dreams

Cold Front

Oh joyous weather when it's cold
For when one sleeps, tis like finding gold
The goose-bumps cross upon your flesh
A breath of cool air, so fresh

Curling up in darkened room

Kaden Moeller

Covered in warm silky womb
A smile, across your face it creeps
As comfortably you lay and sleep

How in the cold you love your bed
The place where dreams run through your head

Resting

Have you ever lain awake
Standing on the edge of a dream
And then made the mistake
Of a slow, but forward, lean

As peer, do you, inwardly
Into your murky mind
And slowly, do you see
The end of space and time

An expanse of worlds, in thoughts
Where endless art doth spring
A canvas without cloth or rot
And a paint the mind doth bring

Out from the heart; the pallet
With colorful shades of red
Which shape the things within it
This place inside your head

The denizens of this realm
Take different shapes with time
Within you, tis a kiln
This melting pot, the mind

To delve into the brain
Through dreams, it is the best
I find it near insane
To think that I'm unconscious

Dreaming

The world is falling
I could be drowning
Is this my world?

Dreamscape

The mind, it is your world
A landscape made from thee
Where nightmares and dreams unfurl
And get to wander free

A place to be yourself
Contained by no single thing
For here you lack no wealth
You are all you need to bring

Here you are not defined
By your sex or your gender
Here discrimination's blind
You are not race or color

In this place, every monster
Is not too big for you
For here, you know you're stronger
And braver then you knew

Oh here there is no sickness
You are not bound to pain
No loved one will you miss
Nor nakedness bring shame

Yes here no one controls your life
Or treats you like a dog
For in your mind you hold the knife
Whose blade can kill a god

In here, you are a warrior
The ruler of your nation
A place you decide what for
It's your imagination

The Dream Catcher

I curl up in my bed to sleep
But I don't want to dream
I cover myself with a sheet
Fearing the midnight scene

The dream master will come unbidden
Drowning me in images and thoughts
And wish these things had remained hidden
These nightmares that he's brought

And so a web now do I weave
To place above my bed
To catch those dreams that would deceive
By placing visions in my head

And though they may descend to me
Like spiders in the night
My web will catch them easily
And hold them there till light

They'll writhe and shriek and kick and scream
As their claws lurch towards my mind
Wishing to manifest, to just be seen
And hold their place in time

Pull and struggle though they may
My web's already won
And legend has it, so they say
Dreams die, when they meet the sun

Perception

Oh who be the dreamer,
Be he wide awake?
Need he be the sleeper,
For all those dreams to make?

Does he have a vision,
Be it foggy or clear?
Can they be a prison,
Does he clutch them near?

Are they only vapors,
Can they be made real?
What meaning be the whispers,
And what do they reveal?

Is anything they see,
In those dreams they walk through?
These parts of you or me,
Be they false or true?

Oh be there any answer
Of who the dreamer be
Or where those dreams occur
Where we will never see

Hole Heart

A man has his dreams
And then he dies
It's stranger than it seems
Thinking of our lives

These many aspirations
That float round in our heads
Ambitions and temptations
Some thought, while others said

Oh every man's a dreamer
And each dream when it's won
No longer special when it's here
He moves on to a new one

Each dream, when it's complete
No longer just a thought
And with every one we meet
To others do we walk

For once our dreams are real
We seem to let them go
They become so trivial
These workings of the soul

So dream the dreamer does
His eyes, always afar
The horizon looms above
He wants to touch the stars

He fills the world up
With every little dream
His mind, oh it won't shut
As it pours forth its stream

Things other dreamers, could not

Have ever dreamed about
Miracles, and what not
What joy the past would shout

Amazing things, these dreams
Such wonders when they're real
And yet, it always seems
These things, nobody feels

For this is not how dreamers work
They look to something else
This yearning in them, oh it hurts
This birthing that they've felt

But one bad thing for dreamers
They don't find their dreams fun
The problem with their dreams are
They can't get them all done

Awake

Sprinkling glass
Upon the grass
I'm in my bed

<u>Gardening</u>

Kaden Moeller

Pricked

Now every rose has thorns
That sticks and stings the fingers
Of the lover's hands, so warm
Their blood, upon them, lingers

For the thorns upon the roses
They look up at their flower
As sweetly, there, it poses
And loved for all its color

And so the thorns, they prick
In envy do they spike
As now they quaintly sit
Dyed red beneath the light

Staining themselves in crimson
Of the one who wants the flower
These thorns, oh they do spite them
They want to be desired

Oh to be beautiful
To be wearing the red
To be wanted, in whole
By the lover they have bled

But oh how we do envy
The beauty found in others
Oh how it makes us angry
How we're not like another

And how we start to hate
The thought that they're above us
As feel we the weight
Of that which makes us jealous

A heavy load it be
Our own standard of perfection
As desire what we see
But know we cannot get them

And push, do we, away
All forms of consolation
As inwardly we say
'I don't deserve affection'

And this, it hurts the hearts
Of those who reach out warmly
And as the bleeding starts
Their hands still hold to thee

The lover and the beloved
Shalt not be rent in twain
And with his scarlet love
He paints over the shame

To put the shade desired
Upon the great despair
A sacrifice required
Of love and all its care

The pain of holding to
Another vibrant life
To carry that load through
Despite the thorns that slice

"Yes every rose has thorns"
These words said by the lover
"But these thorns should not morn
For they're part of the flower"

Spindle

The widow walks with slender legs
Dark shadows midst the green
Sleekly adorn in black and red
Upon her ominous frame

She weaves atop the tulips
A haphazard patchwork quilt
And when her lover courts
It be in her bed's silk

He plays the fabric's threads
A tune his lover knows
With notes mingled with dread
Played through his lover's home

His heart's harp does sing out

Through the widow's silky strings
Strung from within her bowls
The deepest parts of she

And like the blackest angel
Descends the widow's frame
Voluptuous and full
Her body; far from plain

And so she listens to his tune
As plucks he, her sweet strings
There; midst the flowers blooms
His simple notes do ring

And with a subtle nod
The widow accepts his gift
And offers him herself
So he can give her him

And when their love is done
And when his life is lost
The widow lives alone
In her garden of loss

Ménage

To see the bee land softly
And make love to the flower
He kisses her so deeply
And drinks of her sweet nectar

But be this act of tenderness
No expression of the bee's
The bee has only done this
For another lover's needs

A flower, far away
Who never see's his bride
Whose colors are arrayed
But never meet her eyes

Upon a lonely slope
The only green for miles
He lives with little hope
Save his friend, the bee; his tales

He tells him of a flower
Down in a meadow, sweet
A beauty; wanting lover
Who waits there by a stream

And so he sings a love song
And give it to the bee
Who passes such sweet love on
To that flower by the stream

Though never will they meet
Apart will they remain
Their friend, the bee, he shall entreat
Their love twixt them each day

The Honeybee

To my sweetest flower
Collector of the dew
At whom I stare for hours
My pink and tender bloom

Who waits for my attention
And like the honey suckle
Gives me a taste to mention
But only oh so subtle

Your petals fan to me
Your intoxicating sent
The smell, like what I see
It causes doubt to end

If ever had I feared
I let it now be gone
Oh being with you here
And hearing nature's song

I wanted you to know
No other bud could be
The color that you show
In privacy with me

Kaden Moeller

Blooming

The color crimson is thy name
That special little slit
Whose shade be but the rose's bane
And where the dew drops sit

With the fragrance of the temptress
Tis sweet, but oh so faint
It opens but the littlest
And doth test my restraint

Oh how I wish you parted
But fear I'd cause you harm
For once this thing is started
To bud you'll not return

And yet, to see you flower
In radiance and joy
For that I'd wait an hour
And watch you play at coy

But peel back you, a little
To see you more and more
But dare I think you brittle
And wait for what's in store?

The firmness of the blossom
I want to open it
I tremble, anxious at them
Oh such a gift to get

Budding

I'm in love with a rosebud
Which sits upon the stock
Whose plump and turgid tender love
But waits to open up

It stands there, happily
At my fingers light caress
And I, expectantly
Long for its openness

And know, do I, its nectar
Twill tantalize the bees

To carry pollen hither
And spread its lovely seed

I see it swelling, straining
So soon to open up
And then it bursts, proclaiming
Its vibrant tender love

And I, pleased at its flowering
Do gaze upon its bloom
And cannot help my blushing
At what my care can do

I've brought the bud to flower
And smile at my work
Reveling, silently, right here
As its scent and air do flirt

Oh one who seems so thorny
Bears tenderness unknown
A blushing inner beauty
I marvel at each morn

Stopping To Smell The...

My flower's opened up for me
Its peddles, spread so sweetly
A sight so beautiful to see
A sent to breathe in deeply

A nectar, like none other
Tis stored within this blossom
The special syrup of the lover
A honey, sweetest of them

This bashful little flower
Tickled by my attention
As over her, I tower
Giving her much affection

How I love getting dirty with you
Hands covered in the mud
So close, it is, this work I do
I give my flesh and blood

Kaden Moeller

I love to be your gardener
Too care for you, my duty
Those times this task seems harder
Are rewarded by your beauty

But soon you will close up again
And tease me with your bud
But I'm persistent, little friend
I'll coax you out with love

A Child's Family

Kaden Moeller

Motherhood

What does life feel like?
Well, it's warm
And deep inside
Small at first
But promising
Like another spirit is hugging your own

But then
Then it's strange
Like it doesn't belong
Almost a sickness
Kind of
Odd

Hungry too
Often times with funny tastes

Oh, and a restless dreamer
What dreams?
I wonder

Painful
Vary painful and wonderful
A tiring excursion to traverse
Followed by, a happy sorrow

Warm
Life is warm
Holding it
Strange
Kind of
Odd
Hungry and
Funny
Restless and
Painful
Life feels like
You

Parents

There he is
Head on my belly
Eyes closed

Ear listening
Intently

And then, the baby kicks
And his eyes open, and that silly smile crosses his face
As he looks at me
Head still softly upon my tight stomach
His hand's hugging its warmth

"I love our baby"
He says; smile on his face
He's so happy
As his eyes close again and he nuzzles his head against me

"I love you"
I tell him, and he hums a happy approval
He's so cute now; he's such an excited father
"I'm gonna be a daddy" He says
And I pat him on the head; only to run my fingers through his hair
Yet, I feel strange for him

Of the three of us
He is the outsider
He gave me the half of himself, and I kept the half of me
And now; he but waits
Waits for the release of both of us; into this world
He waits, for the first time, to feel our child
He, separated at sex, now sits outside; excited
Waiting to meet what we've created together, but that which he is currently
bound from
He cannot know what it's like to embrace his child, but I do
He does not even yet quite know the baby's weight, but I do

He has no idea, really, of what this feels like
Yet
Look at him
He is a daddy
A father
The expectant one of our child
More so than even I

For I already know our child more now than he knows at all
But he cannot wait to meet them
And while this journey will be shared

Kaden Moeller

This one part, the start
He is only the spectator
And I, I am the mother
Who looks at the father
And smiles

I'm so happy to see him like this
And yes
"I love our baby, too."

Introduction

To this one now in my arms
Someone I'll never know
This tiny life with all its charms
Whom I'm to soon watch grow

Oh smallest splinter, carved
From the depths of mine own flesh
And like the northern star
Now lights a different path

One who shall crawl to me
And follow in my steps
Only to wander freely
Much to my heart's regret

And with each step towards
Tis like ten steps away
As walk, do we, forward
From day to day to day

I'll watch you keep my stride
And slowly overtake
To journey far and wide
And leave me in your wake

Though with me you reside
Know I you won't remain here
I hold you at my side
"Welcome home, my stranger"

A Joy

Babies, when they are born
They bear a little spark

Within their eyes it's stored
Its shine can warm your heart

This ember, though it's dim
With care, oh it will grow
And burn a brilliant fire within
The fire of the soul

Oh these flames will flicker bright
And light their parents world
And much to their delight
They'll watch them dance and twirl

No sight is quite like this
This dancing fiery spirit
A sight one should not miss
So beautiful and intricate

Oh of the warmth it brings
This blaze of life itself
The greatest of life's blessings
A parent's greatest wealth
Though some days it burns and stings
And drains one's life and health

This spirit of their child
Know not they where it will burn
What kindling, of which pile,
Will life's winds cause this flame to turn?

Oh parents cannot control the blaze
So let the fire rage
For this part of life, it's just a phase
The fire dims with age

_IN_

Alone I sit within the echoing silence of my home
Feeling like a tomb
Dead and motionless

The cloud cries out her endless tears, and the wind beats down the trees
"Let me in!" breathed the wind
No sound for my reply

The silence of my humble home was echoing in my mind

"Let me in." whispered the wind again *"I wish to fill your home."*
A long quiet followed my answer of silence in my home

"Silence!" roared the thunder
"Hiss." replied the wind
The door knob turns to open
And my mother steps right in

Cradle

If ever was a warmth
Could match your hand's caress
I know it not, but for
My mind's sweet dreams, no less

To think upon your tenderness
As cradle me to you
Rocking me to quiet rest
Humming a softly tune

My head upon your lap
Your hand runs through my hair
Your fingers lightly scratch
And weave throughout, so fair

Your other hand upon my cheek
And lightly I feel you
Your thumb, it moves so slowly
Conveying love I knew

And as I look upwardly
Into those eyes above
I feel my eyelids weighing
With sleep come from your love

And when I'm off to dreams
You take me to my bed
As off to sleep, it seems
Is where your mind needs tread

Oh such a love can never be
One unlike any other
The only love that comes to thee
That comes from our own mother

Oh

Oh father why go out tonight?
Tell her you'll see her later

But if you do and come home late
You will be in a world of hate

For mother has no more patience
And, your pretense and impotence, she sees

Home Coming

Painful embrace
A pretty face
These scars, they show so clear

Fearful shake
Skin so opaque
Your face, streaming with tears

Holding you
Be not true
We fear, we're not alone

Quiet whisper
My silent sister
Father is coming home

At Night

When the drink comes home at night
It be a fiery water
And floods the house, despite
The cries of any other

And those before its blaze
Curl like paper to its touch
As fall they to the waves
And dare they not get up

Oh as this waterfall
Beats down atop the frame

Of those who beg and call,
And call the fire's name

But as the inferno rolls
And roars atop their cries
It tires and it cools
To coals to sparks to sighs

And where did slide that drink
Left purple burns that sit
As that liquid twould sink
In where the fire licked

And as the fire drips and drops
And leaks back out the door
Though the burning doesn't stop
It will be back for more

Unconditional

To love is to forgive
Overlooking human faults
And accepting the life that's lived
By the one that your heart falls

To love this one before you
No matter what their wrongs
And no matter what they do
You'll prove your love is strong

To love those broad strong shoulders
That deep resounding voice
Those arms and hands, like boulders
And a grip that's like a vice

To love another more than yourself, it
Requires loss of pride
Love, it says submit
And then your love will thrive

To love no matter circumstance
Or any trial of life
To always give love another chance
It is the best thing, right?

To love the bruises on your skin

And the words that cut your soul
To see the one you love and cringe
But still wish just to hold

To love someone as this
Oh it but breaks the heart
But made you a promise with that kiss
"Till death twill you depart"

Confusion

Mama is gone, where is she?
She went out the other day
And now daddy is angry
He yells the words he'd say

*"That bitch thinks she can leave me!?
That she can do what she wants!
Saddle me up with her baby
A kid I don't even want!"*

Dad drinks a lot, I hide
I stay inside my room
And often, now, I decide
Not to use the bathroom

He yells and pounds upon my door
But I'm too scared to open
His voice sounds like a lion's roar
A beast with words, now spoken

But I am hungry, and
I haven't gone to school
So up now, do I, stand
Peering through the keyhole

Open up the door, do I
But then I find, before me
My father's angry eyes
I fear now what I see

But brushes back my hair, does he
With his fingerless glove
And says, he will not hurt me

Kaden Moeller

He just wants to show me love

Purple Paint

While painting with my fingers
My teacher took my hand
On my arms her eyes did linger
As awkwardly I stand

She didn't like the purple paint
And asked me where I got it from
My stomach dropped, and my heart sank
My panting wasn't done

She grabbed my paper, looking
At the swirling blacks and reds
The strokes upon them, echoing
Where the painter's hands had tread

A paint that won't wash off
No matter how I try
A paint whose sting is soft
And which I try to hide

These sloppy blotches, they be
So many places, still
I cover them, so they don't see
This painter's lack of skill

The broad strokes that do make them
So passionate and fierce
And when they start to fade, then
More are splashed upon this painting you see here

"Oh where did you get these?"
They asked me as they stare
Looking away, I say, nervously
"I fell down the stairs"

Childhood

My daddy loves me very much
He tells me every day
As to the bed sheets, do I, clutch
Loving me, his special way

This pain is for my good
He said I misbehaved
Through it's not understood
I work for daddy's praise

He puts his smokes out on my chest
When I don't make him happy
I cut my legs, oh I'm depressed
I want him just to love me

But his love, it hurts me when he shows it
As in the bed I lye
Towering over me, this giant
He makes me want to cry

I'm scared of daddy's love
But I don't want it to leave
And though I push and shove
I want someone to hold me

And then a man in blue did come
He took daddy away
And held me in his arms, so strong
His words were *"It's ok"*

What happened with my daddy
They say it's really bad
But now I feel lonely
And angry when I'm sad

The Weighting Game

There once was a girl who'd sit
And eat ham out of a bucket
And when she was done
She thought it was fun
To return the ham via vomit

A Place To Rest

Home is where the heart is
But what if you're alone?
And feel loneliness
For all you do is roam

Wandering betwixt emotions
Of fear and deepest friendship
Feeling your spirit shun
Your heart, as close you get

As oh, your soul, it aches
Sinking deeply to despair
It fears all love a fake
No matter what is shared

Each smile, but a mask
Each touch, a latent strike
Oh to but feel, at last
Contentment over fright

With every friendly gesture
And every kindly glance
These feelings will not fester
And soon the heart twill dance

For home is not a place
The people make it so
And through their warm embrace
The heart twill mend and grow

Broken

Don't touch, it makes me angry
Or hug me, I'll get scared
Oh the pain that comes with memory
The wretched sad despair

Oh warmth, it does not sooth me
Love, in my mind, it hurts
Behind your kindness, what I see
Could be a monster's smirk

Oh every time I see you
You say the sweetest things
But I know not what to do
The strangeness your love brings

You want to make me happy?
You say things, and I laugh
But can I trust you, maybe

You're but laying a trap

Your hands, they touch me softly
A feeling so intense
And wince, do I, instinctively
My muscles, do I tense

My mind, it is confused
I know not what to do
My intimacy is bruised
I don't know how to love you

And so I sit, and look at you
And smile happily
Though today, I don't know what to do
Someday I will, maybe

Abused

Tonight we were together, for the first time
I am nervous, but this fear is for you
I stand before you naked, bearing what is mine
But you, standing there clad, you don't know what to do

I come up to you, you're tense
As my hands move towards your body
Laying them upon your garments
You look away, now trembling

I slide your clothes off of you slow
Unwrapping my fearful gift
Oh what's beneath, I could not know
As your clothes off, do I, lift

Oh what I find beneath
My heart, it bursts with love
My compassion is released
Your shame, away I shove

The scars, from burns upon your chest
And cuts upon your legs
Of sorrow and pain do they confess
Of a past of flame and blade

But tis not the scars without, that are deepest of all
Rather the ones within, beaconing forth your tears
But my love for you does not dissolve
Beneath this rain of fear

"I'm sorry I'm not beautiful
That my body isn't perfect"
But I, I hold you through it all
My tears I don't hold back

Last night we were together, for the first time
I watch you sleep, your body near
Those scars, they never crossed my mind
Those cuts you keep, they may be deep, but our love, it is deeper

<u>Nature's Wealth</u>

Celestials

The moon and sun, they meet at night
With moon reflecting bright sun's light
Reaching out, across the void
They try to touch, their lives destroyed

The sun can see his lover clear
His pale blue one, oh so dear
He cannot comfort her distress
Too far is she from his caress

Reflecting his light back at he
She does so, so that he can see
That she desires him as much
As flesh desires kindly touch

The space between them, oh so vast
Their hands reach out, and try to clasp
The tragic tale of up above
Of sun and moon, their endless love

Star Gazer

Oh to my pretty blue one
Who hovers up above
Whose face; shines down upon
A sweet cool beam of love

And how I love your smile
That crescent up in heaven
Who lingers for awhile
But soon twill come again

To let my eyes but linger
Upon that special place
Of you, my nightly shimmerer
Though you may hide your face

And while others may twinkle
To take my eyes away
They tempt, but do not steal
The love I have for thee

Oh please fret not, my beauty
Think not of me as petty

Dream not that what I see
Be all I want of thee

So happy you are near
Far closer than a star
Though you may think it queer
I love you from afar

Natural Order

Come with me into the undergrowth
Beneath the canopy
Allow me show you what's below
Where flying eyes won't see

A world made, here, up of the dead
Where rot will feed the trees
Where plants and animals have bled
Beneath their arches; green

Where life, as always was
Will feed upon the dead
Changing how we think of
The way these plants are fed

Nice

Grey bleak drizzling clouds, wet muddy sand
And rainy sets of trees
Damp ground, mud and dirt
Anything that doesn't hurt
Disgusted, they are disheartened but why?
For me its beauty

Ecstasy

The dew drops drip out in the plain
Sweet as nectar, soft as rain
With ripple-less clear mountain lake
A mirror to which the sky relates

And what of the tall majestic trees
Their leaves caressed by loving breeze
Oh what of the thrusting mountain patch

With lava surge and swirling ash
Withheld deep in its molten bowels
Covered over in snow, and winds that howl

And what of the radiant tempest
It bursts forth in thunder claps of bliss
For the best part of the storm is known
In Mother Nature's after-moan

Conductor

The forest is alive at night
Beneath the stars small shining lights
The wolves, they howl in the dark
Their singing spurs the rest to start

The wind plays the needles on the trees
Like strings it strums them with the breeze
The bear supports in baritone
With deepest breath, and lowest moan

The raccoon chatters as the snare
He sets the pace, and combs his hair
The beaver slaps his tail as base
Disturbing lake's once somber face

The crickets play their fiddles low
As the cicadas stroke their Cellos
The tree frogs start their trumpets fast
While bullfrogs bring up the heavy brass

The bats lighten the mood up with their flutes
With high pitch cheeps and chirps and toots
The screech owl sings the highest note
A compilation that he wrote

The mountain lion, who was growling low
His roar now signals the crescendo
The brooks, they babble, and they nod
The waterfalls rise and applaud

Oh man has nature's sympathy
He cannot beat her symphony

Singing

The crow
His song is beautiful
But others find it terrible

Cloud's Eye View

The wind, it takes me round
There by the by and by
With silence all around
I watch the world and sigh

Tis such a pretty view
This quilt of brown and green
With giant swirls of blue
With some white in between

And what spy I beneath?
So many little things
To which I do bequeath
The only gift I bring

I pity those below
Each one so faraway
And yet each one I know
I watch them every day

A tear for those who suffer
And one for those in pain
And I'll add but another
For those who cry in vain

For those who work great evil
And the ones who cry compassion
Wherever my rain falls
It's meant for both of them

Quilting

All life is like a prism
With many different shades
And none are held imprisoned
Rather, spread out they their rays

And blanket they the world
In a patchwork so divine
It makes the mind to swirl
And the heart to beat sublime

Each color be a flavor
A taste of vibrant life
While some shades do be bitter
Some hues taste more than right

No matter where you are
Each color be a refraction
Of the one thing we desire
This life and all its actions

And so the pallet changes
But also stays the same
And if it rearranges
It has no other name

The Rain Dance

I feel the rumblings of the earth
Our home it is, our womb and tomb
And smiling down on us in mirth
Are father sun and mother moon

Both up in the sky they lay
Singing the morning into day

(*Chorus*)
Dewdrops, raindrops, teardrops, falling
Can you hear the voices calling?
They cascade around like water
Whispers to their sons and daughters
Wishing, hoping, praying, begging
That we hear the words they're saying
The veil pierced, they're pouring through
These words, like water, are for you

Feeling deep the pain of nature
As she births forth new life
Her children, though they seem to hate her
Live with her in strife

The clouds above, do they now darken
The lightning and the thunder hearken

(*Chorus*)
The land, it blackens, and it dies
Raining oil, snowing soot
The life remaining, it doth cry
As in horror they look

Seeing a world that cannot cope
A home devoid of peace and hope

(*Chorus*)
Will we heed the words around us,
Or spread the ever growing virus?
Breaking this beauty that we carry
Shattering this sanctuary
Leaving time within a void
Alone, with all of life destroyed
(*Chorus*)

<u>Transitioning</u>

The Color That You See

The rose is red, or so they say
It seems to be the case
That the color, is as plain as day
A sign upon its face

But the rose, it isn't red, you see
This color is but a reflection
All the other colors does it want to be
Except its red complexion

Absorbing all the other shades
The flower is itself
A lie among the grassy blades
Amidst all natures wealth

It exemplifies the thing it's not
To make the others happy
Beneath the sun, so blazing hot
It plays the lover's lackey

This rose, though be it red without
It is not red within
And though its redness gives it clout
Its happiness is dim

But it presses on, amidst the pure white lilies
And the voluptuous violets
Its envy may seem rather silly
Though destiny, it can't pilot

And so the rose weeps deeply
Petals falling from its head
And watches, rather sweetly
As they lay there dry and dead

And for a moment, it holds out hope
To bloom a different hue
And sits their budding, 'pon the slop
Praying that it's true

And as they open up as white
The plant, it holds its breath

But time, dyes them crimson beneath the light
And hope dies its little death

Oh what is worse for the rose than this?
Tis the coming of the pruner
Its individuality, greater, will it miss
And depression comes all the sooner

Oh the deep sorrow that indeed does come
With the shaping of the shears
The forced budding and blooming that is done
To the flower, spite its fears

For like the gardener
We do this, to the people that we love
We work that much the harder
To shape them with our glove

And like the flowers of the field
Our loved ones are quite scared
Of letting their true selves be revealed
This soul they haven't shared

And so they keep inside
The one they really are
And because of their love, they try to hide
To keep this love unmarred

And so reflect they
What they're not
And come what may
They'll hide their thoughts

And this builds upon a great depression
To live a lie amidst their friends
This builds upon a sad expression
And seems to never end

Oh, look at the colors all about
The options on the pallet
The shades, to which, no one's devout
Much like the rose's scarlet

We're like the rose, that I can see
For it's just like I said
As people up and look at me

"I'm not the color red!"

Closet

Oh, I'm someone I don't want you to see
Seems the closet's life is the life for me

So snug is it in that little room
It's safe in there, just like the womb
There are no threats when you're enclosed
To be the one that others chose

To be happy in that little place
That special spot, where there's no face
To which you show your true beauty
The part of you that is the *"Me!"*

So nice is it to hide away
And never have to speak or say
"I'm not the person that you think"
For this knowledge is a bitter drink
So rather keep away that brew
And shut away that which is true

Yes, this must be a healthy thing
To bottle up yourself, and bring
The person that all others want
Who follows you about, to haunt

It's almost like you've no control
And, possessed by your own hyperbole
You try to believe the falsity
But in the mirror, you don't see

That hollow-one you're propping up
The one you say is you, but
The façade is transparent unto you
As you weep before the mirror nude

Being naked before yourself is tough
But coming out is rather rough
A painful pounding of the soul
That beats you back into the hole
A venomous speaking in your ear

Kaden Moeller

This poison drips from you, in tears

This type of hate, that can come quick
Seems to eclipse where love did sit
And with the change of their perception
They shun you now for your deception
And blame you now for all your evil
Of not telling them, your special people

Oh of this trap we set for others
Both our sisters and our brothers
We tell them, love is unconditional
And that this love is not provisional

Oh what a lie this truly be
Why would you be in the closet? Gee
Why won't you say this in your youth?
You'd live the lie than speak the truth

Self-conscious

My reflection, is not the one I want
It's not the me within
This body, my soul haunts
It acts as but my prison

My spirit, its true form
Looks nothing like this husk
So different, and forlorn
For freedom dose it lust

To be the one I am
Rather than who you see
To never, ever again
Reflect one who isn't me

These dreams, they be just that
Fantasy and nothing more
A wish, just to distract
From trials life has born

Oh yes, I see myself
That reflection, dark and dim
You cannot even tell
The person that's within

Beneath The Skin

Before the mirror
I stand
Naked, and looking a
Myself

'Myself'
This body
This soft and slender frame
This person standing here
I hate her

Her body isn't strong
Nor is it broad
It cannot get the girls I want
Only the boys ask me out

I feel my inner skull
The boiling rage within
My fingernails dig deep
Deeper and deeper still
Looking at this bitch
Why won't she go away?

Why won't this skin melt off of me
Molt away
Be shed from me
From soft to hard
From woman to man
I fucking hate her
I hate this bitch too much

I punch the glass
Once
Twice
Three and four times more
And watch that reflection
Crack
Split
And break upon and into the sink

Those glass shards
Speckled red

Shimmering my angry tearful expression
My seizing raging frame
It hasn't changed
It never changes
And I hate that
And I hate myself

I am not this person
Who I am
Deep inside
Needs to come out
Outside
Now!

My quivering hand
Reached out
And firmly grasped
One large jagged shard
And with shivering determination
Start cutting

Cutting
Slicing
Trying to shed
To pull off this
Soft
Smooth
Skin
This fucking shell!

And as I watch my periphery
Darken, and fade to black
I wake up in a bed
I.V
Dripping…
Dripping…
Dripping…

Stitches
Everywhere
My arms and legs restrained
My parent standing over me

I cannot tell them why

Gender

At the psychologist's office
Today
We had a talk
Words were exchanged
And things
Well...
Got a little heated
They called it
"A disorder"
I don't know why that did it
Why I got so mad
But...
I said some things
Things like

"There's nothing wrong with him!
'She' isn't butch or dyke!
He's my son!
And no, it's not a phase!
He's been like this his whole life!"

The doctor calmed me down
He had meant no offence
"It's just the name we call it"

And so...
My son, he sat beside me
Patting me on the leg
And looking at the doctor
He smiled, and then said

"I've wondered, everyday
Why I felt so different
But now
It has a name
Though, it does sound pretty bad"

"Don't despair"
The doctor said
"It happens round the world
Your brain and body don't agree
It's just the way things are

Just take your pills
Once every day
And be the world's best son"

And as we left the office
I looked at my young man
'So he was born a girl,
His identity is in order'

Pretty In Pink

The world feels colder
My bed for two, now one
The pictures on my shelf, a blur
As down my tears do run

My hands, they move upon the things
That once had been my love's
Seeing them, oh yes it brings
Emotions to flashflood

But something now is missing
Her little childhood dress
A pretty pink and faded thing
A portal to the past

As wander I, around the house
While searching I do hear
Whispers, not far out
But very, very near

"Do you like my dress? ...
Why thank you very much...
It was my mom's, I guess...
I know there are holes and cuts..."

Peer now, do I, into the room
Through the crack of the door
My only child from her womb
Dancing round upon the floor

Standing before the mirror
Talking and pretending
While looking, it seems clearer
Whose features were resembling

Those pail wide blue eyes
Like a snowy winter day
And all they do is reminds
Me of the words she'd say

"Our child's very special
A precious little gift"
As in her arms, there nestled
Our baby, in a cradle oh so missed

"So do you think I'm pretty? ...
No I didn't ask my mom...
She died the other day...
I'm really sad she's gone..."

Oh watching this display
I don't know what to do
I don't know what to say
While seeing that pale blue

I open the door slightly
And give a friendly smile
"I think you're very pretty
We'll patch the holes tomorrow"

The smile is returned to me
And then I go back to packing
While thinking of my wife's words, how she
In love, was never lacking

"Our baby's very special
A precious little gift
There's no one like this child
He isn't like the rest"

A Statistic

Daddy said *"No dress up!"*
To leave mommy's clothes alone
He said, I shouldn't touch
Those clothes inside their room

He said, they look bad on me
I know they're rather big

Kaden Moeller

They hang off me all funny
But pretend is my favorite thing

And mamma was really mad
When she found me with her makeup
Her anger made me sad
And now their door is shut

They took all the clothes away
I borrowed from my big sister
The things that they would say
Their love, it comes as anger

I guess that they don't want me?
They say that I'm *"all wrong"*
I cannot be cute or pretty
Because I am their son

But I don't want to be
The person they desire
The person that they see
They do not want a daughter

But I don't want to shave
Or have really short hair
But this I dare not say
I'm feeling very scared

And as my voice, it deepens
My shoulders slowly broaden
My legs, I start to shave them
But still, I feel odd

And so I steal the pills
Of others birth control
Thinking, perhaps it will
Make me to feel whole

But fear I all the more
That I shall soon be caught
And that my family's scorn
Twill be too much a shock

But as these thoughts, they build
A heavy pile of guilt
And with this fear instilled

My life begins to wilt

I don't want to do the thing
That I've already done
To be so disappointing
Away I wish to run

And so one night I thought
'Tis time my mind be stilled'
It's why I went and got
My father's sleeping pills

Daughter Of Acceptance

I found him in bed
He was wearing a nightgown, and a wig
Long black haired, and a note on the bedside
He was foaming at the mouth
Pill bottle on the floor
And I could see he'd thrown up

His body spasmed as I ran to the phone
The ambulance came quickly, and they took him
I sat beside his bed, reading the note

"Dear dad, I'm sorry, I cannot be
The man you expected
It just doesn't feel right, it's all wrong
Everything feels wrong
I know you don't feel right, it's all wrong
Everything feels wrong
I know you don't understand, but I love you
I hope you don't hate me, but I cannot do this anymore
I know it's selfish
But, goodbye"

The doctor came in, he talked to me
Asked what happened, I said I wasn't sure
The police questioned as well, thinking abuse
And I, I just stood there, conflicted

I loved my son, but he couldn't be this way
Others wouldn't understand, I feared for him
But my fear, it had driven him to this

I was so selfish, my child, forgive me
And when his eyes opened, I said to him, my child
"I loved you as my son, I'll love you as my daughter"

Mirror Mirror

Here in his room, away from eyes
A teen boy plays a princess
And dresses up, with clothes he got
From discounted thrift store bins

He pads his clothing carefully
To give himself a figure
And molds himself into a dream
Dreamt daily every year

And when he's sure he's ready
Clothing and makeup right
He looks into the mirror
And poses, oh so slight

And then the clothes come off
So he can masturbate
Using an old hair bush
He slowly penetrates

He does it slow, and carefully
Grouping with his other hand
His eyes, he closes softly
As dreams the brush a man

Oh how his flat chest heaves
And how his legs do shake
Pushing the handle deep
Hoping to satiate

Pushing and prodding hard now
The boy; now in a trance
He finds himself so close
This dream living is fast

His breaths; excitement stuttered
His hips swaying for love
Dreaming of another
Whom he could be his glove

Those hips who wish to deeply kiss
The flesh to which they lust
Who wish to fill that emptiness
In which they vainly thrust

And as his voice; it flitters
In notes of ecstasy
His body starts to quiver
As moans he desperately

And then the sweet release
As strong as he can bare
The boy then crumples up
And feels a slight despair

His friends are meeting people
But he has none to hold
How would they feel towards *'her'*
If he would let them know

A party's going on
Not too far down the street
His friends all would be there
Yet *'her'* they would not meet

But now he couldn't do this
No longer would he stay
And so he got all dressed
To go, go out and *'play'*

"To hell with how they feel!"
'She' said as out *'she'* went
"I know I'm beautiful"
These words were words 'she' meant

And as she neared the music
And saw the people there
She felt herself get nervous
Even a little scared

But she was royalty
A beautiful young lass
And all heads turned to see
When in she walked, a princess

Kaden Moeller

Trapped, With A Drunk

So, ya
I'm at this party
And man
I tell ya
I was hammered, man
I mean drunk
Like you don't even know

And this girl there
She'd been giving me eyes
Like, ya know, eyes
And I
Man
I was so wasted
So like, ya know
I had to go up to her

And she was all like
"Great party"
And I was all like
"I guess"
And we like, sat down on the couch
She was all buzzed
And I, well
I wasn't gonna say no

So like, she straddled me
Ya know
Got all up on my lap
Yea
And her hair was all over her face and mine
And she was all, kissing and licking

Man, my hands
They were wandering
Her jeans were so tight
I mean, man, I could feel her ass right through them
So smooth and tight
Her skin was so warm

But...
Fuck him!
Fuck that rat bastard in drag

I could feel his…
Ya know
And I threw that fucker off

"The fuck!?" I yelled
And that bitch ass freak was all like
"Please wait"
Fuck that!
I ain't gay man
And I sure as hell ain't gonna let that shit slide
Fuck no!

I beat his fagot ass
I knocked that fucker's teeth in
Man, it must have taken, like
Three people to pull me off
They were all like
"The hell is wrong with you?"
Acting all concerned about 'her'

But fuck them
And fuck that fucking tranny!

A Thunderstorm

Have you ever lived through a storm
That when at once begun
It drenched you in its scorn
And caused your heart to run

Those clouds that gathered round
Be thick and dark with hate
And usher forth a sound
That begs your mind escape

A thundering so loud
Followed by crimson mist
As angrily they pound
In a swirling flurry of fist

To stagger aimlessly
Betwixt each thunderclap
And spun round helplessly
As the wind, it hits your back

And when the storm has ended
To be so soaking wet
To cry, for you're not dead
Though you barely lived through it

Missing Person

I was working one night
The graveyard shift
Cleaning the park's
Public restrooms

And
As I moved along
I heard
By the picnic tables
Crying
It was faint
But
The park was closed
And
I was concerned
For the person
But mainly for myself
As the crazies come out at night

But my curiosity
And compassion
They overpowered me
And
I
Wandered towards the sobs

I could see
A person
Back against the bench
Huddled
Legs hugged to their chest
And
In their hand…
Something…

As I approached
They seem to take notice
And

Stood up quickly
Hiding the thing in their hands behind them

"The park is closed"
I said
"I know"
Said he

He seemed strangely dressed
At least
For a guy
Slim tight jeans
And a V-cut shirt
I had mistook him from afar

"What you got there?"
I motioned
He hesitated
"Nothing"
He stammered
"Well"
I said
*"It's very late
And the park is closed to visitors"*

I then
Noticed the bruises
They were faint
But
I could see them
Beneath the V-neck
His left arm
And under his right ear

*"The freaks tend to come out at night
Drunks
Or worse"* I said

He looked at me
He seemed angry
"Do you need the police?"
I asked
"I'm not a freak!"
He screamed

Throwing the thing at me
And ran off

A wig...
A long blond wig?

The kid went missing
Apparently
I don't know where
I still have her hair

Forbidden

My love, my father said no
He refuses to let me see you
To let our love but grow
Rather, my spirit I must renew

I miss your touch upon my skin
Your beautiful eyes so blue
Tugging my heart so deep within
As if to pull it through

You, my Romeo, and I, your Juliet
No matter the poison I shall chew
Never shall I regret
Your love, which I cling to

Oh how I love your strong embrace
In our passion oh so true
A blush across my smiling face
As kiss you that I do

My love, you are Adonis
Oh such a handsome view
I want to be your goddess
And worship love with you

But father says I can't be with thee
Or have this love that grew
For this, it seems, should never be
We can't be one, us two

Rather deny you and I our joy
Oh, this is nothing new
My love, why, was I born a boy?

Was it to keep me from you?

A Father's Daughter

A little girl died today
She was found, bloody and mangled
The police did not know what to say
As they called her father's household

He came down to the station
To identify the body
This bloody violent presentation
Caused now his chest to heave

Collapsing upon the floor
While screaming out her name
The doctor left, and closed the door
As the police held him, restrained

After they had calmed him down
They asked him *"Where'd she go?"*
These questions, and others, he answered now
As his soul within grew cold

After answering all their questions
The doctor came back in the room
Telling him what they knew, these statements
They caused him so much gloom

"The boy that she was with, who
Was with others, apparently
They beat her, and they raped her too
And then, as you can see
They strung her up upon a truck, and drove
Her, over the glass upon the street"

The father, all alone
His world now in ruins
Seeing her lifeless bones
He felt his spirit strewn

He clenched his fists, and closed his eyes
And through his gritted teeth
He moaned forth a father's cry

Begging for relief

"I told you not to do it
To not go out with him
Your love, he didn't deserve to get
For he knew not the you within"

And so the funeral came and went
One day passed into another
The trial, confirmed their intent
To *"Kill that little liar!"*

Sitting in the court room, what he heard he could not believe
"We gave her what she wanted
She wanted to be with men, so we
Real men we undaunted"

"She got what she deserved
She got to live her lie
And then, when we were done with her
We left her there to die"

The father, now at home
Slowly sorting through her things
He'd never felt so alone
Oh, the sorrow that death brings

As through her things he shifted
He found the card of her birth
And trembling, now he lifted
The card up, though it hurt

A painful reminder of a
Precious baby's little hand
His daughter's, his Samantha
Though born a boy, named Sam

Rejection

He's gone, he left me
He walked away
Cursing angrily
The things he'd say

But, I tried

I followed him
Begging to be by his side
To be his kin

But, he left
He's gone
Our gift
Undone

So alone am I
In this sorrow I have made
These tears I cry
They come not from the blade

As slide I thin cold metal
Across my lonely skin
My sorrow does not settle
Nor does it take my sin

The evil of my confession
It hurt you far too deeply
This pain I feel, I hope it lessons
Your anger that cuts through me

Each drop that I do bleed
I pour it out for you
And pray I it makes thee
Happy, this thing I do

Oh I will kill the boy without
For this girl that's within
Letting the blade upon me shout
"Your heart, I want to win!"

This blood libation that I give
I give it all to you
If you can't love me when I live
My death twill prove love's true

And then, I'll shed this body
My beauty won't be fragile
And maybe then you'll love me
For then I'll be an angel

Kaden Moeller

Roommate

This is the story

I came back to drop the groceries off
Because we were almost out
And
I heard her run and shut her door
To her room
And she
She was crying

The hall was dimly lit, and
I knocked on her door
And asked
"What's wrong?"
But she yelled at me to
"Go away!"

And so
I went into the kitchen to
Drop the groceries off
But
There was blood on the counter
And the dinner knife was missing
And there was blood on the floor
Leading to
The dimly lit hall
And she was crying

I went into the hall
Turned on the light
And
There was blood on her door handle
And she was crying

I ran to the door
Pounding
I said
"Open up!"
But she
She didn't answer
"Open up, please!" I shouted
As I heard her weeping behind the door

I went to the phone

And I called the police
I said
"I need an ambulance, right now!"
And then
I went back to her door
She was crying

"Please, open the door!"
I yelled
And then I heard a thud
And she
She wasn't crying anymore

My heart
Overcome with dread
It moved me to take a hammer
And with all my might
I broke the door
Tore off its hinges
And ran to her

She
She had cut
And cut down deep
But she'd fainted from the blood
Her arms were mangled
Shredded
I used my shirt to wrap them

I rode with her in the ambulance
As they checked her body
And they
Seeing the bruises on her skin
Those beneath her shirt
Upon her ribs and stomach
As well as upon her hips
Such a sight, infected me
Making my blood to boil

And then they went to put
The catheter into her
But much to their surprise
What they found was different
Then the girl before their eyes

And then they looked to me
And asked me, if I knew
And I said to them
"No, she's just my roommate."
And then they asked, if I
Knew who might have done this

I didn't know her boyfriend
But at that very moment
Those bruises on her skin
My rage was overflowing
And as the police went looking
I stayed there by her side

Seeing her lying there
I could not stop my tears
I felt so angry for her
Why had he hurt her so?

Those blows he'd laid upon her
Went right into her soul
And as if in desperation
She tried to cut them from her
To take away that sorrow
And live her life without
The part he did not love

Her eyes
They then did open
Upon my face before her
Her eyes
They did well up
Tears streaming down
And my heart
It flew to her
I held her in my arms
While she buried her head in my shoulder

And then I stayed there with her
Throughout the day
And until the night was over

After that I took her home
And while we were in the car
She smiled at me

And then I made myself, a promise
I will not make her cry

A Confession

Across the table do you sit
Staring into my eyes
Holding my hand, as I fidget
Lips hesitating with every try

You lean in close, and brush away
My dark and flowing hair
My eyes are red, and you do say
"What's wrong, why are you scared?"

I chock upon these words I speak
Saying, *"I love you very much"*
These words, they rendered my soul weak
As to your hand I clutch

And then concern crosses your face
My hands, begin to tremble
Feeling alone in this strange place
Sitting across from you

You ask me now, with kindly smile
"Why do you tremble so?"
Oh for me, he knows not this trial
What I must let him know

"Do you love me too?" I ask
You look at me, now shocked
He knows not of my mask
And this life to which I'm locked

Looking at me, you say, in kindness
"What are you hiding my sweet?
What makes you doubt so, in distress?
Think my love you won't keep?"

"Please tell me you won't leave me!"
I blurt out in a cry
You stand, disturbed by what you see

To comfort me, you try

I push you away, while sobbing
"I've lied to you, my love
This one, to whom, your heart is throbbing
Is not who you're thinking of"

But you do grasp my frame
Embracing me, though I shove
While calling out my name
Followed by the words *"My love"*

My mask, it shatters, and
It breaks upon your heart
I say *"I am a man!"*
As the shards, they do depart

You lay there, crying with me
Holding me in your arms, so close
You say *"That's not what I see*
I see the one I chose."

"The one whose eyes, they called me
Whose voice is soft and sweet
The one who's here in bravery
Whose soul I had to meet"

I shook my head, now speaking
"You cannot have just heard
This thing I said, so shocking
My love, I am transgendered!"

But nothing more said you
You held me, and we kissed
No longer was my spirit blue
Your love will not be missed

Cute

I awoke one night to tears
My lover, soft and sweet
She thought I couldn't hear
Her sobs beneath the sheet

"My love, oh what's the matter?"
Said I, under the covers

And wrapped my arms around her
As her body quaked and shuttered

"Oh I am just so sad
I feel so incomplete"
These words, they made me mad
So mad I couldn't speak

"No matter how much I love you
Or hold you close to me
The thing I want, I cannot do
I cannot have your baby"

And then she drew close to me
Her tears, they hit my chest
For her, I felt so angry
She thought she'd failed this test

"My love, you may've been born
The wrong sex to bear children
But please, my sweet, don't morn
If you want, we can adopt them"

Her eyes, they then flash up to me
As if to heaven above
Said I *"You needn't bear my baby*
To know that you are loved"

Utopia

Oh what a sight to see
Young Tammy and John
Who look round nervously
At others at the prom

There's Sally and Cindel
Dancing together slowly
The sweetest two young girls
That you would ever see

And Tom and Todd are kissing
Behind the school bleachers
Their love they are confessing
As they hold each other near

And Steve, the trans-boy king
He hoists up high his queen
Kelly, who's soon to sing
Their school song's new theme

And Reginald, the cross-dresser
He smiles in his drag
His date Erick Guesser
Smiles at the dress he had

The air's sound then is cut
By Elsie's trans-girl screams
As her boyfriend Josh picks her up
They laugh and make a scene

The hall is filled with lovers
Of every shape, size and sex
Each with their own gender
It's separate then the rest

Each one, a happy couple
With all that comes with love
The pleasures and the troubles
That relationships are made of

So dance, do they, about
The great halls of their school
With joyful play and shout
Such love drunk little fools

Oh what a sight to see
This future school be
Where no one there is lonely
Because of *"He"* or *"She"*

A Good Man

Their once was a man with a stutter
Who feared he would someday be buggered
A fear so intense
Of things so immense
The thought of which caused him to shutter

So thusly, he tried to behave
The law, he always obeyed

But then he was framed
They mistook his name
And now he was more than dismayed

Oh this was a bad thing indeed
He was as scared as could be
For he did fear prison
As when you were in them
The practice there was sodomy

But luckily he was acquitted
In his joy, he then overdid it
He wed Maryann
Who was born a man
And finds his sphincter exquisite

<u>Science</u>

<u>Designers</u>

Watching chaos wrestle its partner
Oh, order is grappling desperately
Pound, do they, against each other
As they intermingle sensually

So close and roughly do they fight
Sliding over and atop one another
As grope and grab they in delight
This sister and this brother

And everywhere they roll upon
They smash and smooth it over
This game they play, it can't be won
It's too much fun to bother

<u>Chaos</u>

An expansive flourishing of unpredictability
Responding to uninhibited causality
Spiraling over an endlessly cyclical possibility
Unable to be relegated to passivity

A storm of shattered and endless collision
A merging maelstrom of division
A design corroborated by random chance
Put together by maddening happenstance

Oh how it is that the unknown
Bends and shapes and can be grown
How is it that the nothingness
Can birth forth something so amiss?

<u>Big Bang</u>

My father says we come from stardust way high up above
Does that mean that we are what the stars are dreaming of?

When it was forming in the void
Did it think, *'When I'm destroyed*
I'll be gone, but I won't die, you see
My sparks will make new life from me'

With clashing rocks, and molten ash
Swirling, forming clouds of gas
And making worlds, as yet, unknown
The worlds where our life has grown

So as I lay me down to sleep
I look into the night so deep
And thank the stars up in the sky
For I was born from stars who died

Unending

A vast expanse of nothingness
The all that ends eternally
The endless time of timelessness

Maelstrom

In an endless expanse of everything
What happens there is anything

With time and matter as unending
I think it's time we stopped pretending
That there is something far beyond
This life that we are limited on

So eat, drink and be merry
For tomorrow we die, not the contrary

Neurology

To see the nervous system
Spread wide about your body
Granting unto its limbs
Sensations all for thee

Giving experience
Of what we all would call
Those things which would enchant
Those called the physical

What makes your heart to leap
And runs your blood to cold
Or brings thy ecstasy
Or makes thy rage to boil

This sensual sweet system
Who brings corporeal
To feelings, sweetest of them,
And know that they are real

Ever the more of love
And ever the more of pain
These feelings, they make up
What all of life can mean

Now pull back from your system
Farther and farther still
Until you're farthest from
And look upon the world

Those gleaming glittering tendrils
Now wreathed about the earth
That push away the shadows
When turned from sun's bright warmth

Are giving we a system
That brings experience
Unto another form
The form of our own planet?

To grant our world touch
Caressing other stars
With what has made life up
And grants a happy heart

Oh of the nervous system
And all the things it brings
Should wonder, now and then,
What now our world thinks?

Evolving

Through one great blast of ecstasy
Formed we in the Pleistocene
The greatest shout, defiant spark
Life's expansion got its start

From crawling on the ground so low
To striding towards a greater goal

From instinct did we form and grow
To a thinking mind who works to know

Oh how it is, we cannot conceive
Or even know what we perceive
For we are now but one small step
Towards a goal not to be met

The Super Crab

Oh sweetly be the horseshoe crab
The horseshoe crab, the horseshoe crab
Oh sweetly be the horseshoe crab
A very special crab

He isn't like the other crabs
The pinchy crabs, the crabby crabs
He's nothing like those angry crabs
He is the horseshoe crab

He crawls upon the ocean sand
The salty sand, the burny sand
He crawls upon the sandy sand
Just looking for a friend

The horseshoe crab, he isn't proud
Nor is he loud or in a crowd
He cannot fly up in the clouds
He is a horseshoe crab

The horseshoe crab likes charity
For you and me, and he and she
And though he is out in the sea
He helps out when he can

The horseshoe crab is quite the sport
Although he's short and in a port
He donates blood, out of his love
He is the horseshoe crab

He saves a life and in the night
Crawls back into the sea
Though he is not a trilobite
He is a horseshoe crab

Sand On The Beach

Take a look at some sand, it hasn't seemed to change in over one thousand
years?
Every time, we look at the same old boring sand, always being pushed around
by the water
And becoming, wet sand

Think though, sand used to be a rock, and then became sand
Why is sand boring?

Is it the fact that it is so small, or that it doesn't entertain you?

Did you know that we are sand?
Sand of the world we are indeed and life is our sea

We toss and turn in the waves, and eventually over time we will become a rock
Solid and at our peek, only for us to become sand again

So take a look at some sand, any sand, and realize it isn't as boring as it seems

Objects

The Fragility Of Flesh

A person, though beautiful
Whose sight twill pass the hour
It matters not the form they hold
This person's not a flower

Though both wear; special garment
The raiment known as time
One knows the garment's rent
The other doesn't mind

The person fears the loss
To watch the petals fall
The flower wilts to dross
But does not cry or call

The flower may be pretty
But cares not for its beauty
A person, you or me
We want our sight to please

For flowers don't attract
Others unto themselves
They needn't ever act
To be seen beautiful

But people; they need touch
They want the hand's caress
And beauty brings it much
And helps the love to last

Though both are delicate
And both are beautiful
The one has thorns that prick
The other, hands to hold

The Pretty Girl

They say I'm beautiful, I'm glad
And so I go to them unclad
For them to take my photograph
They promise not to point or laugh

The strobe and flashing of the bulb
I smile warmly, though I'm cold
And with each picture that they make
A bit more of my soul they take

As show me off around the globe
So every man has me to hold
Their perfect little smiling bride
A fantasy, to whom they confide

This picture person, who won't age
And stays the beauty on the page
Whose legs will never show their veins
Whose breasts won't show their mother's pangs

A face not weary yet by love
No signs of time's hard push and shove
Rather they want their porcelain doll
The mannequin me at their beck and call

And so the flatters, they gather round
And shoot me lying on the ground
My legs, my chest, and all the rest
Like butchers they pick out what is best

They say my body is God's art
But does anyone want to see my heart?
I've shown the nipples of my breasts
And other places, I confess

They seem to like all that they see
But they cannot see inside of me
Am I made up of no more than parts,
To be sold at local shopping marts?

Is my body, laid bare, the best of I?
Would anyone want me if I cried?
The lightning of the camera light
It jolts me back with subtle fright

As part my lips now, to seduce
A tool now for public use
As hurry now, I cannot dawdle
For this is the life of the model

Pretty Penny

Where did you get those eyes?
Those dark deep hazel pools
That blend well with your sighs
As round the dogs do drool

Lapping their eyes over
Every silky curve of flesh
A candy like no other
To take in and digest

And though the others stare
Longing for other tastes
Your eyes, they held me there
As did I contemplate

Your hands, they looked quite rough
You worked another job
The money, not enough
And so you dance the rod

You pay the pretty penny
To paint upon your skin
And highlight up your body
To cover what's within

And build, do you, an idol
Who's fashioned from your flesh
Their perfect little girl
From legs to hips and breasts

And pay you for it all
With the strange weight of their gaze
Their eyes do lust and call
In drunken dizzy haze

These prices that you pay
I wonder deep inside
Which one was it that gave,
Away those lonely eyes?

Those eyes that say *"I've broken
Beneath this weight of life"*

Whose loneliness has spoken
With each dance every night

Those puppy eyes, long dimmed
Worn, like those hands so slender
And like those dreams within
A barely burning ember

Those eyes, I can't forget them
They've put me in a trance
As think do I *"Well then
I'll pay for one more dance"*

The Exotic Dancer

The stage atop the candle stick
A fire comes to join the wick
And with its seductive burning light
Draws many to her in the night

She sways and bends around the pole
Her heat melts down the wax to oil
The sweat gathers atop the brows
Of those who watch her dance and bow

This youthful flame so bright and fair
She'll dance because they wish her there
Her body, smooth and hot, it burns
Not to be touched, though viewers yearn

The candle flickers and goes out
The fire left the stage she melt
Leaving her viewers all alone
The fire dresses and goes home

Popularity

So sad now is this girl flame
She's so pretty, yet feels so plain
Isolated from touch and soft caress
Her skin, it burns the hands soft flesh

Her tears are sparks that turn to ash
While her footsteps turn the sand to glass
As everyone around her stairs
Desire they her fiery blazing hair

Looking out deeply, so does she
Staring out at the endless sea
And wonder, does she, then about
If she should douse herself right out

The Juxtaposition

Why be it but manly to fuck every slit
But oh so un-lady like to lust after dick?
So sorry if I've perturbed your so sensitive senses
But I am confused at our culture's strange lessons

I gather, quite clearly that sex, for a man
He's granted to do every act that he can
From jamming his manhood as far and as deep
Into any hole who twill but seek his meat

But strangely, it seems for women, it's best
To never be touched, licked nor caressed
Their virginity, so precious it be
Not one man should dare to ever fuck she

I don't understand, why are men so looked down on?
For if they are virgins, something must have gone wrong
Their phallus is broken, or maybe defunct
Perhaps he has died, and forgot to sunk

I mean, even gay men will fuck something, you see
So men who fuck nothing must be far more than crazy
I mean, women, they're too pure for that
Or rather they should be, and that's a fact

I just do not know, why do we fidget
When people think women lust for cock on to sit
It's like we hate men, deep down inside
That they taint our women with evil when they ride

We hate on gay men because, well you know
They are second best, with only two holes
But men are impure, you know, by default
So men but deserve such sick things, it's their fault

Our daughters are saints, our sons animals

105

Why do we think these things oh so cruel?
We prize one thing while priding another
And yet we still condemn both the lovers

For men are but brutes and women divine
And makes of them both that much less so sublime
It tempers her passions and makes them obscene
And mocks his emotions and feelings for things

For women do wish to indulge in their fires
As much as men do in their burning desires
Yet both are rent twixt each other by differing thoughts
That men are the seekers and women the sought

In A Vas

To be a pail rose
Sheltered, in a glass
Wilting, growing cold
But sitting; in a vas

You are a pretty thing
Though beauty, it won't last
For with time's chime and ring
You'll wither; in a vas

For all the world to see
To but stand back and bask
As watch you die; slowly
You'll sit there; in a vas

Perhaps they'll dye the water
And change thee blue; at last
To make you to the color
They want you; in a vas

So drink in what is there
And burn bright; down to ash
For beauty; it is rare
It sits there; in a vas

A Looker

A flowing ruby red dress
Adorning pale skin
This red, it does caress

The body that's within

Draped across the shoulders
Hanging on the breasts
This garment that's upon her
Stands out above the rest

A color screaming passion
But yearning secretly
Just to be unfastened
And held intimately

This one watching the crowd
This one who's in the red
They look, and say they *"Wow!"*
But nothing more is said

She stands there, oh so still
Is she nervous or afraid?
As watch they, the dress's frill
Kiss long and slender legs

Her eyes, they widely stair
At all the passers by
As some, in envy, glair
At her red dress and sigh

Oh the red provides a contrast
Upon her smooth white skin
A wallflower, beautifully dressed
Is this young mannequin

Paper Midst Fire

Look at what's desired
Look at what you want
Those places you revere
Whose thought but causes taunt

Those pieces; sumptuous
You lust to see revealed
To lick and kiss and touch
This special human meal

Your eyes select the cut
That seems appropriate
And dream do you; to suck
And taste what you can get

Oh feel your desires
They rage as burning flames
And nothing bates those fires
They roll nearly untamed

But you must work the hardest
To not allow the blaze
To move beyond caress
Upon this one you gaze

The inferno of desire
Takes not into account
The person that's required
And makes those places flaunt

For oft we see the surface
And never what's within
So taper thy caress
So as not to burn them

<u>Sickness</u>

Seesaw

Up and down and up and down
My head, it feels dizzy
As up and down and up and down
I feel myself a whizzing

So up and down and up and down
I feel rather odd
While up and down and up and down
My head, it sways and bobs

Now up and down and up and down
I'm feeling rather tense
This up and down and up and down
It causes me to wince

As up and down and up and down
My eyes, I hold them closed
This up and down and up and down
I feel I'll explode

The up and down and up and down
I feel now it slowing
While up and down and up and down
I wish that it'd keep going

Day Off

A little joke I give to you
The comedy that is the flu
You spend all day lying in bed
With painful throbbing in your head

You feel dizzy, and off kilter
Your stomach acting like a filter
Decides for you what's in your gut
The rest of which you will upchuck

You sweat yourself until you're soaked
As sandpaper goes down your throat
You cough and wheeze your body aches
You feel hot, but get the shakes

Oh what a joy, this feeling sick
So funny, no one laughs at it

Desire's Disease

A stiffness, has come over me
The sweetest sickness one can see
An overarching turgid pleasure
Pulse taller, do I, when I'm measured

My head swelled now with pounding throb
In blissful nausea sways and bobs
Taunt skin so tender to the touch
The slightest stroke could be too much

Try I to calm my drooling face
This pleasing panic's everyplace
Bringing great lightness to the mind
A burning madness so sublime

My body twitches and it tingles
My senses blend and intermingle
The tension now has reached its peak
Now come the seizures that I seek

And feel, do I, a welling up
Flood breaks the leaking door once shut
And writhe in awesome agony
As I do gush forth ecstasy

And then unconscious do I fall
My body limp, no longer tall
And now, with tearful frothy bliss
Reach out to you now for a kiss

The Title Of The Poem

My sticky fingers, so unclean
So dirty are they from my dream
They drip down drops that fall quite wrong
Splattering in patterns thick and strong

The scent come from these hands of mine
That stench of life some find divine
Wash them, do I, as best I can
This fluid which I cannot stand

My head is light, my hands are shaking
I try to calm my stomach's quaking
And breath, do I, my deepest breath
As off to bed I go to rest

Sensations

Together, now with you
I find I can't recall
A thing I once well knew
But seems away to fall

Across you sit there, in your dress
That pretty pale blue
And as my fingers kiss your flesh
I don't know what to do

I'm greeted by the needle's point
That pin's caress, that grew
And took from me what once was joint
And rent it right in two

Your skin, to me, but pressure
And hate I that it's true
Your warmth was such a pleasure
To feel that silky smooth

Though happy you are near
And that your love shows through
I grieve that you are here
And I am not with you

I feel farthest from you now
When I confront this truth
This sadness weighs upon my brow
And takes from me my youth

This barrier between us
A wall so cold and blue
"A fate, oh so unjust"
I hear you softly coo

Though at the door I stand
And knock, though no come to
Upon your skin, my hand

It won't remember you

A door others can't open
A thing that I should do
And yet, the lock is broken
My home, become my tomb

And so I stand there waiting
At a door I can't go through
My heart tis not abating
In loneliness it broods

For it was far too soon
To lose you from my touch
And stand outside the room
Whose door's forever shut

The Changing Room

I'm in my room, devoid of sound
And look, do I, at my white gown
Standing there, before my mirror
My throat lumps up a bit in fear

The thoughts race round inside my mind
Each second seems a private lifetime
My memories swirl about, a blur
About my deeds, and what they were

These nervous tears, hold back, I try
They drip and drop down from my eyes
My hands, shaking and damp with sweat
I haven't come to terms quite yet

My emotions, uncertain and unsure
The truth, however, is quite pure
Never before have so few words
Mean more to me after been heard

My family waits outside the door
Mother cries on my father shoulder
They want to be in the room with me
But I fear being the center of all they see

My stomach turns upon its side
I want to curl up and hide
Standing, my legs quiver and tremble
Signs of an earthquake of the mental

Upon the door I hear a knock
The time has come upon the clock
My man is waiting down the hall
And now I answer that man's call

I don't want to feel this anymore
And so I open up the door
I feel naked all around
A symptom of wearing the gown

The Smiling

How does one deflect pain easily?
That's simple, through dark comedy

You walk on out towards the stage
Your buddy says *"Hey, break a leg!"*
You fall down stairs and there you lay
At least that luck, it was obeyed

Or what about that one dark night
When you were held up with a knife
Then you were stabbed right in the joint
The least you can say's you got the point

Oh look at these silly things
We tell ourselves within our dreams
But we cannot see through smiles and laughs
The sorrow we bare upon our backs

The Best Medicine

Life, it is so beautiful
And yet, time, you hear its tick
Each a knock by death upon the soul
Felt deeply by the sick

But say they, with a smile
About the steady tapping
"At night, it keeps me up awhile
I hope death's bones aren't cracking"

"Arthritis must be a killer
His joints must be so dry
I sure hope while he's here
He gives rest a little try"

The humor of the ill
So dry and dark it be
The wittiest of pills
A tonic of bitter glee

For laughter is the better
Of all the medications
It's good at cutting fear
To make light of one's condition

This medicine, however
Tis not for those that hurt
It is for others, rather
It's meant to heal their hearts

Yes, the humor of the dying
It's meant to ease the pain
Of others, who are crying
As they watch their candle wane

Oh, the jokes from shallow breaths
The last roar of the lion
A heckling of death
Like saying, *"Well, come on!"*

These little quips, so quirky
Are acts of great compassion
The death throes of empathy
These simple little actions

Easing others into a world
Where they will soon be gone
They know this is a hurtle
That no one wants jump on

And though, their heart, it rends
Death's hand twill soon take hold
But hope, do they, it ends
Not in tears, but with a chuckle

<u>Friendship</u>

Come To Me

When I was crying
Did you hear me?
Did you come to comfort me,
Or perhaps you walked on by?

If you did, did you give a glance back,
And hesitate return to me?
Did my sobbing keep you up at night?

When you thought upon my tears
Uncomforted and lonely
Without a friend to hear

Was it some pain?
You'll never know if you don't ask
And investigate weeping

For misery loves company
And company, compassion
For when you comfort sorrow, see
Those tears, now, you can end them

So never pass those crying
Without a thought or helping hand
Give unto them compassion
And raise them up to stand

Best not to be haunted by
"What happened to them?"

Words Can Draw

I haven't come to make a friend
I've only come to speak
And if my words cause some to lend
Their friendship, then we'll meet

And intertwine our thoughts, will we
Our minds twill intermingle
And bring some souls to jealousy
That words can make us whole

That meaning can be found in speech
Whose strangely human sounds
Like barks and quacks and shrieks and squeaks
There's something to be found

Oh when we listen earnestly
To others when they speak
We find that who we're meeting
Is not the one we think

For every book has title
But what's inside, distinct
Can bring you both to smile
And sorrow soon to drink

So if my words can find thee
And make of thee a friend
I hope that when you meet me
You'll stay until the end

Holding Hands

The warm sensation of a life
Connected to my own
A piece of heaven, oh so nice
It's like I've found my home

A feeling of completeness
In places where I'd groan
And worry, in my weakness
The thought, *'Am I alone?'*

But no longer am I dejected
My heart has only grown
Much more than I'd expected
Much more than could be known

You've taken what was hard
What once but seemed a stone
And sculpted out a heart
From the kindness you have shown

A feeling so sublime
In our time we take to wander
It swells the soul to shine
And makes the spirit kinder

And so we walk together
Through both the highs and lows
So nice to have another
Who's brave enough to go

Stopping Next To Another

When kindness glances at you
And blushingly give way
A gift you never knew
That you'd receive today

Come from a stranger's hand
Who, by chance, passing by
Relinquished something grand
That would alight your eyes

A simple pleasure, really
Not some great sacrifice
But something more than nearly
That gave your heart delight

Perhaps a word of compliment
Or maybe an embrace
A subtle slight event
That left a special grace

Something that made you say
"Thank you" though you're entranced
For what they left, dismayed
At that lone gift they'd grant

A Friend

Do you need a friend to stand with you,
To carry you, now black and blue?
You needn't stand upon your knees
You can, instead, hold onto me

Do you need someone to stand up strong,
To be there when you sing your song?
You do not need to run or flee
Instead, you can hold onto me

Do you feel afraid when you're alone,
When you hear the silence in your home?
Alone you need to never be
Just reach out, and hold onto me

Are you ashamed of who you are,
Do you think your life at best a scar?
Don't be ashamed of who you see
Because, you can, hold onto me

Together We, Us Two

Together, we are rowing
Down the river, dark and blue
Neither of us knowing
Where stop we our canoes

Beneath the tree's soft canopy
And the twinkling beams of light
Reflecting off the waters with glee
Making the shadows bright

Yet farther do we travel
Us two, do we, together
As the waters, they do babble
This soothing song we hear

But then we came upon a parting
Two different tributaries
One, away from the forests shading
The other, beneath the trees

And betwixt these two new paths
You nod your head to me
To take the one where shade is cast
The one beneath the trees

And so we two did part
You took the one with sky
I know, do I, in my heart
You'd rather you could fly

An Embrace

You've fallen, and you've skinned your knee

I look at you and sigh
Come reach up your hand to me
I'll hold you while you cry

Your first love has left you
You ask the question *"Why?"*
You look at me, oh what to do?
I hold you as you cry

Oh on your wedding day
Tears coming to your eyes
So happy, you can't say
I hold you, and you cry

Your children have been born
And no matter how you try
Your emotions are a storm
I hold you while you cry

You come to me, I'm ill
And seeing through my lies
You find that what I have, it kills
I hold you, and then you cry

You sit beside me, holding my hand
As on my bed I lye
You see now I am too weak to stand
You can hold me as you cry

As in silence, there you sit
Watching me slowly die
As you despair, I will, in spirit
Hold you while you cry

Beside The Phone

Waiting
It's been three days
She'll call, right?
She will
She said so

I mean
After that night

121

Kaden Moeller

It was amazing
Everything I could have hoped for
She was perfect
And
I so wanted things to work

So
We had laid there
And I
I didn't want her to leave
I just wanted things to stay this way
But she
She had to work
And
I gave her my number
And she gave me hers

And I called
I called the next day
No answer
I called the day after
Nothing
Maybe she needed some time
Maybe she was working
Or tired

She'll get my messages
I made sure to tell her
"I want to know you
All of you
I want to meet your family
And maybe try of a life with you
Please
This 'just friends' stuff
It doesn't work anymore"

She'll call
Please call
Why won't she call back?

Barnyard

Kaden Moeller

Jingle Bell Hop

We're going round and round again
My partner, he and me
Batting him over floor with my hand
I chase him happily

He giggles as he rolls away
And I peruse his tune
Calling after him, I say
A simple little *"mew"*

His shiny face reflecting mine
With black and fuzzy whiskers
This waltz of ours is so divine
As you roll over and over

I knock you to and fro
And chase you round the rug
And then I pounce upon you, so
As to give you a hug

Chips And Dip

My dog's paws smell like corn-chips
Those crunchy tasty treats
The funny part about it
Is that it's on her feet

How did this come about?
That scent, oh so divine
When it's around my house
It means it's party time!

With friends and food abound
That smell is everywhere
And comes such merry sounds
With chips smell in the air

Those sights that smell does bring
Are full of happiness
And yet my mind won't bring
To me a single guess

Why does my dog have fredo-feet?
The answer I don't see

For what she steps in, it seems to be
Only her own pee

My Pet

My person's very funny
He acts quite strange indeed
And always entertains me
With all his funny deeds

Like when he throws his ball away
And I go get it back
"You don't dislike this ball" I say
As he tries again, I laugh

He makes such funny sounds
When he wants his attention
So stupid, I can't frown
Are these sounds that I mention

And when he holds me close
I think he feels lonely
So silly, cause of course
I will not let him leave me

My human, sits for hours
And stares at his strange boxes
While I look at the flowers
As round the bee now buzzes

And so off to bed we go
And at his feet I slept
For what he doesn't know
Is he's mine to protect

Donkey

The ass brays night and day
It cares not what the hour
Bringing sound that dismays
And makes you think it foul

The rudeness of its call
Twill cause all about to fidget

It makes the talk to small
As there are snickers in it

No matter how you try
To silence such a sound
You find it will defy
Till blush you all around

For oh this rogue is daring
It cares little for the shame
Of company, it's uncaring
It sounds forth all the same

Sometimes tis low and long
Others, it's high and quick
But if you clench it wrong
Careful, you may just shit

Early Riser

Just before the morning, the cock rouses awake
In preparation for, this awkward scene he'll make
Getting up, so slow, until he stands proud and tall
His face, so blushed and eager, he likes to make his call

And as the dawn doth break, up in that sky so red
The cock, excitedly, does up and raise his head
And crows, does he, quite happily, the song that's known as life
A song that wakes you in your bed, and from that dream so nice

You look down, and you shake your head, again the cock hath crowed
And as you now doth leave your sheet, to bed the cock doth go
He lays his head down softly, happy he's sung his song
And though sometimes he's inconvenient, you like to sing along

Pony

I've come to ride my stallion
He waits at home for me
As open I his stable pen
His eyes look wildly

I slide his saddle on him
He fidgets gleefully
As feel I his turgid skin
Tensed in anxiety

Spreading my legs, into the stirrups
I mount him, holding tight
And revel as he roughly bucks
I break him with delight

And as he calms, I lean in close
And stroke his sweaty main
My hands run down his chest, I boast
Upon my happy horsy's frame

And so do I dismount
Legs quivering a bit
A thrill I can't discount
I love this bronco's kicks

My mount, he is beside me, standing
And nudges me with love
I smile, face now blushing
And give a playful shove

It was a happy ride
We both thought it was fun
The pleasure, he won't hide
He prances round, high strung

We two, we are good friends
Closer than most can be
And though our visit ends
I smile as I leave

Now off to work I go
The day has just begun
In happiness, I know
We've time for more, we're young

Self-interested Representation

The scarecrows up and file in
The words they speak, hollow within
Their actions are a pantomime
Exemplifying petty crime

Their speeches, they go on for hours

These worthless words which time devours
Making a war with what they say
Inciting the march of the macabre

The crop outside awaits protection
Fooled are they by their deception
They won't be protected from the crows
The crop, so stunted, it won't grow

With stalks razed high, they beg and plead
The birds watch, perched on scarecrow's sleeve
Agreed are they, between the two
The crop is theirs, that's why it grew

Each crenel tis meant to be used
Threshed, crushed, eaten and abused
It matters not how much they eat
There is no way plants can retreat

This bird business, it is quite cold
Their song is cruel and quite bold
They change the world not for their need
But rather their unending greed

Consume will they every resource
There's no appeal or recourse
They put themselves above the rest
Opposing them, the greatest test

This type of life just cannot be
For it doesn't take great eyes to see
The crows will die if they don't stop
Their abuse will soon dry out the crop

For when you take too much away
Strangle, will you, the future day
The only way for all to live
Can only happen when we give

Animals

The pussy is out prowling
She's looking for a playmate
Slinking, as she's growling
The night is getting late

The cock, he's sleeping soundly
He's calm, as there, he slept
But atop him pounced the pussy
He then became erect

He squirmed round as they tussled
She writhed atop his head
Anxiety enveloped he, they bustled
Both of them blushing red

But as the dawn did break
The cock did crow his song
The pussy then did make
A purring oh so strong

And up together did they curl
As they both went to sleep
She had her fun, this kitty girl
Now both are counting sheep

Red Petals

In a place farthest from home
Surrounded by shouts and screams
These cheers of what's to come
Of an abysmal scene

The crowd, they rain but roses
Upon their sacrifice
This strong standing; broad soldered
Lone one, whom they'll entice

And comes his strange opponent
With a flamboyant flare
This one he's never met
As cheers run round the air

And here, in humble fear
Stands our confounded friend
Who knows not why he's here
Or what they'll do to him

He may look like a mountain
But looks can oft deceive

Kaden Moeller

His wants aren't greater than
A pasture long and green

And then the pain, it jolts
The depths of his long back
And the cheers volume but bolts
As round the hands do clap

And then the fear wells up
As his turgid muscles tense
His mind is puzzled much
At his strange predicament

They hope his fear twill make a sport
For their long sacrifice
To appease the blood god more
With this entertaining vice

But our hero is too terrified
To fight or run away
He know he cannot hide
And so he looks; dismayed

He stares at his attacker
A look upon his face
Of open naked fear
As screams bounce round the place

And then another spike
Another, then another
And though the pain is high
He doesn't even bother

He looks around; dejected
Despair upon his face
And at the one who stabs him
This person in this place

And the Matador; he goads
And presses deep the spike
But his opponent, oh
The bull, he would not fight

He would not wild spin
To the crowd's horrid delight
Rather, he stared at him

For the bull, he would not fight

And with every single hit
Though it brought his face to fright
He would take every lick
As the bull, he would not fight

And the crowd, it did grow restless
With silence speckled 'bout
To watch, in such distress
Died down they their blood shout

And the crimson caped bravado
Of one of the two in sight
Began grow slowly cold
As the bull, he would not fight

With scarlet raining from him
Our hero takes a knee
The pain and those round him
Have worn and wearied he

He but lays down to rest
In red and crusty mud
He's more than in distress
He wears the cape of blood

And there, the Matador
He stood with all his might
As he looked there on the floor
At the bull, who would not fight

And the crowd, they sat in silence
As if almost in fright
As the Matador cried, yes
For the bull, would not fight

And as our hero laid there
And took in his last sight
Red petals rained the air
For the bull, who would not fight

Kaden Moeller

<u>Love</u>

The Needle; Midst Hay

To the mate that I shall find; my friend
And that mate that I shall find; again
Mayhaps you vouchsafe what's yours to me
And I'll embrace what's come from thee
No, never, be it said of you
That you are not worthy to woo
I'll chase and play
We'll waist the day
And let our lives
Meet twixt the night

Satisfaction

The painful pleasure of desire
She licks at me with loving fire
Oh how my lust is taunting me
With lips pursed, just for me to see

How giddy is my heart when wanting
Such ecstasy is oh so haunting
My arm goes out to grasp her hand
Just out of reach, I try again

She giggles as she steps away
I give her chase, we laugh and play
Her naked body tantalizing
Frustration, boiling up and rising

Her curves caress my eyes so sweetly
They motivate my life completely
Oh how I wish to touch her so
I hope I never catch her though

A Desire

Oh, some days, wish that I could dream
And dream a dream untold
That one beauty would come for me
And in our arms we'd hold

I'd run my fingers down the back of those locks of angel hair
So deep and dark; raven black

133

And I'd breath the scent in deeply
Wishing; never forget I that

And I'd go limp and frail; loose from weariness
No shame in it at all
And I'd forget to play the part men play
And stop standing so tall

I'd hold so close, and I'd be a child again; wanting love honestly
And there, my protector, would speak softly
Whisper words of comfort; strong words of love
And I'd look into their eyes and cling them close to me

And the fear that's in my soul; though wish it rise
My lover will quash with a word
And I will feel secure and without want
Just at the thought of what I'd heard

And I could be uncovered
Devoid of barriers
So that they could see me
And I could see my lover

Ascent

The one thing that love is
Our thoughts often prevent
Us seeing it, clearest
That love is only patience

To size up the peaks above
And swallow up our doubts
To grasp within our gloves
The rocks that start it out

A waiting to get to know
And once the thing is known
To not to just up and go
And with others to roam

Though we will slip and stumble
Our footing we will find
As some rocks, they crumble
Their footholds now don't hide

To take the things that come

The good, bad and annoying
The pleasure, pain and fun
And every other thing

And dangle there, attached
To but a thread of rope
And though you hold it fast
It is a desperate grope

To stay when they are angry
And hold them when they're sad
To dance when they are happy
And forgive them when they're mad

Oh to survive the avalanche
Those few that come, in time
It is, at but, a random chance
That you'll be left behind

To tolerate their habits
Both good and full of vice
And but try to cohabit
And live one single life

And as you weather tremors
That come from deep within
You try hard to remember
That they come from the mountain

Accept the past that's with them
And hope the future's bright
To hold them close until then
Until that breaking light

And grasp you to it firmly
Now that you're high above
To fall would surly kill thee
When in the heights of love

And take what comes with age
What has been made familiar
And now seems but to say
"What have I now to offer?"

So climb a little more
Though your body be weary
The view it holds in store
So very few are worthy

To desire happiness
Upon the other's face
And work so hard to bless
This one that you embrace

To look off of the mountain
And see horizon's end
To smile at the climb, and
Enjoy your mountain friend

And remember that those wrinkles
Be the cost of loving you
The patience that they hold
That's deep within them too

And though those heights you scaled
You never were alone
Your life too, had no trail
Though now it be well worn

The great work that is love
A labor of the heart
Whose heights be high above
And yet, this climb, we start

Powerful

Love; a word for the strong
A word of predestined loss
A gift, once unwrapped, doomed to degrade
Though be it the highest cost

But try to lift its weight
When you, alone, but one
Attempt a thing for two
You find it can't be done

The hearts that love the deepest
They know the depths they dive
And fear, do they, the greatest
Of what will come someday

For love, its weight is greatest
Upon its approaching loss
When know you soon will miss
What once was near your heart

And when the burden's gone
Your soul is not relieved
For missing that someone
But brings the weight of grief

And so I tell you now
That when you fall in love
Remember that you vow
To someday lose someone

Aroma

Oh what be beauty's fragrance?
Be it sweet or bitter?
Does it linger, this scent
That smell; which draws you near

A lure in the air
That hopes to catch some love
Something to draw you near
And hopes you'll stay quite long
Though it may fade, you fear

Something to fascinate
To stimulate the senses
That says, twill satiate
A perfume to caress
And sweetly perforate

Oh how our hearts do track
Those signs that beauty leaves
We tend not to turn back
As sniff, do we, the breeze
And hope we soon to catch

Outside Looking In

How can one speak of love in depth,

Without at first having this love met?
This fantasy of fallacies
A lie that never was to be

The youth bask in their joy like light
As they mingle closely in the night
But what they fail to see is this
The light will take away their bliss

It burns away all their delusions
Making them think on their new union
It will seem less a fairytale
With each and every new detail

They'll see each other different then
Merely as close and kindly friends
Now how do I know this to be so?
That's what it means to learn and grow

The Youth's Lament

When someone lays there lonely
It be bad for their health
They want someone to love they
But they must love them-self

To be content inside
Accepting who you are
And bridge thee that divide
That at times seems so far

And when your heart is ready
To draw someone to you
But keep your spirit steady
And let it shine right through

This person that you be
Is someone you must show
The one that they must see
And then to get to know

It be the hardest thing
To let yourself depart
Allowing love to bring
A softness to the heart

So tender will it be
The slightest touch twill sting
But soon twill bring you glee
And cause your mouth to sing

Now laying with another
Your head upon their breast
To listen to the lover
That beat within their chest

Then, will you ask the question
Wonder will you now?
Does that love that you get from them
Make you complete somehow?

Or is it that your loving
This action that you do
To them you seem to bring
Reflections deep in you

Is this love made for them,
Or be it for yourself?
Oh do you love this friend,
Or be they but your wealth?

To be with one is one thing
They're rendered a possession
No matter golden ring
The true test is to love them

Lost And Found

I think I'll go down to the pub
And adopt myself a stray
To find a soul for me to love
If only for a day

I'll search through the silky smoke
And read the lonely eyes
Of those which drink has soaked
And whom time's weight has tried

Those faces who look out
With expressions oh so sullen

But whose spirits seem to shout
'I just want to be taken'

Though each one has a house
They do not have a home
As inwardly they grouse
'I feel so alone'

Each one be damaged goods
Worn in so many places
Used and misunderstood
Be every of these faces

Oh such a wide selection
Of lost human companions
Familiar with rejection
But waiting for adoption

What I Know

Oh know I not your fantasies
Nor all your deep desires
But your hands, want I, on me
To lift my spirit higher

That I have never seen
Those people that you've hurt
To me you seem most clean
No matter what you work

I could not know your father
Had done some things to you
This person I see here
Let's not those scars show through

Those animals you cut
That rage you aired, so true
I do not know that much
But I know I love you

Walking Through The Park

I found something, the other day
Twas sitting all alone
Looking rather down and grey
Like a slowly sinking stone

I said *"Hello, how are you!?"*
The response, an annoyed stare
Those eyes, they were confused
Asking, *'Why was I there?'*

"Beautiful day" I said
"Too bad there no one to share with me
But your face, just like mine, it read
I'm stuck in solitary"

I chanced a nervous smile
And received a blank expression
But after a little while
Some words came, in succession

"I'm going to leave right now
So please, don't try to follow"
The words that came next, wow!
They were, *"Come back tomorrow"*

I found something the other day
And unhappy little dove
I don't know how, I cannot say
I think that I found love

From Afar

I saw you standing there
Your eyes, they glanced at me
You seemed to fear my stare
And so, I looked away

But you, you blushed for me
You knew of my conundrum
That I saw you, so pretty
But words, I hadn't found them

You moved a little closer
Looking the other way
My heart, beat all the faster
I don't know what to say

With every inch towards me

Kaden Moeller

I feel the panic rising
The more of you I see
My eyes, I feel widening

You're standing here, before me
I feel like I will die
As look, do we, now nervously
I smile, and say *"Hi"*

Chasing The Wind

Let us chase the whirlwind
Together my friend
Let us fall in love
And bask in this moment called life
Gripping each other together
Flying and falling as one
Dizzy and filled with vertigo
Propelled and pursuing at once
This temporal existence
The briefest ripple; to be gone in a moment
We will embrace; we will love
We will embrace; we will weep
Coming together as two
A pair upon the path
Chasing the wind, for the fun of it
Both wondering where our paths end
Where they will break apart
And leave one lonely traveler
Lost with a broken heart
Let us chase the whirlwind
Together my friend
Let us fall in love

The Lightning-Rod

Pray for the one who falls for me
That as they plummet down
Rocks cleave them not asunder
As fall they to me; like the ground

And wish for they I catch them
And hold them close, and see
That though they fell, their heaven
It somehow is with me

For though the fall be far
And though the fall could kill
They come, though not unmarred
Despite the fears instilled

So pray for that poor soul
Pray they find who they need
Pray when they fall they know
That all they'll get is me

Am I worth falling for
Or be they fools, indeed
Who could not find one more
Worthy for their needs?

Oh pray I catch them safely
And hope I they don't mind
That when it is they see
Who caught them, they are fine

At First Sight

I feel myself falling
The wind rushing through my hair
My eyes, I feel tearing
As see I you standing there

Now rush, do I, towards you
Plummeting down in fear
I don't know what to do
As downwardly I near

My heart, its beating fast
My eyes, taking in sights
I do not want to crash
I wish to stay in flight

Your eyes, they look to me
My mind, it just goes blank
I know not what you see
I don't know what to think

The world, it seems so quiet
As the wind whips round my frame

You are so beautiful, and yet
This fall could cause me pain

I'm falling now, it's true
Like a shooting star above
Now will I crash, or will you
Catch me with your love?

A Rush

A feeling, what is this
My heart, I feel it flutter
Oh as your lips move near to kiss
I feel my lips but utter

"Why?" it comes out silently
As if twas never said
This question, though it pours from me
As scream it in my head

And then your lips warmth comes
I feel my passions surge
Oh what is this, I stand there stunned
I cannot find the words

I feel this thing within
I don't know I can describe it
My soul, it isn't dim
It's been chained to a commit

My heart, oh it is racing
Towards the great unknown
Your lips, mine are they gracing
But my heart has never flown

This new type of horizon
A star rising before us
As hurtle we towards the sun
I know not what waits for us

It feels almost like fear
But instead, I find I want it
I hold it to me dear
Enough, I cannot get

It's like I'm falling fast

Faster and faster still
As to you do I grasp
As my heart do you fill

My head, oh it does swoon
My mind is drunk with love
I know not what to do
As our spirits soar above

I look into your eyes
And like glass reflecting me
My passions do I spy
The same ones that you see

Oh hope I that you feel
The same way that I do
I pray this kiss, a seal
That signs myself to you

As hold you close to I
My eyes, I dare not shut
"If this be a dream" I cry
"Oh please don't wake me up"

Shaking Hands

How many times
Can you meet someone?
How many times
Can one seem strange?

And be
To you
A different person
A soul you've never seen

Yes, when their anger comes
Or when their passion's bright
Or when their tears do run
Or when their feared with fright

Oh, how many times
Are they new?
Yes, how many times

Kaden Moeller

Are they strange?

And when those moments come
And how many times will pain
Be the sole one who greets you
When you meet them again

Oh why those nervous glances?
Why hesitate the touch?
Do fear you all the chances,
That love is not enough?

Yes fear do we the stranger
We shun who we don't know
And want we what's familiar
To never let them go

But how can one hold to
A sprite of shattered glass
A million peoples are we
Reflecting what was last

And so the question
How many times
Can you introduce yourself?
How many times
Can you learn to love?

Blind Date

Oh have you met poor Richard?
A man so sensitive
His emotions come much quicker
Than the credit others give

Yes, Richard seems so strong
He puts on a good show
And yet for all his brawn
Love seems all he knows

Yet often does he stand outside
Being quite hesitant
He's not so bold, he often hides
He thinks the view's unpleasant

And yet when Richard does come in

146

He is the life of the party
And think we differently of him
We think him bold and hearty

But Richard, he is shy
And so easy to hurt
It won't take much to cry
Please, no one be a jerk

So, know that he's attentive
And that he listens well
For love is his incentive
He lives under its spell

So now that you've met Richard
Oh, by the way he's blind
That redness in his face, I've heard
Is him saying *"Please be mine."*

I hope you can be friends
His nerves may make him sick
But when that sickness ends
Would you please call him Dick

Comparison Contrast

"I can't be with you
I can't
You're way too out of my league!"

"Why say you this?
My love
Why this do you believe?"

"Just look at you
Now me
There's no comparison"

"What do you mean?
My sweet
What's wrong with your person?"

"You're kind, and vary gentle
Not me

I'm rough around the edges"

"You need my soft touch, for
Then we
Will get where we are headed"

"But I'm so shy
Unlike you
Outgoing and so smart"

"But you follow me wherever I may go
It's true
You have a lovely heart"

"You cannot degrade yourself with me
Please don't
You can do better"

"What other person could there be
Who won't
Leave me for another?"

"You will be happier
I promise
With another far more hansom"

"How happy do you think I'd be?
I mean
Where would it come from?"

"Oh please don't settle, not
For me
Look at you, you are pretty!"

It's ok for you, you know
To say
That you're in love me"

Rosy Lens

Oh I have found a perfect mate
Whose hand, I'm soon to take
And now I cry
"It's no mistake
That you should be with I!"

"I think you see them dimly
I'm sorry, please forgive me
But love be a strong wine
And too much makes you see
The other as divine"

But you know not our joy
Our love, would you destroy?
Do you look down and think
"Poor boy
Your naivety doth stink"

"That rosy rump
Still takes a dump
Upon the porcelain throne
I'm tired of hearing all this junk
Good day, I'm going home"

Happiness

If only all my dreams,
Twould be as sweet as you
And shine, twinkle and gleam
As gems of deepest blue

I'd never wish again
For all my hopes come true
To just but hold your hand
And feel the love that bloomed

Oh never will I want
And ever will I rejoice
And quaff from thee; a fount
Those sweet words from your voice

To live with thee, a life
Is worth more than all things
To be there in the night
With all the joy it brings

To ever hold to you
And feel thy tender touch
Tis not a dream, tis true
This truth seems far too much

Strange Desires

I want to be your angel
In whom you can believe
I hope this isn't shameful
To ask to meet your needs

I want to be your pillar
The one who holds you up
Though I'm not always there
I won't leave, no matter what

I want to be your pillow
Where you can lay your head
No matter where you go
I'll sooth you with the words I've said

I want to be your anchor
To hold you steady through the storm
And though the waves may rage and roar
I'll hold you, safe and warm

I want to be your neighbor
So that, when you need
A place, an open door
To go to, it is me

I want to be your friend
Just to receive your care
I don't want this to end
Your presence, I want it there

Oh all these strange desires
I know not what they mean
My heart, it never tires
It beats my love I streams

Holding

Dear one
Allow my touch
Dear one
Gift my clutch

Near one

Make me whole
Near one
Take my soul

Gift me
With thy love
Gift me
To thy blood

Hold my
Life to thee
Hold my
Fear from me

Ever so
Kind and sweet
Ever so
Behind my feet

Dear one
Hold me close
Dear one
Hold me most

A Sunset

As sit I, on a bench
Held in my lover's arms
And feel, do I, the wind caress
Me sweetly with its charms

"Oh tell me what it looks like"
I say unto my darling
*"Describe to me the sweet sight
That nature is expressing"*

And so the words did come
Oh cherish, did I, them
The warmth that I felt from the sun
Came from rays that were golden

That gold, apparently
Got mixed up with the clouds
That sat over the sea

Kaden Moeller

Who copied it somehow

And make, did it, a pallet
These watercolors in the sky
As swirl there, they, lit
By the golden multi-dye

A churning mix of colors
Orange, purple, and red
As round the leaves now flutter
And autumn rears its head

The water glints and glistens
Sparkling on every crest
As carefully, I listen
To my lover's beating breast

And then the sun sinks low
And lower, till it's gone
Oh this now do I know
But wish that I was wrong

My lover speaks to me
Telling me that we must go
Saying *"I cannot see*
It's dark and very cold"

Oh all those sweet words to me
Those colors in the sky
That painting of the sea
And the sun that hangs so high

These words of what I'm feeling
That I can't picture in my mind
Words that have no meaning
To a person who's born blind

Lovely

The evening sun is sinking low
We sit here in its afterglow
Its golden beams bounces off the lake
The time is getting oh so late

We sit and talk about the trees
And watch the wind blow through their leaves

I smile and you shake your head
We really should be off to bed

The moon has risen in the sky
We start our trek back, with a sigh
And comment, do we, of the stars
How they seem close, but are so far

And so go up, we to the house
I say goodbye, and move on out
This love, it has no word or passion
Speak it, do we, through deed and action

Behind My Eyes

The most important thing you be
To someone like myself
So much so, I do not believe
There could be greater wealth

To have you is enough
And everything I do
I know it isn't much
But all of it's for you

And how I toss and turn
On many sleepless nights
My heart, oh how it yearns
To know that I've done right

Every smile on your face
A sign of your approval
And every line a tear doth trace
I find the world so cruel

And when you're close to me
I only want to know
Who is it that you see
In this one that you hold

The love I feel within
Be in my deepest place
Why can't I let you in
To see behind my face

Kaden Moeller

Life Sentence

I've set myself up to fail
I've sentence myself to love
And bound to me travail
And sorrow yet to come

I've dug for me, a grave
Which I twill fill with tears
To burry to whom I say
"My sweet, I love you, dear"

A time I've set to come
Though I do know not when
Where I twill watch this one
Depart me; without end

And not a thing to do
And not a thing to say
Except to dread and rue
That one so fateful day

But since I've dug the hole
And time, I see, is passing
Dare I now forestall
To tell you what I'm feeling

My love and passion do I give
And hope it be enough
To make that memory of the grave
Seem it twill not be shut

But in the quiet of the night
When I do watch you sleep
I fear that one day's morning light
When you won't wake for me

My Love

I hate not seeing you
I hate being alone
I hate not hearing you
I hate not having you home

I hate not touching you

154

I hate missing your listening ear
I hate not tasting you
I hate how you make me fear

I hate you most of all
I hate your denying me you
I hate your leaving so soon
I hate waiting until tomorrow
I hate this loneliness and sorrow

I hate you
I hate waiting for you
I hate thinking of you
I hate dreaming of you
I hate not loving you

Swimming

Was ever there someone
That you loved more than thee
And craved drink deeply from
Until you could not breathe?

To drown yourself in them
Submerged deep in this other
To take delight and swim
Throughout that living water

And let that water ripple
Cross that once somber face
Oh let your light touch trickle
And cause their heart to race

Oh let your swimming satiate
Those once so stagnant waters
And let those waves proliferate
Within that stormy lover

And let the sea but toss
And let the waves but churn
But swimming's not a loss
In a sea that you do yearn

Devotion and desire

They make a mess of thee
And yet they light a fire
That burns amidst the sea

The Price

Dear, how I love you so
And yearn for tender touch
Oh but the hammer blows
From my lips be too much

I curse the tong within
This chisel of my malice
And tremble in my skin
As now I hide my face

Each tear shed from your eyes
A precious little gem
These diamonds that you cry
I force you now to spend

I wished them stored away
And never to be spent
Why do I make you pay
And charge this wretched rent

The tax of being with me
It seems too high a cost
Oh how I deeply grieve
These precious stones you've lost

And yet you still draw near
Having paid the awful price
Those diamonds, oh so clear
They glisten in my vice

Helplessness

What horror be unknowable,
Yet seems, does it, familiar?
It is, that when to one you hold
You know you have no power

They say they love you deepest
And so you do they cleave
But yet, to your distress

You fear that they will leave

That someday a dreaded truth
Twill cross their lovely lips
That they do not love you
And leave you there helpless

And so with all the strength you have
You give to them you love
You offer them your open hands
In hopes they will not shove

You help them everyday
Beneath the hot sun's light
In hopes to claim a prize, they stay,
To hold them in the night

Your arms are not a prison
They be but an embrace
That if accepted by them
It means that they will stay

But being with another
No matter what you do
It still carries the horror
That they could leave from you

Free Will

Love is letting go
To love without control

Giving one freedom of their voice
Allowing them to make their choice

Remaining with them when their wrong
And not casting them off when hope is gone

Oh love is very hard indeed
But love, I fear, is what we need

Labor Of Love

I'm afraid of marriage

"Why?"

Well, it's just
The hormonal love that we experience
It only lasts for about a year
Then, were really just friends again
Friends, together in awkward living arrangements

"I know you're scared"

How can I keep you?
You won't be blinded by love anymore
You'll see me as I really am
And I'm afraid you'll leave me
Afraid you won't love me

"So you'll just have to show me
How much you care
You do know that kindness and helpfulness
They create hormonal responses too
They don't last a year, but a few months or weeks
Can you be kind once a day?"

It won't be enough

"You'll never know until you try
Love is both noun and verb
Show me how much you care
And I, I will reciprocate"

I'm scared

"Do you think,
That I don't share those fears?"

Anonymous

I'm writing this for someone else
For the one without a voice
The person whose inner self
Is not as confident in their choice

"I love you more than words can say
As this poet knows quite well
It is my heart that you doth slay

I'm captured by your spell"

"You came and found me in the dark
Broken, blind and lost
And with your kindness warmed my heart
Melting away the frost"

"That loneliness that I once had
Once shrouded in despair
It now is gone, no longer sad
Your love has made me care"

"Without my shell protecting me
Skin tender to the touch
More vulnerable than I used to be
To you I hold and clutch"

"I'm not sure what I'd ever do
If you ever left my side
My life is centered around you
Your love is but my pride"

I know no other way to say
What other people want
But, inside, I know they cannot stay
Or they will die and haunt

Caves

There can be love
In places dark and deep
That up above
In the light to which we keep

There is much hate
It stands but masked
Telling us, lovingly, that love can wait
It knows no such thing, it can't be tasked
Prove yourself
Is what it asks

In darkest places
Way down deep
You prove your love

Kaden Moeller

With what you keep

Proposal

Will you come
Come
Come with me, together
And will you be
Be
Be with me, forever

Submissive

I give to you my porcelain heart
This smooth white human gem
A fragile peace of art
Be this pail blood basin

This gift I give to you
My most valued possession
Is all that I can do
To show you my affections

I cannot give the world
Or promise you the moon
Nor make the stars to twirl
Or make the sea to swoon

Offer I, but what I have
Know I it isn't much
Not gold or gems, rather the bland
Porcelain, to hold and touch

I know, now as you feel it
It has a couple cracks
To you, my heart I've lent
Oh please don't give it back!

Becoming A Parent

Oh two of you, my parents
The halves who made me whole
But to whom fate would grant
No baby girl to hold

But how you loved your son

And dreamed him dreams so high
That he would meet someone
Who'd touch the endless sky

And as your child, I
Did work to make it well
To show my inner drive
To you, oh who could tell

And then the day did come
When someone found my heart
And back to you I run
Know not I where to start

"Oh joy of joys!" I say
"My mother and my father"
A gift from past once prayed
"I bring to you a daughter"

The Contract

And so, you've signed
And agreed
The right to receive
Both; dreams and nightmares

You have agreed that
You will take any call
Be it night or day
And answer
Knowing
Anything could be said

You have agreed to
Hold both life and death
In your arms
When the time comes
And be powerless to both

You agree to use
All of your strength
Every ounce
To do everything you can
But know that

161

Kaden Moeller

Your decision
Is not the final one

You have agreed
Both of you
One to each other
To be wed

Ring Around

On the playground

You stumble, and you skin your knee
I see you fall, come up do I, and kneel
Your eyes, now tearful, look at me
This pain you know, now do I feel

We lay together

Your eyes dry, they deeply stare
Into my soul, I find you glancing
My hands, they move, and brush your hair
Grasping my hand, rise we in dancing

In flowing dress

We circle round, laughing in joy
I hold you close to me in bliss
You're no girl, and I'm no boy
And heal, do we, our pain in kiss

Lovers

To see the bride there smiling
Oh such a pretty lass
Her eyes, oh they were shining
Like leather after swamp-ass

And her groom's a man's man
With muscles large and plump
His skin is tough and tanned
Much like the rhino's rump

Giving his daughter off to he
Her father's tears were showing
Watching the rings exchange

162

His mucus, it twas flowing

The bridesmaid though, it seems
Stands out like a hole
She steals the show so sweetly
With her great bulging mole

The flower girl stood smiling
Within the heat so muggy
Her button nose and bucked toothed grin
So cute that she was ugly

Her mother sat in shock
Just trying not to brag
Her face, so worn by love
Looked like a wizened hag

The best man stands there rigid
With his one lazy eye
And a happiness as livid
As a man about to die

So happy was the crowd
An occasion so memorable
This of family and of friends
Just like a funeral

"Speak now or..."
Says the priest
Then up the crowd does stand
Not to hold their peace

Here Comes The Bride

There, right there, down the isle
In a procession of flowers and joy
A gift wrapped white; she smiles
At I, her groom; now a boy

And everything comes in a flash
My hopes for our future; my dreams
Along with what's of us that's past
Those days and these nights so serene

Kaden Moeller

My knees, oh they do but buckle
As one hand now but covers my face
A gift oh so beautiful
Who wrapped herself for my embrace

I cannot believe she's for me
I cannot believe I am loved
I've never felt so happy
It's more than I could dream of

And comes she up quickly to me
To hold me; the happiest man
I must look oh so unseemly
It seems I can but hardly stand

"I love you" is said by my dearest
"I love you" again and again
She then wipes my tears with her dress
And brings me from child to man

And so we say our vows
Here in this place, together
And so then cheers the crowd
As watch we join and wed here

Conjugation

Now stand, do we, betwixt
Our passion and our fear
Where now our lives do mix
As stand both do we here

A subtle glance between
Our blushing fearful smiles
As here we do now glean
Our greatest test and trial

Oh we two best of friends
Who will not stand in wanting
Our lives now do we blend
A mixture, oh so daunting

A game now do we play
Of love, and the tears we'll cry
The rules are, to stay
You win the day you die

164

To work between the boundaries
Of two competing souls
And somehow forgive the frailty
Of the one you grow to know

To hold in warm embrace
And listen to their heart
To, with its beat, keep pace
And forgive them from the start

Accept that we will learn things
That now, they be unknown
The baggage that the other brings
Is their life now made known

We will see many special things
And we'll tell many lies
And feel, will we, the things they bring
As live, do we, our lives

A special hope this be
But not one made on faith
On trust and work and love do we
Come together in this place

With all these things in mind
We say our vows with courage
Our love, it is not blind
It's but one part of marriage

Honeymoon

I wish I could keep this moment
This one special time
I wish I could keep it and lock it away
To visit it from time to time
And remember you this way

But, most of all
I wish I could keep it for you
I wish you could remember how happy you look
How perfect you are
And I wish you knew all of it forever

Oh to give this to you
The knowledge of how much I care
How much I love you, and love looking at you
That smile, right now, I am so happy
You're so happy

I wish I could bottle your joy
And when times get tough
When I fall short of your expectations
And I most certainly will
I can wash that taste of failure out with this

I so wish I could capture this moment
To visit it with you when things got bad
To hold you to me as we dream of youth together
Holding close and thinking on this moment
How I wish it were so easy

I find this desire strong
And yet, I cannot do it
I cannot capture this
Can't keep you in this moment
So, I best enjoy it now

Moving

Today, I just moved in
With my other half
And with a nervous grin
I try hard just to laugh

As in, I drag my trunk
Filled with my memories
My throat, oh it does lump
This trunk's not just with me

So to, in do I bring
The suitcase of my dreams
The handle, oh it stings
It weighs more then it seems

In also do I carry
My pocketbook fears
With help, they are not scary
So long as you are near

So I unpack these things
A little at a time
What is it that I bring?
In this baggage of mine

"Oh I hope that you're not angry
It's in all shapes and sizes"
"Oh honey, quite the contrary
You know I love surprises"

The Conundrum

How do I say *"I love you"*
Anew but once a day
And make you feel in full
The joy of yesterday

When we were younger lovers
When we were all but perfect
Before we knew each other
And on that love reflect

If only I could kindle
Those wild un-tempered flames
Who were both brave and bashful
And were not balked by shame

Oh how can I remind you
Of what brings you to smile
To let your heart renew
What time passed, back awhile

Like echoes midst the vapors
Of times long fading kiss
A feeling, both of us, neither
Can claim we cannot miss

So how can I but clear
That fog, and give a view?
A special love reminder
And make you feel renewed

Oh but to do this once

Kaden Moeller

Each day; us two together
A challenge, though not one
That I would shirk from; never

Hellenism

Oh my love
How can I express, to thee
My heart
My soul
My inward being
Has wrapped itself around you
Embraced you

You'll never be separate from me
If you should die, I will go with thee

You'll take me with you
Down to the grave
For even if I still yet live
My soul will die, and
Will follow you

I will not be apart from thee
The underworld won't keep you from me

Not death
Nor deepest chasm
No gulf is too wide
No path too narrow

I will never be apart from you
No matter what the fates may do

<u>Contemplation</u>

Kaden Moeller

Going Clear

Clarity! Clarity! Come for me
Clarity! Clarity! Give me ease
But wrap your arms around me
And sooth my inmost parts
To let me travel gaily
And lighten up my heart

Clarity! Let me wander
Clarity! Allow me ponder
To put my thoughts upon the page
And draw up places yonder
As let me take the center stage
As imagination's founder

Please think me not a mad man, clarity
Please think me not insane, clarity
For I desire thee the most
To hold you close to me
And be the one who, of you, boasts
Of deep intimacy

So take me, sweetest, clarity
Allow me, grace, clarity
And let me but once more
Be stricken by your presence
Please, of me, don't abhor
And to me don't relent

Contemplation

I want to be alone today
Don't want to feel happy and gay
I want to sit and slowly descend
Into a madness without end

I want to feel pure despair
Alone, with no one standing there
To die a little more inside
And wish, so hard, that I could hide

Surrender, will I, my life to flux
Whose god is change, its truth and crux
Oh I am not on the rock, so grand
But rather on the sinking sand

170

So here I sit, dark and silent
My solitude is harsh and violent
Just let me sit here in darkened mood
Let me fester, rage and brood

The Villen

I want to be a monster
A beast; the worst of which
Whose presence would devour
And make the mind to sick

To be the source of more
Than fear or trembling
To be the greatest horror
That life could surely bring

Whose sight causes distress
Whose voice conveys but terror
Whose words are uttered; best
When in the dead of winter

With a soul like placid tar
And eyes turned but a void
My scenery but char
The ash of the destroyed

To be but lacking empathy
And never need compassion
To take pleasure in cruelty
And know not the lack of them

To be what fear is made of
A weight uncompromising
That sinks the spirit with a shove
And brings the eyes to dying

To be a darkness; deepest
Where shadows fear to tread
The most ominous presence
That's ever to be said

And when my enemies

Look but towards my frame
They feel their spirit freeze
In cold and cutting pain

The dread that I bring with me
Should be but stark and thick
And bring to my heart glee
As you but run from it

And I, I know no boundaries
No limit to my wrath
I find no moral quandaries
In clearing out my path

I'll search and find a foe
Whose worthy of my fire
And bring their world to cold
As it be my desire

My service to myself
Is that I hold no idol
Except for what you've felt
My love is what I do

The Meaning Of Life

As I sit in somber mood
Upon the deepest bits of me I brood
And try, do I, to lift me up
To put some cheer into my gut

I try to help those I don't know
To build them up and watch them grow
And this did please me great indeed
But didn't fill my restless need

Rejoicing over my enemies failures
Crowing over the loss of their hard labor
And though I cackled long with glee
It still did not quite satisfy me

So than I chose to build my mind
Learn, did I, all I could find
And so my wisdom grew, and yet
So many things I could not get

Sitting, I ponder, what to do
The answer, in my mind, I knew
Your life is not for anything
It's like a song, whose words you sing

A Good Buddy

My misery is my company
In whom do I confide
She's always there for me
From her I never hide

She sooths me with her sorrow
And consoles me on my knees
With her there's no tomorrow
There's only what I see

And though my sight is blurry
My vision now obscure
I never have to worry
I'm not alone with her

The best of friends are we, oh yes, indeed
Our depth goes far beyond
Any relationship that could ever be
This bond of ours is strong

I don't hate her, this vengeful one
Who doesn't like my joy
She doesn't leave me alone with fun
She knows time will break my toy

No matter how I push her back
Or say that I'm not lonely
She'll fall with me into the crack
Oh, what loyalty

Masochist

Has ever but there been
A type of misery
That you could revel in
To bring thee ecstasy?

A type of torment, sweetest
That ever was to be
So much so that your flesh
Wish not part from this feeling

What be this pleasure to thee,
Can you but safely say,
That this sweet misery
Is something that will stay?

A Time

I love sadness
It's like depression
They are the things that are always there for me

That falling feeling
Or wretched pressure
The horror you know, but cannot be

The greatest raiment
And loosest cloth
With eyes dressed in tears as blurry and smooth as silk

Of the truth
Or unpleasant fact
Its bitter sweetness, course as silt

The lovely wandering
The empty shell
The weight atop from a love relieved

A certain time
Time of grief
A time experienced, and not believed

Chained

My shadow, like my soul
It has been chained to me
And like a marionette, I hold
Its strings, dancing for all to see

Eclipsed, is it, by many things
And covered up by light
As painfully I pull the strings

Pulling them left and right

Tis like a dancing slave girl
Skin bruised, with all laid bare
Her chains, they weigh the world
A load she cannot share

Her veins, they are the strings
Pulled out to make her dance
Oh the pain it brings
Pleas, of which no one grants

She's but a novelty
A toy, a child's puppet
No matter every scream from she
Her possession, do I, covet

And every day she tries to leave
Every attempt, a failure
As over her chains and strings, she grieves
While dancing for her jailer

This prison in which my spirit dwells
This jail for my will
It is a type of cosmic hell
For should either depart, it kills

Loneliness

I asked my spirit the other day
"Do you know what it's like to feel alone?
To be amidst a crowd, and say
I feel I'm unknown"

The crowd, it towers over me
As shrink I smaller still
My words, they seem as whispers, they
Fade and come to nil

Oh no heads, will they, turn
No eye will glance my way
My skin, I feel it squirm
They hear not what I say

175

As loneliness encroaches with the crowd
The people fall away
The words, though they be loud
They hear not what I say

Speaking the language of the lonely
Of the invisible
As cry out, do I *"Oh, if only!*
Can't you see my soul!?"

But hear they nothing of me
No matter what the words
It seems I'll never be
Listened to, or heard

To my spirit, this I told
And then I asked her, dejectedly
"Like I, do you feel cold?"
As look, did I, at she

She looked out at me, smiling
Knowing I felt forlorn
And then she said, while sighing
"With you, I feel warm."

"I'm with you always, everywhere
You never are alone
So why is it that you're so scared?
You are where I call home"

"You are not small to me
You are my castle walls
No matter who you want to be
I'll always hear your call"

But the loneliness, it did not leave
And I but looked away
I'm missing something that I need
Though she hears what I say

As sit together we
Right next to each other
Laying your head upon my knee
You'd be unhappy with another

<u>Passion</u>

Kaden Moeller

Standing Still

Eyes upon you
Strange pressure

A feeling of lonely company
The fearful sensation, of being seen

Shame

I'm naked
And you see
What is it that you feel, for me?

Beautiful And Terrible

Of both the fear and joy
That comes when being loved
A terrible ecstasy
That both of you lust of

You want to feel pleasure
And yet there's fear and shame
You are so self-aware
Of your now naked frame

You want to touch the other
But you don't understand
Why do they call you lover,
And, to you, extend a hand?

Oh you, you do desire
But also know yourself
And feel you the ire
Of being loved and felt

You feel so unworthy
Of this strange special gift
You think yourself so dirty
And do not understand it

The privilege of such a thing
To be loved and in turn
Reciprocate this feeling
Towards the one you yearn

The beauty and the terror
That is intimacy
To know that what you bear
Another calls lovely

Getting It One

So, Steve and Mary Sue
They are about to do it!
What they're about to do
It makes them squirm a bit

Yea, they are all excited
Though a little bit embarrassed
To be naked, though distracted
By the other one, undressed

Yes, Steve was sporting something
A bulbous growth, so swollen
It made funny his walking
Though helped speak words unspoken

And she, so slender, smiling
The object of his love
Though she, down there, twas glistening
And slimy like the slug

And both were there, so sweaty
So much so that they stunk
For the other were they thirsty
But both already drunk

So floundered they awhile
Deep in their murky lust
Oh most days they'd revile
The smell of other's musk

Though he knew not all the ins and outs
He'd certainly studied well
The material had been brilliant
A graphic manual!

And bounced they, up and down
To and fro, side to side

Making the monkey sounds
Those moans and shouts and cries

The sweat, it travels down
The long arch of the back
Until it went and found
The start of the butt-crack

His grunts and groans, so guttural
Crescendoed in highest pitch
He was quite happy, though
She was sore, that was it

A Sacrifice

A woman lays before me, unclad
An offering is she, so glad
A nervous joy upon her face
She's with me in this special place

As I survey her naked flesh
Embarrassed, is she, but also blessed
I lift myself above her frame
And plunge into her a swift sharp pain

Her eyes tear up from this first blow
As from her now, the life's blood flows
Her body now, it tenses up
Her hands reach out for me to clutch

The ritual is now complete
Her sacrifice was so complete
Her gift was not to what's above
But rather me, the one she loves

Excitement

I love to look at you
How your sight sets me afire
I know not why tis true
That you spark my desire

To see your sweat laced thighs
And wish to glide upon them
As to make wide your eyes
That I might fall into them

And let the incense of your scent
Caress and waft round me
Until intoxicated, and
Made meditate on thee

To let my hand slide cross you
To grasp all that I can
Though futile, it is true
I'll always try again

And how I taste your love
That strange sweet pungent fruit
As sweat, it glistens off
And twinkles upon you

And I'll bathe in your beauty
For why should I refrain
To love you totally
Is more than I could claim

Men

Drops, manly drops, so small
They bead forth top the slit
A clear little purl, balanced precariously
Shining as a fire upon a turgid torch
Glinting beneath the soft beams of love light
Evening beams, night beams, soft light
This gem of desire, secreted in lust
Teeters, its formation too large
And so it slides, gently, softly, slowly
Down the exterior of this manly aqueduct
Until it lightly caresses the reservoirs beneath it
Only to drip from them to the ground

Oh the scent, the love scent of a man
So heavy, as his body, so reflective
It conveys the weight of him, his love, his desire
All about him does this
His body, his scent, how he makes love
For even if he were passive, his body surges
He pumps, his own body, without his control
And only as a man does he do this

Every motion, voluntary and involuntary
Makes him a man

Strained to the utmost, he longs for love
His manly frame desires embrace; fears loneliness
His mindscape is awash in insecurity
He does not wish to be without, he is vulnerable
And how he loves, he loves so strongly
Holding his beloved, breathing their sweat
He loves them; feeling their warm frame
Pressed against his chest
Oh how this makes him feel, a man
He knows himself when he is with his lover
For he knows his love, and he loves them

His passions, how he flexes them
How he, with all his strength, works to be embraced
To have his body cradled
To feel the warm acceptance of helpless joy
As he feels the pressing of his lover's arms, legs and depths
To be fully free and totally bound
Restrained, by loving hands; to stay
Unbound, by his nature; to fuck
His loins, they press, deeper and deeper
As if to become one, to go inside, to indwell the lover
To be curled up again within another; total embrace; total acceptance
And as he thrusts, his moans; they sing
A song that manhood knows
"I cannot plant my love in you, but I can sow my seed
For oh, I wish that sowing proved that love would grow in thee"

And he is joyful, and he is ashamed
He is strong, but so afraid
To have and to hold, is pleasure
But, to be held and cared for, is love
And men want love, need love, crave love
To know one looks at them; at night
When they lay there asleep
And with compassion in their eyes
Will lightly touch their cheek
For men, they are not monoliths
Not stones, or frozen hearts
They are flesh and blood, and they wish you knew
Wish you could see, that they long to be taken
To be longed in as much as they long
To be loved as much as they love

They but only desire their own desires returned upon them
To be precious in another's sight

But, as a man, we are unsure of our desirability
Even amongst ourselves
But, that beauty, that strange beauty of men
The knowledge of their inmost soul
Knowing that a man's confidence is as emotional and ephemeral as the wind
That in his depths he is as uncertain of being loved as he is of the length of his
life
A man is only as powerful as his lover grants him
For he is stronger when he feels their love upon him
And weakest when he is farthest from it

His heart, pumping, priming his masculine organ
Pushing, pulsing and flaring with delight and pent up desire
His blood, loosed from his heart; the source of his love
It jubilantly dances throughout his vessels, and floods the aqueduct
Bringing to brimming his bounteous reservoirs of lust
He is ready, yet he restrains, attempting to prolong the act
His love making, he wishes his partner joy immeasurable, pleasure unceasing
But how his nature scolds him *"Release!"* it cries *"Release!"*
"Children, make more children, fill the earth with them, your children!"

But men are more than such desires
And their love goes beyond their lover's sex
Their simple mortal coil; the body
Men love, and make love, in great strength; regardless and with joy
They seek a beloved whom girds them for life
Who surrounds them with affection and soft warmth
A warmth only a resting body beside can deliver

Sweat, sweet sweat lapped up, midst seething breaths
Tong tasting and searching all places
To know, to know in deepest region
All parts of the beloved
As his un-abating piston primes his partner, as his heart does his manhood
And all is finished
His sex spasms and splashes, a syrup, running its thick essence through and
upon his lover
It's sticky nectar wiped and sliding midst the fingers of the one so loved
So loved; as to impart himself upon, into, towards; in passion

How men wish bask in the cool silence of sex's after-moan

The delirious act, now a loving embrace and a tapering of lovers' excitement
The sweet sprinklings if *"I love you"* mixed with soft raindrops of kisses
Arms round one another, bodies still closely pressed
Their sweat, slightly clinging them together
And a placid mind, free of the fear of loneliness

Oh, this is what it is to be a man
To be a man; so vulnerable
Wherefore such strength?
Are we not just as all, people awaiting another?
Yes, we men know this
That we are strong, strong when we possess the one thing unattainable by might
Strong when we have stumbled across the affections of another
Though we cannot understand
How came we by this treasure? We knew not where to look
But love is there, and we want it
Love is there, and we need it
Love it there, and men chase it, we chase it; to be captured

A Drink Of Fire

Oh would you light me up
And set my heart ablaze
Your sparks, oh let them drop
To light this dark malaise

And make my feet to flight
To rise up with the smoke
Unto the highest heights
As passions do you stoke

To shout, from rooftops, gaily
In joyous anxiety
For you, you make me happy
Oh just to be with thee

My eyes, they lap you, lustingly
They drink you deep and long
To quench what now is burning
But this fire be too strong

And so I quaff and chug
To keep the fire low
And calm this blaze of love
Relieved as we two hold

Grabbing At Flames

To grasp lust with the lover
That temptress made to flesh
Who taunts thee like no other
To feast upon the breast

And drink deep from the fount
Sprung from thy lover's passion
To drink until made drunk
And still desire them

And have, both as you slept
Wake neither to distress
Rather, hope, in has crept
A joyful playfulness

And as the dawn but breaks
And slides across the skin
Those sunbeams loving licks
Alights their bashful grins

To sweat desire from thee
And pour it out like water
To cool passions now made free
Those flames sprung from the lover

And wash, will these sweet raindrops
As sprinkle they upon
As from the one begot
Now cleansed from lust, so strong

Oh happy be the coals
Beneath a summer rain
Still burning, not so old
But knowing they will wane

Loving

Oh sweetest be the nectar
That beads upon the flesh
Of those who call you hither
Thy tender lover's sweat

And best be the embrace
That covers all around
And leaves thee not a space
To cool thy body down

And then that burning in your chest
It moves within your belly
Then where the two of you connect
And swells inside of thee

Tis like you're dying to impart
Not just a piece of thee
But all the contents of your heart
Do wish to fill their body

And as your soul bursts from you
To blanket theirs with love
You wish that it was true
That they were blood of blood

Though tender be the lips
And supple be the flesh
It is the taste one gets
Of who they are tis best

Security Blanket

My boy, my sweet boy
A man made playful before me
And I; his greatest joy
Do tantalize and tease

And he is everywhere
Upon and in
His scent doth pierce the air
As he deeply groans within

Oh, such fragility
My lovely one
My boy; so thick and manly
Wishes love be upon

He loves me
Pressing, gripping, groping
To have all that he sees
His heart but only hoping

What he wants
His greatest desire
Tis not but to vaunt
But love; that, he requires

He loves more, my embrace
Than any he could give
And so, now, do I grace
To him a love so vivid

I grip him close to me
With all of me at once
And in his eyes I see
Bliss hit him with brunt

More than his loving me
He wants his love returned
To cease feeling lonely
And end the lover's yearn

He wants to be desired
To be held in acceptance
To be something required
For someone else's existence

His touch, to him, is something
He wants me but to yearn for
No, not just that pleasant feeling
But the person behind the pores

To him; he isn't pretty
So what makes him beautiful?
I find him rather silly
He's vain and yet so bashful

And as my boy lays next to me
Arms round me; hands cupping my breasts
I feel his steady breathing
And sense a slight distress

He's ever such a child
And yet he is a man
I give a subtle smile

Kaden Moeller

And lightly touch his hand

He's no more grown than I
I just find that it's funny
That men aren't meant to cry
And yet they're frail things

Making Love

With lustful passion in her eyes
She grips me tightly with her thighs
I drink in the sight of silky flesh
Sliding my hands across her breasts

She runs her fingers through my hair
The scent of skin floats in the air
Her sweat drips off her curves like rain
Cooling my passions burning flame

I bring her close to me, she gasps
Her breaths are quick, and oh so fast
She quivers in waves atop of me
Her body bathed in ecstasy

With eyes now wide, we deeply stair
And think, do we, of what we've shared

The Dance Of Life

Warmth begins surrounding me
As deeper I go into she
A pressure that I can't describe
A pleasure confirmed by her cry

This strange dance that we now perform
And expression of the love we've formed
Conjoined together, that are we
As tightly are you gripping me

I grasp now tensely you to I
Released now are we, with a sigh
A strange numbness washes over us
Our eyes reflect our naked lust

You blush, and turn away in haste
A smile creeps across your face

188

I pull you up to me so close
I've gave you much, but not the most

Your lips form words that I do miss
As silence I you with my kiss
Desire you to me do I
We give the dance another try

A Moonlit Night

My dark night laden beauty
Oh such a frame so fair
And skin, lush, as I smoothly
Breathe in thy sweat-laced air

Your lips; the softest pillows
Part slightly at my touch
Revealing those white perils
Whom make thy smile up

And lose myself, do I
In the auburn jungle of your hair
In which sweat drops from thy
Bring forth a wild and fragrant air

And drink I; deeply of you
From lushes lips so fair
As your ashen palms hold to
My sweaty lust; laid bear

To let my hands sink in
To those supple midnight hips
And feel the bed lust lays within
When passion stops its fits

And now those smooth firm chocolate thighs
Do tantalize my fingers
And taste you, do they, as they glide
Upon the damp interior

The humid sweetness of the night
I find, just like the day
Is beautiful, and brings to light
Our passions, light and gay

Kaden Moeller

Manhood

Oh look at all the dewdrops
That formed upon your skin
Condensed from you; so soft
Withholding trepidation

And look at how your flesh has flushed
So tender, firm and ripe
A fruit which yearns, but to be touched
In middle of the night

But what also of your eyes
Glossy and moist within
Who twinkle, gleam and shine
As emerald diadems

To listen to your voice
As it but comes out in breaths
And hear it guide my loins
As feast I on your breast

For you but bring to me
No gifts of rock or stone
Yet, oh you make me greedy
When we two are alone

I want to fill the earth
With children birthed from you
And every day to work
To ever fill your womb

My god, to watch the dewdrops
Now glisten in the sun
No gem, no gold, no rock
Gleams as your sweat does run

Milking

I am here
Between my cutie boy's thighs
With those curly little hairs
I've come to hear his sighs

I've laid myself upon

The alter of masculinity
To worship and to fawn
My loving deity

I cradle, now his manhood
Tucked softly in my bosom
Embraced, in mammary love
My man now revels in them

He's splayed; back on the bed
His hands but reaching out
Clawing the sheets soft spread
As coax I, his love, come out

I smile at him, daringly
Bringing his face to flower
I find that crimson cross his cheeks
The pleasure of the hour

And now the subtle spasms
That cause he press to me
His love is stirring in him
To plant in me his seed

But I do slow his pace
Loosening my embrace
And watch, as flushed, his face
Pants and prays my grace

I gawk here, at his tip
So ripe, about to burst
It's flared, so hard, his dick
Leaks syrup for my thirst

And I envelope him
Into the tightest hug
His hips go mad, and then
His lust released its love

His fuck sprays onto me
And glistens on my breasts
As feel still, do I, him twitching
There in my loving chest

His body, then, it loosens
His tension's been released
As I stare at his semen
I can't help but think deep

'This is a part of him
This man, the one I love
If I twould put it in
What life would we make up?'

'What whole would then be made
From our two separate halves?
Oh what am I thinking?
This is his birthday bash'

Numbers Game

With supple lips, we faintly kiss
Places nor often touched
Our loving licks do bring to bliss
Though never oft enough

Tis like our skin reached deep within
And found our heart twas wanting
As they reached in, by passed our sin
A feat far more than daunting

And this did say, in strangest way
They'd found our inner beauty
Our flesh made gay, as do we play
Sweet music made from we

As dance us two, our sweat laced dew
Does slowly slide between
The lonely parts of you, not yet carved through
By tong, those sweet ravines

A blush between, and so it seems
That we be not quite proud
Should some have seen, this funny scene
Would we go take a bow?

What Is Happening?

Oh of the life within thy breast
I bury my face in thy chest

These breaths thy breath be not the same
You grip me tight and call my name

Oh is it that my love for thee
Be not that it ever leave from me
These passions of thy mortal shell
Render not my life a living hell

A Bath

A dream, one night, did have I
A woman, naked, did I spy
She called me forth to wash her body
And so I did, in melancholy

Clean every inch of supple flesh
Why did I this, I cannot guess
Her beauty, oh, it was unending
Yet my actions, not descending

I looked into her eyes deeply
And felt, did I, my fear and pity
She was so beautiful to see
No passions did arise in me

This dream, that which, some may call sad
The best dream that I've ever had

<u>Philosophy</u>

Law

This is the law
The law of the land
A man kills his vice
And cuts off his hand

Dancing

Wisdom is dancing with me
In such close proximity
Brushing her hair against my face
She keeps me in flirtatious pace

Her eyes give me seductive glance
My heart's the drum-beat of the dance
The sweat beads trickle from my brow
Our bodies play, they sway and bow

As sparks of pleasure flash about
No memory comes of being without
No worthy life could ever be
If I could never dance with thee

And so I hold you, we embrace
I do not wish to leave this place

Everything

To be nothing, what does that mean?
Be it as frightful as it seems?
To be a void, without a place
Being blank, without a face

To be empty, without a soul
Be but a shell, a living hole
To see yourself as everything
For tis what it is to be nothing

Knowledge

Much I do not know
My mind, it needs to grow
To cultivate it, like a crop

And nurture every little thought
For as they spring forth, and become deeds
Actions fulfilling wants and needs
Expressing forth what's in my head
Things well remembered, when I'm dead

Certainty

I am unsure
They say it's a sin
What's the answer?

Convention

I'm here to catch men of intellect
They're hard to find, much less get
Gathering them is much like herding cats
Or catching a swarm of swirling gnats

Their individuality prevents this thing
The sparks between their minds can sting
And yet these sparks can set ablaze
The minds of those now gone malaise

Oh yes it is a funny sight
To watch the greatest minds unite
And then be spit on and ignored
By those who do so for the Lord

And so it matters vary little
These sparks and all the flames they kindle
They are a blight unto belief
Disproving them would bring relief

But little do they understand
That reality makes one demand
With knowledge, ignorance dissolves
Now learn from it, and just evolve

Secular Morality

Chaos I've come to wrangle thee
Your lawlessness will not take me
Straddled atop your mighty frame
Break you, will I, and make you tame

You buck and writhe, and throw your back
Spectators say I can't do that
But as our battle long ensues
The cheers slowly eclipse the boos

And those who said it can't be done
They fold their arms and frown the fun
The bronco keeps on bucking still
I hold on tight with all my will

But the stallion twirls wildly round
And off I fly and hit the ground
The crowd grows silent and concerned
While naysayers scoff, noses upturned

So there I lay, some think deceased
And up to I then comes the beast
Deep into me this void now stares
This untamed abyss into which I glare

Round me, this nothing trots about
Up do I rise, the crowd gives shout
Mocking stands this madness free
But its master will I be

Some still do say *"This you cannot do!"*
So do I rise to go round two

School

How is it that one can learn?
A simple answer, one must yearn
Learning comes from a desire
A spark that kindles a great fire

And once the flame takes hold within
That mind shall never then be dim
That fire will then become a blaze
A flaming all consuming haze

Want, it will, to touch and burn
And spread throughout you like a germ
Let it blossom deep inside
To bloom into your secret pride

To move inside you and infect
Every thought you let it get
Don't let your mind wall off the flames
Let them rage, wild and untamed

For so long as knowledge builds you up
No door before you will stay shut
You'll see the world with different eyes
And see through, will you, the many lies

Words Of Wisdom

Our words are broader that you think
They're fluid water which we drink
For when words are rigid and don't adapt
They then are used to ignore the fact

It isn't about the definition alone
Its tone, syntax, the mouth, their home
It's what's between the words that count
The strength of the words we ride and mount

We can't be blinded by our speech
We must be wise when we beseech
Our abstract and complicated thoughts
A thing that only words have brought

Spots And Blemishes

What is perfection?
The answer is quite simple
There can be no rejection
Or even spot or wrinkle

No one could criticize
The thing that's now supposed
Not able to divide
This door that should be closed

It would be evident
And need no speculation
All eyes, when they're present
Would give no alteration

But it would not be beautiful

It would be but a fact
So indisputable
That no one could change that

However, there's no problem
Because there are no perfect things
And we are better for them
For that's where beauty springs

No True Scotsman

I know the true Scotsman
I have seen him
Met him personally
Nice guy

He's helpful; kind to strangers
Always considerate; thinking of others
Give what he can; selfless
And he is as we all should be

He is human
And not just any human
The kind of human who tries to be humane
The only kind of human we want

So, when we say
Of some other soul
"You're no true Scotsman!"
We're saying *"You're inhumane!"*

So, yea, we've all met the true Scotsman
And I must say
We meet true Scotsmen everyday
Humane humans

Come And See

Go down with me; my friend
Let us go down into that molten pit
Let us burn our palms and knees as we slide down the rocks
Let us sear our flesh as the vapors of heat rise round us
Oh yes, descend, should we
Into that hopeless place; that land of despair, long ignored

Oh let the flesh, red raw, protest our ever quickening sliding; into the pit
The center, where we wish wander, is a lonely place; of darkness
Where all of man's contemplation and sorrow weighs heaviest
Where all of life's truth is laden as a heavy vapor
And bask in that airless fog; as your flesh melts from you
Oh, let us go down into the pit

Masculinity

Kaden Moeller

Secret Admirer

What if it were, by fate
An unrequited love, gazed upon you
Looking, with longing and admiration
Desire seething in them, a sorrow so pure
And you knew them; you were friends
Best friends, so close
But they, for fear and knowledge
Never told you their love
How they wanted to, wanted to burst
Loose those pent up waters; raging
Allowing their lips pour forth
Their turbulent emotions
Cascading and crashing round you like rapids
Attempting to chart passage round those feared stones
Of your rejection
To reach you, to speak to you, to have you
Yet, they never speak
They let you go; about your life
Watch you take a hand
And wonder if their silence was wrong
If you would have loved them,
If they had but spoken
But they didn't
Because they are not quite desired
For you, the one they love,
You want the opposite sex
And they are same

Curious

'He's really very pretty'
You say it to yourself
As you watch him, and you see
Who he's standing about

He gets the girls he wants
And they want to be got
They show him as they flaunt
And strut around a lot

I've never looked at guys
Until I had seen him
And now I feel strange *'Why?'*
I do not understand

But girls, I do like them
I do, I really do
So why do I feel strange, and
Like looking at him too

I've never felt so awkward
And yet, I do not know
Of these things I have heard
But, what if he were told

That Night

We were together
You know
Just
Hanging out
Friends
We were talking
Just
Talking

He laughed
Oh how he laughed
I always was good at that
I knew how to make him smile
To
Bring him joy
I knew how

But then
For some reason
The silence lingered too long
It hovered
Loomed over us

We were still smiling
But
Nervously
Something had changed

I don't know when it happened
Was it two days ago
When we stayed out later than we had expected

Kaden Moeller

Or was it a year back
When we couldn't stop talking to each other
I don't know

He moved in close
Too close
The kind of close that scares you
That
Causes your heart to run
I wasn't sure
I both was exited
And scared
Angry even
I both wanted and feared this feeling

He touched
Just touched
Nothing obscene or sensual
Just placed his hand on my shoulder
Just conveyed what I now knew

And
For what seemed and otherworldly age
We gazed into each other
I know not what he saw in me
But it was what I saw in him I wanted
And so
I
I touched him back
And removed my guard

And how he clawed my clothes
He seemed rabid with desire
And I
I had no idea where to start
I floundered with belts
And stumbled on pants
But he quickly dashed such impediments
And then
For the first time
I was naked
Naked before a man

This realization
The feel of the cool caress of the air kissing my skin
It brought me clarity

The haze of passion was cleared away
For but a moment
And I stood
Hesitantly
My hands both shaking with desire and trepidation
I was to be his

He noticed
And his ravenous temperament abated
Coming up behind me
Draping his arms about my shoulders
He whispered
Soft
Soothing things

I felt him
I felt his pressing up against me
And though his words were calm
His body
His magnificent manly body
It spoke
It said to me
"You are the object of my desires
You are that which will make me whole
I want you!"

And then
With excitement and anxiety
I motioned him my readiness
And he
So gently
He kissed me as we moved

My back
Arched
And how strange it was
To feel him
To envelope him
It was
It was odd
Uncomfortable?
Painful?
At first

To him
This idea
I had just realized
I'd given him my first
My first experience
Given him
My virginity

His motion
As it quickened
I felt things
Pressure
Pounding
Throbbing
My heart quickened in excitement
I was somewhere else
I was at the peak of arousal
Never had I felt this way
I felt pleasure eclipse all other sensations
No longer was this strange
All shame and embarrassment
Melted away in this embrace
I felt
Like nothing ever before
And I collapsed
Breathing heavily
Quivering endlessly

And he
He too was tired
And we lay together
Listening to each other's breaths
To the slow tapering of our hearts
And we held one another close
Saying not a word

I turned over
And looked at him
He
He could only smile
Turning his face away with a blush
And I giggled
He was cute when he was embarrassed

And he
After a time

He slid his hand across my face
Caressing the stubble there
And felt I then ashamed
Felt I
I had not done what I should have
To look well

But he
He but continued
Running his hand over my cheek
"How's my pretty boy?"
He whispered
And
How strange it was to hear
Yet
I was warmed by it
And oh so comforted

We lay
Long and quiet
Together
And
I must admit
I had never thought, that
I could be this happy

A Work Of Art

We were together, and
He looked at me
Held out his hand
"Do you like what you see?"

Eyes down cast, they glanced
At me, and blushingly
He chanced
"Do you like what you see?"

His legs stammered to and fro
As he stood there nervously
His voice, it quivered low
"Do you like what you see?"

As tremble, did he, cold

Hugging his lonely body
Begging me to hold
"Do you like what you see?"

Oh to lay your body bare
And stand naked for me
I see you standing their
And I love this one I see

By Another Name

Just today; a special day
With nervous in his eyes
My lover gave away
A special bloom, to I

No, twas not a rose
No scarlet did have he
Rather gave me those
Some think not beautifully

He gave what bloomed o're corpses
Twas all he had to offer
In blushing loveliness
He gave me a black flower

What many say aren't pretty
And others call as foul
To show his love for me
He gave to me his all

It lacked the rose's nectar
And had a different scent
And he did slightly shudder
For fear I would reject

And I, ever so moved
That he would give to me
A part of him, to prove
A special love from he

He gave me his black flower
And though it is quite common
He could not give another
Has he but one of them

For though they bloom year round
And no one lacks their presence
I find this gift, somehow
Means more than averageness

For many say no joy
Nor pleasure could come from
A flower from a boy
My ever special someone

But they'd know nothing of
What we two share together
Of your sweet gift of love
Oh such a pretty flower

You needn't gifted me
Affections from your heart
But how I cling to thee
And hope you don't depart

I love this gift you've given
Don't think it isn't precious
Worth more to me than diamonds
Is your sweet hand's caress

Remember will I; always
This humble little present
And how, away you gave
Something the heart has meant

Oh such a subtle joy
As there you blush and cower
Just like a schoolboy
I kiss you; for the flower

Marriage Comes To Florida!

Its wedding bells!
Wedding bells all around!
Its winter time, but the sun is out
Shining high and fine

Do you hear them?
Do you hear the chime?

As tears flow, light and gay
Pleasure that those beloved would know

The restraints are broken!
The captives freed!
Abandoned lay the shackles, happily
Unbound; need lovers struggle?

Cry out, proclaim!
Cheer loud in mirth and glee!
For couples pared, now come together
Embraced, with lives to share

Oh faces, blushing!
Smiles, wide!
Be proud, applaud them all
Intoxicated; make mine calibration loud!

To all the brides and grooms
And all the grooms and brides
And grooms and grooms, and brides and brides
My arms are open wide

Taken Back

One day, out of the blue
Came a knock upon my door
My man had come back to
Beg, plead and implore

"I've changed!" He said to me
"I'm a very different man"
He said it with great glee
Like it was something grand

"Don't tell me you've found Jesus"
Said I from slacking jaw
"No?" said he, in earnest
Relieved, I said *"Thank god"*

And after a time or two
We decided to be wed
And off, like a foreskin, we flew
To Vegas, blushing red

As we went to the alter

To leap up off that ledge
We found our leaping faltered
Morally, Elvis won't do gay marriage

Mighty Fall

I see the one I love
The strongest man I know
Who looks at me because
Of what we have been shown

This man, whose muscles rippled
As swept me off my feet
Whose beads of sweat did trickle
When our passions first did meet

Whose firm and tempting chest
Twas where I'd rest my head
Oh those so supple breasts
That my caress had tread

That heart that beat within
And lulled me off to sleep
As there my mind would spin
Dreams, temptuous and sweet

Oh your embrace twas more
Than kindness in a touch
It caused my heart to soar
Though never high enough

But oh, to see you now
Shaking here in our bed
As fear around you crowds
And echoes silent dread

To lay beside you, helpless
Unable to relieve
That weight, that great distress
A load to never leave

But you are not the only one
Who holds a weight, in part
For as I watch your setting sun

Kaden Moeller

I bear a heavy heart

And though we hold together
It doesn't break the cold
That icy frozen dagger
Who only death could hold

As bask I in the twilight
I hold you at my side
And as it slips to night
I know my love has died

Emotions

The Human Condition

We are all, contradictions
Every one, not one is not
We look back
The things we see
What sights

We change
Change more than once
Flexing and shifting
Building and falling
Starting again

If you were to meet yourself
Before and after
How disappointed would you be?
Should you be disappointed,
That you've changed?

Change; a constant thing
You can always change
We all do it
It's nothing new to us
We; chameleons of the soul
We will always be a different shade

Embracing Life

I wear the uniform of mourning
Wherever I may go
And let this dark adorning
Enjoin with mine own soul

I look upon each tranquil spot
And know that death stood there
And reaped what once was vibrant
Until its husk laid bear

I see the passing lives
Who whirl round about
And like the wind; will fly
Until they taper out

Each breathing body, soon,
Will someday breathe its last

And leave an empty room
Where once a life was stashed

To know that it's inevitable
That tomb; oblivion
Can make some weaker hearts grow cold
And even fear the end

But I wear funeral clothes
And wander bout the earth
With what the mortal lover knows
The secret of life's worth

And so I let the tears to fall
And let the heart to leap
Emotions; I will feel them all
Though knowing I can't keep

Motivator

Magnifying that which we love
Showcasing our passions
Giving out a great show of
An elegant distraction

An over powering affiliation
So total and complete
The greatest form of motivation
And common for deceit

Healthy it be, in moderation
One should not overdose
Succumbing to its inebriation
Razing it up, a toast

For then if we're not careful
It kills those we hold dear
Who is this strange council?
It is your good friend fear

Gets Your Up...

The thing about hatred is
It is a beautiful servant, but a cruel master

It can motivate you to be great
But is a poor wise man or speaking pastor

So long as you are not its slave
It can allow you to attack the horrible
But should it rule over you
It will destroy your soul

Hatred is not really so bad
It allows you to covet what is good
I think people just don't see it so
This part of us is misunderstood

Hate is a part of all of us
One of our most useful tools
It marks the fights for human rights
And reveals all the fools

So hate, you see, isn't quite so bad
When guiding it responsibly
You can achieve a great success
And further a good for all to see

Anxiety

Why is it, that I hate everything?
I hate all of it
I hate my friends, because they distract me
I hate my family for the same reason
Yet, I hate not seeing more of them
I hate being alone
I hate feeling isolated and without connection
But, I hate the effort of being friendly
I hate having to maintain the upkeep of love
I hate having to worry about whether or not I should call
I hate having to take their feelings into account
I hate knowing that I could hurt them
I hate being vulnerable
I hate everything
It just never ends
I hate it
And it drones on and on in my mind
Over and over
I hate this
And it never ends
Some days, it's less of a problem

But, it's always there
I hate it

Personal Conversation

Well now, friend
Its been awhile
Since last we met

As I recall
Our last meeting was a bit, one-sided

Upon our meeting
I must confess
Not much light was there
In my world

But you
Deciding that what was there
Was indeed, too much
And so, you
Snuffed out
The only candle guiding me

You, plunged me into
A world of endless night
So black
Empty
Devoid of light

But
Your soul I caught
Only a glimpse

That dim coal
Faded ash

And that little light
Did I follow
My spirit stoked itself

As step
By step
I perused thee

Kaden Moeller

My hate, burning
Around me
Illuminating the darkness
You cast me in

My rage
Closing in, around
Your dim little spark
What was your soul
Eclipse you, will I
As anger grows

My vengeance
A thirst unquenchable
And you
But a drop
Amidst my inferno
Though you will
Not satisfy
But leave me in
Tempted thirst

The drop that you are to me
I still yearn for
Desire you
Rather than the sea

For you will never put me out
I won't forgive
What is that?
But to forget those
Who suffered most
To desire my own pleasure
In the forgetfulness of forgiveness

No!
I'd rather burn than be doused!
My flames will consume thee
Rage untamed will they
And overtake my soul

For forgetting is unforgivable
This bitter blood that courses here
I quaff it not to quench my thirst
But rather

To rectify my resolve
Finish my revenge
Oh no sweetness comes
Vengeance is unending
An action never to cease

No solace
The journey, is rough
The fruit, is bitter
The rest, is restless
The end, is endless

Spite

Beyond my happiness lies your sorrow
A place which I reserve for tomorrow
A malicious special little prison
An artistic expression of sadism

I'm building up my plan for thee
How shall I express what's within me?
What shall I do to reflect my depth
Of which I feel cannot be met

I think I'll show you what's within
A venomous bit of private sin
The part that infects the body's soul
A part that with the passage of time will grow

I'm going to hunt, and track you down
I'll wash you in my hate, to drown
But death, it will not come to you
I'll let you live, let that be true

You'll never die while I'm around
But torture you down to the ground
And make your life a quivering heap
A worthless mass of mobile meat

Oh this torment shall bring me pleasure
Beyond any and every possible measure
I'll crow over all of your woes
And as you cry, my joy, it grows

I'll see you suffer beneath my will
You'll beg release from my dark chill
But never will I quite be gone
For all your misery makes me strong

Now you may say to me *"But sir!*
Give me relief from your harsh words"
But you sir, just don't understand
I love this art done by my hand

To My Betters

Sincerely, I hate you
I hate who you are and what you stand for
Lying as ever you do
And gaining from it the more

And people let you do this
And you walk around with an air of, false respect
Treating you honorably; to my distress

Oh I hate you, and all you are
To take away that veil of respectability
To rip it wide; ajar
And let my hate go into thee

With the barrier removed
Come crash the waves upon
With nothing now to hold to
And nowhere left to run

Oh let the laughter rise
In scorn and hateful bays
And as it climbs the skies
As more rise up; in waves

To watch them break against you
Crash into you with glee
And break your soul anew
Now wracked with melancholy

And keep that laughter rising
To a whirlpool of rage
From it there is no hiding
It follows every day

The Sweetest Thing

Oh be it all
The greatest joy
When none other pleasure grasped
Think I then of nothing better
Than the dish, I serve, of ash

I do not wish mine enemies
To die nor be made vapor
I want for them to stay
To live longer than all others
And watch them fade away

I want that affluence they hold
To slowly slip from them
To watch them grasp desperately
As all they love grows cold
And all their world ends

And see I them there weeping
As clutch they to their fame
A dead and rotting thing
They claim it in their keeping
Their rotting molded name

To see them losing all they've built
Yet thinking their foundation
It must be strong
Oh but their wrong
As love I see it wilt

To watch them live to see
Death in obscurity
As try they wretchedly
And oh so desperately
To cling to what they grieve

To die a death so slow
One racked with isolation
With all their tribulation
A sorrow that but grows
As they will lose their patience

Oh and I hope they know
That at their funeral
The crowd won't be much of friends
Rather just those they fooled
Who'll meet them at the end

Yes this be pleasure, sweetest
The sorrow of their groan
A type of joy unknown
The best revenge, it be this
To never let them go

A Cold Spot

Revenge; is an ugly thing
Violent, but oh so sweet
Its catharsis, so relieving
Yet oh so short and bleak

If revenge were more like vengeance
That moment it's released
That happy recompense
Would keep our heart relieved

But never it be lasting
That second of our lust
To make another sing
That painful song, so just

The fires in us dim
When vengeance is doled out
And yet they rise again
They'll always be about

An Atheist's Lament

Oh how I lament when evil dies
Naturally, of course
Who live their lives completely
And flourish vibrancy
With no hell to greet them at their death

I cannot help but weep
To cry out bitterly
How much I find repugnant

And yet, none shall be punished
They'll live in lavish luxury

And how I feel helpless
So sorrowful and angered
I feel it deep within me
And yet I have no respite
No way of finding justice

So grieved unto my soul
And so I only wish
I wish sincerely, from the depths
With all my being
This thing I feel within

For every liar out there
Who deceive the mind for money
And every murderer
And those who kill by way of indifference
Every large living apathist

I hope so strongly
That you get all you wish
And all your plans succeed
And you get all your dreams
Sleeping well and long

I hope you smile broadest
And find someone you love
And love them deeply
Deeper than anyone
And feel that love returned

Oh let you soak that in
And marinade yourself
In all of that emotion
To give you happiness
And your mind, entitlement

And let that joy be taken
Not quickly ripped away
But rather, let it crumble
Let your house burn down around you
And let you watch it all

Watch what you built dissolve
Go up in smoke, destroyed
An incense, oh so sweet
The failure of your strength
To protect your dreams, brings me joy

And then, to see your family
Licked clean of life and love
That fire burning them away
But you will watch
You will watch them vanish

And languish, will you, in agony
Your body sick and lonely
Fading, dying, slowly
With no one to hold you
And no one who cares

And may you live long
Longer than any other
Let you live alone
Despised by all you trampled
Held in distain by society

And let the cobwebs grow
Throughout your rotten estate
And let the people forget
You ever existed
And let your accomplishments fall away

And may your last breath
Be painful and filled with fear
A cry, mournful and terrified
And may it be a curse
Upon the day you were born

Lament your very existence
Regret your life, in whole
And see that you were wrong
And wasted your life
And the very breath you had

And I, I will morn you
I will deeply regret your passing
And pound my chest with rage

And shout bitterly to the heavens
So painful will it be

For you left too early
Your misery did not last nearly long enough
A minute, an hour, a day, a week, a month, a year
Oh how sorry I'll be not to bask in your sorrow any longer
My hate, now stifled against you

Your entrance into oblivion
The final escape
No justice lies in death
The only justice there is
Is in life, and we must dole it out

Righteousness

Oh when compassion comes
It often comes with rage
The anger at the ones
Who lash the weak, depraved

A sorrow for the vexed
But tis mingled with anger
My tears for the depressed
My hate for the tormenters

And when the beasts attack
They do so with intent
And tear flesh from the backs
Of those so innocent

And those, they think it wise
To never back, repay
Those who would demonize
And with their words, filet

But my compassion's earned
Along with my distain
My heart, oh does it yearn
To find and cause them pain

To tear at their illusions
And rip way their respect

And heap upon their delusions
My hate they will regret

For all the pain they caused
To cause that much the more
So close to them I'd draw
To watch them live in horror

I'd bask in their despair
And love their lamentations
To watch them weeping there
So happy that I've hurt them

And with a glee, perverse
A malice like none other
I'd revel in this curse
This thing that they deserve

I bay this forth, in sorrow
Oh how it pains me so
That it won't come tomorrow
My vengeance, they won't know

What Is Best In Life?

Over the misfortune of others, do I gloat
Their pleasure do I chide
And when I hear their saddened croak
It swells my heart with pride

I quaff the misery of their tears
Moistening my dry throat
So that my crowing, loud and clear
Grows their sorrow, I promote

This causes me to smirk
Happy to hear their wails
Though it doesn't always work
It never completely fails

Well, in my mind, to whit
Tis a splendid way to behave
And that's pretty much it
Then it's a clear run to the grave

<u>Daily Life</u>

Kaden Moeller

Bad Day

A turd floating in the water;
Things have been better

Hymn Of Sincerity

Oh life, if you had ears
I'd say these things
Asking you, with tears
And joy, as I would sing

I ask thee not for ease
Nor wealth, abundantly
Nor rule by decree
Or endless ecstasy

I want to be someone
Who smiles shine upon
And bring the world joy
With all that I employ

I'd like to love
If it's too much to ask
To hold them close
And hold them tight and fast

And make a friend or two
Along the way
To turn their world from blue
To light and gay

I beg of thee, oh life
If it is right
Give me not much strife
And not too dark a night

Oh how I wish that you could hear my words
That we'd commune together, closely
But I know that one plea you not have heard
And I feel ever so lonely

Oh life and love, to be with you today
Is better than a word that I could say
And though I know I'm coming to the end
I'd like to think of life, my dearest friend

The Painter

While cruising through the skies
A bird, he thought, deposit
A special little flyby
With a nice white peace of shit

To whitewash my windshield
Twas such a thoughtful thing
His generosity unveiled
Twas all that he could bring

My eyebrows were perturbed
As my windshield wipers squeaked
Until his helpful turd
Was smeared where it was leaked

So furrowed I my forehead
And went and got a cloth
"Those damn birds!" I said
As I wiped that whitewash off

And so the next day came
My car, I looked at it
Oh every day's the same
They're all just full of shit

A Single Parent

Twas when the light did greet me
And much to my alarm
I found myself tucked sweetly
Within my father's arms

Unsteady feet did fall
But strangely came no harm
A warm embrace twas all
Within my father's arms

The tails that he tells
As late at night he yearns
I end up sleeping well
Within my father's arms

He has the strongest will
As silently he morns
It's cold, but there's no chill
Within my father's arms

As off to bed I go
He hangs up all his charms
And sleeps with none to hold
Within my father's arms

Adolescence

This pimple on my face
This pink and yellow spot
It seems so out of place
This early form of rot

A bloated puss-filled patch
Of soft and sickly flesh
A place decay is stashed
And shows itself compressed

This bulbous blemish that I see
It stains my white smooth skin
And seems to make the rest of me
Feel ugly deep within

For deep inside ourselves
Our bodies be at war
Between the parts controlled
And others that want more

Each pimple be a victory
A triumph for my health
The dirty bits pushed out of me
So that I save myself

It's such an ugly thing
As there I see it sit
I know that it will sting
But someone has to pop it

The Idol

Now comes upon the stage

The novice singer, sweet
Though she may be in age
Her talent now we meet

She sucks the air in round her
Her face a fiery red
The room so still, you heard
The pin, dropped, shake its head

Then does come the sound
Billowing forth in glory
The noise, it was abound
Clearing minds of inventory

Her voice, twas like a fart
From Santa's rosy cheeks
A song; sung from the heart
But with a sphincter's bleats

Oh did the crowd protest
The only way they could
Their voices did attest
Her lack of being good

But on the singer sang her tune
Ignoring their distain
She did not know that she was through
She thought the crowd insane

And as she then did leave the stage
Heading out into the street
Seeing a talent show sign for the next day
She thought *'I should compete!'*

Bartender's Parable

Today, I man the bar
And prep to tend my patrons
To mix their tonics, hard
Till memories be gone

This stretcher where I shake
And stir these different brews
Each similar to make

Kaden Moeller

Yet all the same use

I lace them with sweet joy
That lingers but a little
Until it is destroyed
As happiness is brittle

Then comes the bitter aftertaste
Of gayety made to misery
Unlike pleasure's fast pace
It lingers long in thee

The more of it you drink
The worse the pain becomes
Until tis all you think
And then one day it's gone

The pleasure of the lover
Who stays, there at your side
And then one day it's over
That day, the day they died

And matter little, does it
All joys that came before
As know you will not get
To go back for some more

Oh when the tap is empty
The aftertaste remains
I, your apothecary
Lead you out into the rain

I close my shop, and you
Now well soaked in despair
Stagger slowly through
The streets; lit by dusky air

And know you well, that pain
It never truly leaves
It lingers on the name
Of those whom you bereave

Oh yes the drink of life
Tastes of sweet bitterness
And though you hold it tight
It leaves you just as fast

I look out in the street
And watch the vagrants cry
Until they fall asleep
I drink not, wonder why?

Boulevard Parkway

I love to walk the loneliness
The sidewalks moist with rain
Beneath the neon signs
Of pink and green
(Dripping, dripping, dripping)
In the dark streets
And staring down the alleys

To watch the cop cars slowly pass
And leer at me
Midst the forgotten
The night women, drunks and homeless
Passing them; the night shade
A shadow, at home amidst the streetlights

And down the peer I wander
An empty place to glance
Out at the crashing waves
Into the vast expanse
And watch the water twinkle
Beneath the stars above

And look out at the bonfires
Speckled upon the beach
With what the young do
The drunken dance
As I, standing over them
Wonder at their vibrance
And pay them one last glance

Out there amidst the crowded
Twix fires on the beach
Tis not the place for me
And so I walk the streets
Through dark and dirty places
Those not so safe to be

Those, some say, ugly spaces

I am the midnight wanderer
Wracked with insomnia
Who loves his city's streets
And those places long forgot
Where many tread lightly
Though rarely they be cops
Down the boulevard to parkway

Sun Bathing

Upon the beach, one can sit
And run the sand grains through your fingers
Their coarse texture, upon the skin, it sticks
As you marvel at its figure

Each grain; a wonder
So small, yet oh so rough
And yet slides through the fingers
As water to the touch

Oh you could hold a handful
And yet; what be it worth
For sand's not beautiful
Or rarely causes mirth

Each grain; a stone to heft
Though small they be in weight
There is much more sand left
Than wonders you could make

If sand were loved; as gold
Then wealth would never end
No soul would be a pauper; no
To want, no one would bend

To watch them roll right off the skin
And settle on the ground
And know each grain's now lost in
The dunes abound around

To slip between the fingers
Each grain, with its caress
Reminds you, sitting there
The water's kiss is best

Inhibitions

A vivacious vixen sways
As drunkenly she stands
And slurs the words she says
As fumbles, she, her hands

Chastising those in line
Those standing behind her
Other's patience, she grinds
As the casher's life, she stirs

She insults the checker's hair
And calls the manager fat
As at the pedestrians, she blares
She's unpleasant, that's a fact

And so she staggers out
A relief, if there ever was
For she is drunk, our minds do shout
'She knows not what she does!'

So I am next in line
The casher looks at me
And says *"Would you waist you time
Lusting after one like she?"*

I said to her
*"She's not for me
After what I heard
And there isn't much to see"*

*"Besides, no matter her looks
She holds no sway on me
My passion she won't cook
When I can get that online for free"*

She laughed, and then she said
"No wiser words were spoken!"
And then I bought my bread
And kept my eyes peeled, for that crazy girl's sedan

Kaden Moeller

Alarm Clock

Click, ding, bing, ring
The pictures in the yearbook
Click, ding, bing, ring
Each face a different look

Click, ding, bing, ring
There's Tommy Ravencar
Click, ding, bing, ring
He's our school's football star

Click, ding, bing, ring
And the shy Selena Quall
Click, ding, bing, ring
A flower on the wall

Click, ding, bing, ring
Suzy, Tammy, Ted, and Todd
Click, ding, bing, ring
Each one of them said I was odd

Click, ding, bing, ring
Today they're gonna see, what it's like to be Ronald Stroll
Click, ding, bing, ring
My backpack's packed for a long day; I'm going off to school

The Don

I'm here to get my chest of meat
My tasty tender little treat
Coming this far was no small feat
Long had I traveled on the street
And sit for hours in my seat
Until up I stood, and beat my feet
Towards a man, built quite petit
He gave to me my chest, discreet
And off his list, my name delete
Driving, do I, over concrete
To gathering, where people meet
And open my chest without deceit
Now let us all sit down to eat

Playing The Game

The dealer has cast the cards

And the bets have all been placed
Now, though the game's not hard
Each put a steely face

And now the game begins
This test of luck and chance
Though you can bluff to win
The hand improves your stance

Now, this deck only deals
Hands that both win and lose
And no matter the reveal
You won't know what to do

And pony up the dough
Will every person, still
With every card, a show
That reveals our lack of will

And so our money wanders
With every single hand
And like every losing gambler
Say we, *"Deal the cards again"*

Please

While we were walking, down the road, looking up at the stars
I didn't see headlights, coming from afar
All I heard was a horn, and the screech of tires
Now you upon on the floor, as I shout, my eyes afire

(Chorus)
Please don't take my girl away from me
She was scared
She didn't know
Girl, I'll be here
Don't let me go

Now the driver gets outside, he's running up to me
As I hold by baby's hand, crying till I can't see
Oh please I cannot be the one who lays you down the rest
As I clasp you in my arms, and up against my chest

(Chorus)

Oh we're flying down the highway, under the blue moons beams
The engine roaring through the darkness, drowning out my screams
As we near the city lights you let out one last breath
There is nothing I can do but scream into the face of death
God
Please don't take my girl away from me
She was scared
She didn't know
Don't leave me here
Not all alone
God take me fast, and take me now
I'll take her place
I'll go to hell
Please don't take my girl away from me

Talking Over Venison

You're not eating
Tis time
Looks like you're ready to discuss

"It's different now"

Of course it is
Even the taste should be

"Was she scared?"

Well, yes
Death is a scary thing
But it need not have been

You missed your shot
It didn't kill her
It merely wounded
Maimed

It was the pain that
Brought the fear
The pain that
Told her to run
The pain that
Told her to live
But she could not
And we
Took that life

"I'm not hungry"

Oh son
I remember my first time
My father
He was so proud

But I
In the back of my mind
It's still there
That strange feeling

But you
You did good, son
It was your first time
Mistakes were made

Remember, this is why I'm teaching you
Violence done not for pleasure
But for purpose
So that you may kill quickly
So that death is not accompanied by pain
By fear

*"I don't like hunting
I don't like killing"*

Nor I son
But
Tis life
To live
One must take life
We kill so that we live

Each life taken with our hands should not be wasted
No drops of life's elixir should be spilled
For each life we take
But stays the hand of death
For but a little longer

For death collects his dues
And we do pay
The currency, another

But with every year
The debt goes up
The price becoming high

In life
We are hunters
And hunted
Predator and prey
No one is above this
We are all vessels
Of life's special brew
And we are desired
By others who do seek it
Who, just as we
Wish to take our life
So as to extend their own
Piling on the lives of others
In these mass graves of our meals
So that we
Can stand atop the bodies
So as not to join them

But yes
Someday, we too
Will be but part of the foundation
Of another's life
Of whom we made
Our deaths building their life's kingdom

So this is life
My son
Us predators and prey
Tis why I respect my kill
With a quick and painless death
They need not feel the fear
For without the pain, they will not get it

"But death itself
It's horrible
You're eaten and you rot"

Son
What fear of death?
The fear of non-consciousness
Of eternal oblivion?
There is no pain in this

No suffering
Or sorrow
Tis merely
Over
Do you remember the womb?
Or before?
No

My son
Eat
Let not her life go to waste
Don't throw away her gift
Do not spit on the life that gives you life
If you truly wish to honor her
If you wish to be grateful
To show remorse
Eat

A predator kills to live
He does not live to kill
To waste a kill is
Indignant and ungrateful
You dishonor life
But to eat
To be thankful that you may live
Celebrating the life of the dying
Honoring their final act
Providing life in death

This is good
To eat your kill and know this
So yes
It is different
And twill forever be

Eat son
Don't show disrespect
For someday
We will be the vessels of life
That others will drink from

So please
Eat
Live while you can

Because death
He comes
For everyone

Home, Sweet Home

Welcome to a home
That is yet not your house
A place that you can come
And feel warm all about

Where those you love indwell
But you can only visit
And feel slight pain, as you can tell
That time has aged all in it

To feel you have left
But only yesterday
But when you look at it
The years have passed away

The youthful company
Once was there
Now but a memory
Home has shared

And feel you that hollowness
That so slight empty pain
Of what growing up truly is
To leave home yet again

And know, in silent sorrow
That upon every return
Upon every tomorrow
For home is where you'll yearn

To leave that lovely company
That gave you life; so gay
Departing from your family
But wishing you could stay

Expectations

If life doesn't meet me halfway
I swear to you, I'll make it pay
Because it owes me oh so much

In fact, my presence is enough

So hurry up and give to me
What it is that I want from thee
If you don't know that, you're a fool
For you're supposed to be my tool

Repetition

A little king I met one day
He smiled, and then he had to say
"I'm not so happy as I look"
As stood he there within the brook

He told me of his new found passion
Doing nothing; as his action
He then spoke of his misery
How every day was boring, you see

But I spoke to him in simple heart
In change, get will you a new start
But he got angry, called me mad
What a fool, oh so sad

For what is it to be content?
It's being ok, with your consent

Boring

I've been to every mountain top, and seen each mornings glory
And swam in every lake and stream, like from some a children's story
I've been everywhere, anywhere even nowhere is a place to be
Having docked, and set my moorings, in every port and sea

I've done it all, and must confess
Not once have I not been depressed
The mountains are far too still for me, and the waters they won't stop moven
Some say they are majestic, but I say they needs improven

So if I get to heaven, and don't see something new
I won't resist, I'll be quite pissed, and snap my harp in two
Hell sure ain't much better, it smells like rotten eggs
And with that much fire, I have no desire to walk in it with these legs

Kaden Moeller

So here I sit, on this dark night, staring at the stars
Oh what the heck, I'll cash the check, I'm going off the mars

<u>Heart's Journey</u>

Kaden Moeller

Gifts

Oh every hug I give
Was given unto me
Their love has helped me live
And so they'll now help thee

A gift of warm compassion
So simple, yet so strong
Oh what is stored within them
A treasure; wearing long

Those arms which wrapped round me in love
Twill lift thee up anew
And raise thee stand above
To lift up those beneath you

You'll feel the strength of those
Whom you will never see
The love they gave in droves
To those long gone from we

The strength of their embrace
Reached here though time and love
May it ever keep your pace
And give thee but enough

Social Animal

The heart's a social creature
Who travels in your chest
And lets your outreach bear
Warmth to thy hand's caress

And bring does it a softness
Unto thy scarlet lips
A tender silky smoothness
That brings love through thy kiss

Oh how it makes the legs to run
And cause the spirit fly
As blood marches to the drum
Of the heart that beats inside

So pound, the blood band does
This life sustaining tune

The first there ever was
The music of the womb

And so the heart, it gives
To every limb about
And through them its love lives
But never returns to it

For the heart, it's only generous
It never keeps a thing
The strangest part of us
The best part that we bring

Facial Muscles

A smile can alight your day
And cast the morning fog away
With twinkles from the depths within
A stranger or one's deepest kin

And make a rainbow from the drear
As given from that ivory, near
And here to for upon the path
Which seemed, last moment, dry dead grass

Twill lift your heart and bate thy soul
To chase such joy as we may know
To bring sweet pleasure to a glance
That may; a moment, leave entranced

Twill lighten burdens upon brows
And make thee happy in the now
Though it may be but momentary
That moment twill be more than merry

For though it lasts the shortest while
Your spirit never hates a smile
And though it fades as fast as breath
It leaps a beat up in thy chest

Chaste

A virgin of passion may I be
But no virgin am I to love

The heart that swells until it bleeds
The lover's tears of blood

My soul doth pant after the wells
Those springs of others scarlet
And wish to drink, and so to quell
My bleeding heart now slit

Pray, my spirit does
Not for my heart to dry
To receive enough donations
So that my love won't die

So long that I receive
So to, I keep on giving
And fill the other cups, though cleaved
So they may keep on living

Sharing my love abound
I hold my cup aloft
But never will I drown
From this blood I share, not quaff

So no, no passion do I know
Of this, I'm not familiar
But my love for you doth overflow
A bleeding I don't fear

And so I do doll out this drink
Tis like a marriage toast
And happily now do I think
'I hope I gave the most'

A Grave

That empty space within you
That oft you wish to fill
Twill never brim or overflow
But rather cause thee chill

No, love twill not abate it
Nor will companionship
Nor vengeance satiate
What this hole here inflicts

This void within you now

Is what you want from life
The thing to which you vow
To conquer through the strife

But as you keep on living
That hole but yawns and gapes
You try to fill it with the things
You think will satiate

But nothing fills that hole
No; not even a god
For he's sucked in as well
Into that endless maw

That hole; your desire
That emptiness; ambition
A thing that but requires
The moments of your attention

Oh how it vexes thee
That hole in your heart
And brings a fear, to see
That death can fill it up

Trek

When down the winding road
At once I spitted, clear
That I was not alone
And someone else was here

Though know I not whence they came
Or how they caught up to me
They seem to know my name
And speak intimately

And I, slightly confused
Though not unhappily
This person I've come to
They follow close to me

And as, we two, together
Traverse the trail ahead
Life's storms that we do weather

As doggedly we tread

And as the weather wears us
Carving beneath my eyes
A new level of trust
To this one at my side

And when we're hunched and weary
We rest beside the road
This person here with me
Will stay until we go

Road Home

The path is vary rocky, and will often cut your feet
Your mind, twill yearn for a pillow and a blanket made of fleece

But once you've crossed the river, of all your broken dreams
And through the forest, past, beyond the wind still screams

But once you've made the last step for love, life, fear, and hate
You'll see yourself in bed, scars on your feet instead

There will be no glory honors, no parades for you to join
Just an average house, in an average town, with another road to travel on

The Fogotten

The Loneliness

What is more painful,
The pain we suffer from our afflictions,
Or that pain within thy soul
Knowing there's no assistance?

Is the hurt from the experience,
Or the fact that you're alone,
That apathy enchants
Those who should make thee whole?

An agony unbearable
To be invisible
That no one cares or knows
And leaves thy spirit cold

The trials of one's life
They can be overcome
But tis a harder plight
When you're the only one

When left to languish; lonely
Without a friendly hand
To but extend to thee
And pick thee up again

It is a foul thing
To be left in the gutter
Knowing others could bring
Relief unto another

Oh be it misery
The chains of solitude
Which separate from thee
What other souls should do

Manufactured Consent

When poverty grips you
It be a vile embrace
One not accorded to
Consent or loveliness

It holds you face-down in the bed
And straddles you angrily

Then grips your hair, and lifts your head
To whisper viciously

"You're mine, you'll smile for me
And keep yourself respectable
Fail to do these things, you'll be
Somewhere far more than painful"

His weight atop me, hurts
I'd cry, but I'm too scared
And as he violates my dreams, his words
Smother me in despair

"Keep up appearances, responsibility
Work hard; be with me
Trapped for eternity
In grinding poverty"

'Oh help me, dear God, help me!
Please someone get him off
He's too strong, oh my frailty
Please someone help me up!'

These screams, they be inside
As I put on a placid face
Keep up appearances and hide
It's expected, it's my place

Rap

I am going to write about mundane things
I will not talk deeply today
Ignore will I the important
Because I am going to write about mundane things

I could speak on the behalf of the child
Who, just the other day, was beaten black and blue
And then went to school in the same clothes as the day before
But no, I will write about mundane things

Like my sexual conquests in the bedroom
Not the rape victim down the street
Who, yesterday, had a flashback, and
Broke down crying in the middle of the road

No, I will write about mundane things
Like my desire to legalize certain drugs
But forget will I the addict, who
It just so happens is eighty pounds
And tomorrow will sell his body for just one more
Yes, just one more hit off the pipe
But this is not a mundane thing

Instead I'll rhyme the word nigga with nigga
And forget about the trigger, that
Was pulled to take the life of the emancipator
Yes, the dead who lie and wonder
Who sleep and say *"Where have my people gone?"*

I could speak on these things
But I, yes I, will write about mundane things

Not the homeless man beat dead last night
No, he was just a parasite
Who, though, was looking for a place to sleep
Was found in the street, by kids
Yes, just children, a bit too drunk

I mean, what am I saying?
I thought I was writing about mundane things

Limerick

Whenever you roll up a blunt
Your growth, it surly will stunt
Then you'll get angry
And others will see
And they will all call you a runt

A Prisoner

The room I'm in is much too small
It sits right next to concrete hall
I have barely what I need, instead
A toilet, a bed, and bars of lead

Oh and at night, the sounds you hear
The grown man's strength, transforms to fear
A cold and dismal place
The doldrums stretch across the face

I'm not really wanting to be here
But no one wants me to be near

Chained Gang

Upon a lonely highway
Midst trucker-bombs and cigarette butts
The ex-cons work all day
Bent down, and picking up

From cans to plastic bottles
And bags or newspapers
All of it, they will shovel
Into trash bags, piled near

A job, they only one
That didn't ask the question
A thing they needed done
And they would also pay them

The price paid for that puff
That long drag off the blunt
The law said, twas enough
And so their future's gone

Life now spent in the gutter
Where dirty water runs
A punishment so utter
And never will be done

Battle for Dignity

In the land of median
The homeless make their stand
They hold their cardboard shields
With the well worn cups they wield

Standing midst the fray
The traffic of the day
Attempting but to tame
One heart; for merely change

An onslaught, thick and full

Kaden Moeller

And fraught with more than peril
They stand there, lonely knights
Shunned and called parasites

Each one has family
Many were military
They fought for this great land
And now they seem ronin

Each day; a fight for bread
A war just to be fed
To clasp and cling one piece of need
That shrinking shard called dignity

So stand they; staunch and gallant
Not shabby; be they valiant
It takes great courage to be seen
In the lowliest of human scenes

In the land of median
A land so close at hand
You mayhaps yet battle there
Beneath the sun's hot glare

Street Side

A mother and a son
Walking
He's very young
Perhaps five
And she
She's holding his hand

That grip
That warm hand
I remember it

Like seeing through
Foggy glass
Peering back

Yes
When I was young
My mother
She held me
Just like that

With that same smile

Yes
I remember
Our warm house
Her baked foods
A full stomach

Yes
Laying in my bed
Her beside me
Her soft voice
Reading

I remember
Her warm arms
That full embrace
With sprinkles of kisses

Oh, it's their
In my mind
Like a mist
Blanketing these happy thoughts
Making them as but dark silhouettes

Yes
Those days
I remember
Oh, so long ago
And then the mother
She gives the boy something
And he looks around
His eyes then
Finding me

And breaking from his mothers grip
He walks on up
And from his little hand
He gives
A dollar

He smiles
Saying
"Have a nice day."

And back he goes to mother
And then they walk away

Oh I remember
The memory's but a shadow
Oh how I miss my mother
Oh how I miss the past
I miss those days
Those long before
These days

I am homeless

A Rainy Day

Whist drinking in the rain
I watched a little lizard
He was so small, green so plain
Staring at me, licking his eyeball

And I gawked at him too
Whilst drinking in the rain
And I wondered what he thought of me
Though surly not distain

Me; with my tattered mane
Of hair long thick and greasy
Whilst drinking in the rain
And clothes full of holes

I must look quite the sight
For he stairs without refrain
And here I sit, just thinking
Whilst drinking in the rain

The Backpack

Out and about
I wander to and fro
The streets
Though seem they free
There's no place I can go

So every curb's a job
And every cent a bone
Thrown

As if at chance
To ones like me
Who roam
And every precious thing
That my hands
By chance
Do grace
Join me in wandering
Though they may hold their place

Tucked away so safe
Packed like precious gems
These things I love
They trace
Sweet memories that end

A family picture here
A well worn book beside
Each one, to me
So dear
A faded joy I hide

They weigh upon my back
This lightest part of me
As wearily I stride
These well worn sidewalk cracks
And think on them sweetly
These dreams within my pack

A quarter of a bottle
And less than half a stype
A lighter
Old and battered
To light the smoke
So awful
And yet
Each be I grateful
To have these things at all

I fret
But I am able
To know my luck
Though small
And while the homes are closed to me

The parks are welcoming
A shower
Warm and wet
My glee
To clean myself again

And so, I leave outside
My mobile treasure chest
In bushes
Safe
They hide
And cause me less distress

The droplets
Like the rain
They flood my senses well
And wash away the pain
For moments

And as I do go back
To find my house again
The bushes hold no sack
My life
It has been stolen

Suspect

A homeless man is standing there
Beside the road, upon the pavement
His eyes, far off, they stare
Begging for meager cents

I'm tempted to give to him
But wary of he, am I
I know not to give into his tin
I suspect him as a lie

Perhaps a panhandler,
Or just a worthless beggar?
A one who won't work harder
To make himself much better

Or maybe he's a robber
Who wants to steal from me
To take all that I've got here
And get it all for free

A lazy leeching mooch
Who wants to never work
I'd hate this oh so much
From duty does he shirk?

That man, just standing
Lonely and unkempt
His cup was not demanding
To be filled with but one cent

Oh all these things he could be
Tis a hard thing to judge
But as I walk beside he
I find my hands do budge

My wallet, I unfasten
As his cup, do I bless
Fuck it, I'll choose compassion
If I fail I pass the test

On The Steps Of The Capital

I wonder what it's like,
In the big house?
I wonder what they think about
And why
What would it be like,
Being the boss of the big house?

Knowing that you can go
Wherever you want
See
Whoever you want
And people know you
You can do things
You're special
Because you're the boss
Of the big house

I hear the boss
He can set you free
Make you clean
Because the boss has the last word

Man, if I was the boss
I'd pardon Jimmie
I'd get him out, back on the streets
Back at home

Cause, Jimmie didn't do nothing
He was just smoking
Man, I'd let Jimmie go
Hell, I'd let everyone like Jimmie go
Cause I'd be the boss
The boss of the big house

Prepping For Work

The madam puts my makeup on
And long hair on my head
A pretty thing; men lay upon
And take me off to bed

She feeds me just enough
To keep me nice and thin
And lets the boys play rough
Their toy; it is my skin

And I, no longer scared
I sometimes cringe a bit
Though fear, it isn't there
The reflexes don't quit

I've learned to do my task
To be just what they want
They needn't even ask
This skill I often flaunt

And as she paints the lipstick
Across my tender lips
The madam slightly smears it
And slaps me just for this

But I, I make no sound
I sit quietly there
For being slapped around
Leaves me no worse for wear

She will not cut me, yet

I'm still a pretty thing
The customers I get
Much money do they bring

But I'm a grownup now
A whole fourteen years old
And now I wonder, how
Long will my beauty hold?

The other boys are younger
And the girls needn't worry
But I, because I'm older
What will become of me?

But I forgot this question
As I hurry off to bed
For customers are waiting
And what more needs be said?

American Beauty

A young girl walked my way
Though youth, from her, was gone
As she walked amidst the cars
A song, over the radio, played
'The stars and stripes forever'
And I watched her march on by
Car after car

Her pale blue wide eyes
With bags of weariness
Those amber waves upon her head
Now grimy and unkempt
A couple bruises were there too
Those violet violent blooms
And I could not help but gaze and say
"Oh what happened to you?"
And as the song crescendoed
I read her tablet clear
"I'll take what you can spare"

But like each motorist
I looked away and sighed
And passed that girl by

Had I not a dime to spare
And waned that mocking song
That I, the wage slave, heard
And thought I long upon
That girl at the curb

Matches

I'm cold and I'm alone
No place to call my home
I stand out in the street
No shoes upon my feet

My stomach, it is empty
People, they don't see me
Am I dead? In eternal sleep?
Perhaps a ghost without a sheet?

I must be invisible, that's why they cannot see
Or even hear my begging plea
I am cold, and so alone
I guess the grave will be my home

Living Nightmare

Oh when I saw her there
So naked and so thin
Once hidden, now laid bare
Now shown upon her skin

Her hair, so long and fair
Before her face, it draped
Her eyes, sunk deep, did stare
As her lips parted, agape

The veins in her arms and legs; collapsed
They proved themselves unable
To take the thing this girl grasped
And deeply drink the needle

Her belly, not a pleasure
To handle or caress
So sickly thin to measure
As likewise were her breasts

The spark of life within

Twas dimmer than I'd guessed
So much, I feared the wind
Would blow her out, no less

Who is this strange one here?
What is it they have done?
Oh dare I draw them near?
Away now, could I run?

With quaking hands and trembling heart
I move to do the thing
That could I not do from the start
Towards me, her to bring

Her eyes so dead; her body still
I hold her in my arms
Her head, now on my shoulder, brings chills
And causes great alarm

Oh what have you done to yourself'
And why have you done this to me?
You've thrown away your health
For one more drug laced dream?

I bear to look upon you
As there you shake and shiver
I don't know what to do
For you, for my big sister

America Looked At Honestly

On the streets, you see the real America
Not the one painted over
Red, white and blue makeup strewn about
Covering the blemishes and bruises
No
You see the nation unvarnished
And you know

You see the veteran; abandoned
Begging on the street corner
Hand out, mind rattled, in need of help
Sitting there on the sidewalk
A look of exhaustion in their eyes

Kaden Moeller

Under a billboard saying *"The Few, The Proud"*

And though you cannot see the sex slaves
You know they exist, just behind doors
Visiting customers, looking tranquil but
Feeling tumult and fear
They're not quite like the prostitutes
But both poor kin together
Souls dispossessed and desperate
Ever the poor among us

And you can see the overworked
Their eyes, dead and tired, looking out
Smiling plastic smiles, as fake as the economy
Though others; pupils black, the size of dimes
Go to the back of the store for a quick snort
And then it's on to the third shift
Standing and selling disposable joy

And then there are those who've given up
Sitting placidly at home
Who've made a bed for sloth, and his partner despair
And watch the news all day; drinking their life away
Feeling the weight of inactivity
That sorrow of idleness unbound
And you see them walk round the block at night
Insomnia gone awry; ashamed to be seen in the light
For fear of further loss of dignity

Oh, those poor persons, most of all
Who search for work all day, walking, driving, writing
And getting the same old *"Talk to the manager"* speech
Every day, their drive dies a little more, and every day
They wonder what went wrong

But let us not forget the workers, who've worked a place
For years, and years more, and still only make base pay
Who ask for a raise, and get only a chuckle from the boss
And watch their years depart them, with nothing to show for it
Ever the worker, ever the slave

Yes, this is America, you are poor and should be ashamed
At least that is the message those with wealth say
"Work hard and you'll succeed" yet there are only so many hours in a day
How many jobs do you need, to appease the god of the market?
How much of your life need you give

To live a life worth living?

The Lash Of The Coin

It cuts to you the cost
A cat of nine tails so perverse
And lets the sufferer to speak
Through screams by which they beg release

Wielded by the invisible fist
They tyrant Want; it is his whip
It pays the price; the wretched wage
The cost it be to rent a slave

A servile bondage at the gains
Of contract's vile slavery chains
A voluntary association
Birthed from desperation

The Hiring Process

"Sell yourself"
Said the interviewer
"Tell me why I should hire you
What about you will make me money?
Why should I consider you over others?"

I twitched, just a little
The verbiage sounded wrong
"Well, I'm well qualified
Done it for years
I know all the ins and outs
I work well with others
Quick on the learning curve
And am happy to do it"

"But what about you is different?
What makes you better than the other candidates?"

"Well, I've never met the other candidates
So I don't know
I know that what I've presented to you is all I got
I am what you see
You see my resume, over ten years experience

Kaden Moeller

So, I guess, if there's someone else with more than me
Well, they may be more qualified"

*"No, you've got to sell yourself
Tell me why I'd want you"*

I twitched again
"Like a product?"

*"Well, yes, kind of
What would we get from you that they couldn't give us?"*

"What else do you want?
I can do the job, it's what you were asking for, right?
Isn't that enough?
What else could you possibly want?
Isn't that what you want?
You asked for someone who could do these set tasks
And I agreed that I could accomplish them"

*"Yes but, what else would you provide?
What extras are we getting to improve our interests?
Remember, sell yourself"*

"I'm not sure I understand
I'm not for sale
You're renting me
Buying my time of course
But renting me"

"So are you saying that you don't want the job?"

"Well, to be completely honest
Do I want to have to rely on you and your company for my food?
My shelter? My livelihood? My prosperity?
No, not really
But am I forced to do so because that's how life works?
Yes
So, in that case, sure, I want the job
So, do I have it?"

"No"

"Why? I've met all of your standards"

"You just didn't sell yourself properly"

"Because I'm not for sale"

"And that's the problem"

Nietzsche's Lament

When the poor man sleeps
Out in the streets
It is the death of God

When a child starves
Midst passing cars
It is the death of God

When a woman dies
Midst labor cries
It is the death of God

When a family weeps
For a loss so deep
It is the death of God

When people suffer
From another
It is the death of God

When nature dries
And slowly dies
It is the death of God

When one is raped
With screams of hate
It is the death of God

Does no one know
That God is dead?
We see the tombstone there
Carved; with every crime there read

An all-powerful loving God
He must be dead
And we have killed him

Kaden Moeller

Trials Of Life

A Trail

They say when unborn children die
They leave no trail of tears
For they have never graced your eye
Nor did they live in fear

They never walked the path of life
Nor cried an earthly year
They never knew a day of strife
For never were they here

No hatred have they known
For that they'd have to live
For consciousness to grow
And meaning: it to give

They've never lost a loved one
To time's cruel advancing years
Their heart's never been broken
And caused their eyes to sear

And so; my weeping darling
With an empty crib so near
You've not that luxury
You'll leave their trail of tears

An Abortion

Oh mother of a child
Who never was to be
And bears the weightless trial
Of a womb far more than empty

And father of the soul
That he will never see
And now is left, the cold
Of silent vacancy

With quiet tear-filled touch
And pain-filled downcast frame
In their arms, do, they clutch
A couple brought to pain

Kaden Moeller

Two people, here alone
So far off from this world
And as their spirits groan
They wonder, boy or girl?

Oh how they feared the blame
And harm someone for life
And make them feel ashamed
For their one moonlit night

And with a light sad kiss
That has not lost its charm
They leave with only this
Broken hearts and empty arms

A Fearful Feeling

I've noticed, that my touch
Brings not your skin to flower
It does not make you blush
Or playful; through the hours

Yet, if you were but cold
I'd anger; but forsooth
The greatest horror of all
You are indifferent

You'll go through all the motions
And when our lust is spent
It won't matter at all
We are not intimate

Remember, do I, fondly
Of when I'd make your breath
To notes of ecstasy
Whose tune would not relent

But now; tis sighs and shrugs
More like annoyance; grieved
There's nothing left of love
You just put up with me

I hold you in my arms
But I'm more like an object
Like mattress, string and yarn
I'm just part of the bed

This feeling terrifies me
I don't know, but I dread
I'd never thought I'd see
Our love, here lying, dead

A Divorce

For though, at first, we felt compelled
Our lives; to bind
We found; as we grew, parallel
Our limbs won't intertwine

We, two so close, have grown apart
Though be we both together
And now, as every conversation starts
Each word feels old and weathered

No longer intrigues spark
That which brings remindedness
Rather, just but the start
Of why this love won't last

And yes, the feeling's tough
And something that denies
A type of truth to love
That seems to realize

A gulf has grown between
Our closest of embraces
And this brings us to see
That we two must come to face this

A heart, it cannot beat
When it be rent in twain
Its music; it must meet
A special note; so strange

And though we are together
We find; that deep in spirit
We're nowhere near each other
Our passion's gone from it

There be no rage; in truth

We've just grown separate ways
Know that I do not hate you
We two just cannot stay

What Love Looks Like

With breaths so deep and quick
And muscles tightly clenched
A bloody flowing slick
With thoughts, fearful and tense

Her hands do tightly grasp
The hand of her young lover
And though in agony she basks
His company is like no other

She looks at him, teary eyed
His face, to her, a blur
He smiles, giving compassionate sigh
Knowing it's hard for her

Then comes the final surge
And agonizing cry
He speaks to her kind words
Tears streaming from his eyes

Gone now, the physical pain
All they can do is morn
She hath travailed in vain
The baby was still born

You Need To Sleep

I want to ease your pain
I hate to see you cry
And so, without refrain
I tell to you, a lie

Oh this untruth interjection
Of mine, your eyes, it seems to dry
And with this word injection
The pain, it passes by

And with your sorrow lessened
I sit there by your side
And watch your new expression

As in relief, I sigh

I tell you *"Go to sleep"*
Your eyes close in reply
"Tomorrow you will meet
Our baby boy's blue eyes"

As drifted you away
Grip your hand did I
These words that I did say
Were worthless goods to buy

As lay there, did you, resting
You slept, but I did cry
They couldn't stop the bleeding
My wife is soon to die

Bleeding

My eyes are really heavy
"I'm getting very tired"
It's getting hard to see
Oh, your words I hear

"I know"

"I feel very cold"
Your hand's warmth fades somehow
But your arms wrap round and hold
And you whisper to me now

"I know"

"My head, it feels dizzy"
The world, it spins in circles
"I'm really very thirsty
Oh please don't let me go"

"I know"

"I feel very scared"
I heard myself now cry
And though you wouldn't dare
I say *"I'm gonna die"*

"I know"

Breaking

My broken heart, it weeps
It burst of all its love
And now it only leaks
Its mournful tears of blood

Oh every tear poured forth
With its incessant pounding
It flows without remorse
And fills my lungs to drowning

Each drop, a tortured yearning
Each drip, a mournful sigh
For though my heart is burning
Its tears seem not to dry

So bursts the levy forth
To flood my inmost depths
The pain twill run its course
And float my deep regrets

So let the tears to come
This anguish twill I ride
Upon this sea, come from
This broken heart of mine

Mainstreet

Kaden Moeller

The Right To Life

You are conscripted from the womb
Thrust out into the world
This involuntary human bloom
A sand grain made a peril

Your only right, it is to live
Ask not the question *"Why?"*
This life that others, to you, give
Is forced for you to try

You can't reject this offer
You do not get a choice
You cannot leave by volunteer
You'll answer life's invoice

Awake you now into this dream
A seed, at random, cast
And with or without fertile stream
You'll grow, and grow up fast

Ignore the pain of living
Walk it off and do not cry
If you are to have misgivings
Tis that you're born to die

But you cannot go back early
To the nothingness of the tomb
You have the right to live, for we
Pulled you, screaming, from the womb

Children

The latch and key
Behind the door
Our children play upon the floor
But we don't watch them
Take their steps
For money calls
With much regrets

The latch and key
Behind the lock
Our children study beneath the clock
And wait for us to come back home

Exhausted and so tired
To sit across from them in despair
As childhood expires

The latch and key
A turn of the knob
With girls women, and boys men, how odd
Where was the time to love them
In moments long ago
Those precious parts of life
That oh so quickly go

The latch and key
Beyond the arch
And empty house, an empty heart
I worked for every dollar
To give my children the life
That I never had
Alone all day, till night

The Rock Or The Hard Place

I got the letter
It was in the mail today
'Foreclosure'
'Eviction'
My god!

I sat at the table
I must have cried
For quite awhile
'What am I going to do?'

When my girl's got home
I wiped the tears as they walked in the door
Gave them a hug
And hid the letter

I sat with them
Watching something
I can't remember what
My mind
It just kept saying
'You can't let this happen

Your girls can't live out on the streets'

I put them to bed
Kissed them softly
Everything will be ok
"Sweet dreams"
I said

I stayed up
That letter staring at me as I held it
The streets
They were no place for children

And I
I could not protect them from the dealers
With no home
No place to stay
No shelter

I thought
Long and hard
And thought
'I could go to Big Mike'

He was a pusher
But he respected his people's families
He had the best reputation
Only hurting those he deemed responsible for stealing from him
Never their families

The thought then crossed my mind
'What if he, thought I was stealing?'
He'd kill me
He'd leave my girls fatherless
He wasn't a man of charity
Though luckily he found prostitution and pedophilia beneath his line of work

But
The reality of the streets
Others did not think so lowly of such trades
And they would snatch them away the second my eyes had left them
They cannot live out there

I looked in on them
Sleeping so sweetly
Tossing and turning

So small and fragile
My girls

And so
I locked the door
Took that long walk
Down second avenue
To *'Big Mike's'* late night convenience store

He manned the register
King of the night in downtown
And like everything else

He knew I was coming
He knew his city
He knew his people
And without so much of a lifted brow
Gave me my route
Told me my clientele
Assigned me my *'overhead'*
And sent me out on the beat

'It's going to be ok'
I thought
'Everything will be ok'

Money Makes A Mate

Finances make a marriage
Love is good; yes
It helps
But money
Money is what people argue about most

Money is power
Money is strength
Money is security

Love may be unbreakable
But money helps it stay unbroken
In fact, it may be the shield that saves it

But money itself is only one part
Of the equation

It's the self-worth that comes with
Earning a lucrative living
A paycheck that contributes to the couple
That gives succor against the tyrant of want
And makes safe the future of the partnership

So, marriage, is a financial construct
It is a blending and binding
Of one's debts and one's assets
Love is part of it
Children can be involved
But money is all of it

If a couple is in want of money
The marriage is in danger of collapse
If one person in the pare earns nothing
Than the marriage is fragile

Money is dangerous
It can make any friend an enemy
Too much makes you drunk
Too little makes you rabid
But enough allows you to live

Money is stability
Money is structure
Money is responsibility

To be the primary bread winner is a weight unlovable
It makes you to a brute
Who holds the club of coin
Over the one you love
Or; who never hold's them long enough
Not to fall in love with the job
To become so estranged that
Coming home is more awkward an experience
Than staying at work

So, marriage is, what?
If money makes a marriage
If financial stability means
Divorce will lesson
Then, money, for lack of a better word
Is a fulcrum which is required

Economic stability

A living wage
Security

The opportunity for prosperity
In the fertile ground of a social contract
Guarding against the tyrant of want
A strong marriage
Is both loving and economically secure

Bread Line

Oh of this line of workers
Or rather unemployed
A people who are eager
To earn their bread and joy

But there be but one opening
For every fourth person here
No matter the papers they bring
Twill bring them no more near

And these hollowed positions
They're only temporary
And those lucky to keep them
Will work, but only barely

The pay, oh it is low
When measured to the past
And if it ever grows
It never twill grow fast

Security is unheard of
And scarcity, the norm
So that we push and shove
And fight just to be warm

Oh what a wretched thing
And no hope, so it seems
Always coming and going
With never enough time between

Over And Over

I was doing the laundry

Kaden Moeller

Cleaning
When
From nowhere
My stepdad asks
"What do you plan on doing with your life?"

I said
"I don't know"
The answer
Though honest
Wasn't good enough

*"You're twenty-six
And you have no fulltime job
Where's your future?"*

"I don't know"
I said

"How many jobs have you applied for?"

"Seven in the last week"

"Prove it!"

"I can't you have to apply online"

"You need a job!"

"I have one!"

*"That is a dead end job!
Its only thirty hours a week
I mean a real job
With benefits!"*

"You think I don't know that?!"

*"We don't need a maid around the house
Go out and find a job!"*

"I have been looking
But
There are no jobs
Everyplace I apply only wants part-time work
They won't hire full-timers

I mean
I apply
But it's like throwing darts in the dark
And then
I go ask the manager
'Are you in need of a worker,
Someone to do a job?'
And then
Without fail
A bemused look crosses their face
And they say
'Then you applied online?'
I say yes
'Then why are you asking?
We'll call you'
The discussion ends!
They; like the job market
Are currently too busy to hire
And I
I am just one more under-employed person
Like millions more

"I know it's tough"
He says
"But..."

No
He doesn't know
He, and many more
They haven't a clue
Every person my age
All who I know
They
They're all looking
Seeking
But
Like I
Not finding
Work
And so
I help around the house
Because
I don't want
To be useless

Unskilled Labor

Why am I less than you,
Because I scrub the floors?

You; at your desk
Me; on my feet
We work; our hours, our lives
You sit; and type and gripe
I stand; moan and complain
Your backside, sore
My legs, the more
Yet I'm held in distain

I clean the toilet-bowls
And mop the floors all day
Wipe windows, glass and metal down
And scrub the grout
Yet, strangely, I don't matter

"Unskilled" they call my labor
Yet, seems they need it, desperately
The garbage doesn't remove itself
And you; there in your cubicle
Your typing is so valuable
While I, the janitor, seems so reprehensible

They need the jobs be done
Both required are they
We both were trained to do it
Yet my job, lacks the respect

I come in every day, faithful to my task
Yet, because my job's not pretty
Such dignity I lack

An Old Man

The hands of age upon
A man, but once a boy
Whose work-cloths be light beige
And youth, now long since lost

Who punches twice the clock
For only half the pay

And pays the highest price
For what someone else owned last

His brow, tis beaten deep
Plowed by the stress of life
Ten hours work, and then
A light level of rest

The grind of constant drudgery
It leaves no time to dream
Because of this, this young man can't
Be bothered beyond the line

Oh told was he, so often
His life would be much better
Than what he lives and sees
That dream becomes a crutch

And so he tells himself
He hadn't worked enough
That now he lives in hell
Because of the work he shirked

Be he not responsible,
For how his life has turned?
This lack of joy he got
All of it is his

Self deprecation be
The walls enclosing him
This great unfair position
Is he justifying

Like sin, no matter its size
Each action be equal to hell
That's why he deserves this
As he meagerly thinks through

For oppression's upkeep is simple
The people crushed beneath
They'll keep to their distress
And think that it's a must

The Crew

I work with two men here called Willy
I don't think either's from Philly
As with them I roam
Never quite alone
In this building that is slightly chilly

These two men who do work with me
These two men both who're named Willy
They both are in charge
Though neither are large
They're tall, but I'm wider, really

So clean up, will we, chicken bones
And sweep off dirt, grass and stone
To clean, so they see
That we are cleanly
That they won't complain on the phone

And so after work I go home
And rolling my eyes I do groan
What's Willy call Willy?
Now please, don't be silly
Willy calls Willy, Jerome

Economic Value

Seven-Twenty-Five
Is what an hour of my life is worth?

An hour
What else has happened in an hour?

I've walked the bounteous fields of grass; miles long
Hearing the wind rustle its leaves

I've basked in the pail beams of moonlight
Beneath the pines of the forest

I've spent the last moments of loved ones lives
And embraced them tearfully at their last

I've laughed with friends on the beach
As we joked of our missteps

I've tasted the sweet nectar of the lover
As we laid together quietly

I've held a child in my arms
Gazing into those wide wondrous eyes

I've lost myself in silence
And garnered the wealth of contemplation

I've felt the ecstasy of exertion
And the pleasure of running through the wilds

I've stood by the seashore
And allowed the wind weave through my hair
Felt the ocean spray against me

Yet
I find my labor
Seems worth less to me
Then those moments
Why?

Wage Slavery

The grind, the grind, the grind
Every Day at six
The grind, the grind, the grind
Till one in the afternoon
The grind, the grind, the grind
Then eight at night to three
The grind, the grind, the grind
Everyday all day, every night all night
The grind, the grind, the grind

Those days of dreams and sleep
Now shadows in the night
Like shadows, they don't keep
They vanish in the light

When once was young
Now old am I
When once I hoped
Despair and sigh

The grind, the grind, the grind
Each minute of the day
The grind, the grind, the grind
To waist your life away
The grind, the grind, the grind
And let your dreams to fade
The grind, the grind, the grind
With each and every day
The grind, the grind, the grind

Working Illness

My heartbeat is rising again
And my palms are sweaty
So I make my way to the janitor's closet
To spend some time, silently crying
At work

This seems to happen now
When it never happened before
I know what it is
No days off in four months
Sixty hours of work a week
And other responsibilities
Along with exhaustion

So I let the waves come
And I hug myself, alone
Waiting for the panic to subside
As I bring my breathing down
And attempt to calm my mind
Now flooded with the thought
Of no end in sight

It's not like I even live off the money
It's barely enough to rent on with a roommate
But, it's all the work I could find
And I'm still poor

The crying has stopped
I wipe my eyes
Put on a smile
And go back to work

How You Look

The weight of life
Weights most upon your eyes
Your shoulders too, despise
And wish that it were light

Though bearing up under it
The tears it makes
Though things it brakes
No stronger get

They heal not
Rather they show
A portrait; slow
To ready rot

The burdens placed atop people
Many, unnecessary
So arbitrary
And, often, mostly cruel

So light could be the load
If we would stop and see
If we could make it be
And lessen what we hold

To divvy up our burdens
Midst every one of us
Twould seem a weight so small, a weight, the weight of dust
No strain to stand

We need to live
We live but once
And life; it haunts
Our eyelids

Killing Yourself

Oh heart of hearts, why
Needs ask they my dreams to die?
I'm wed to them, and they are me
To sever us leads fatal bleed

Kaden Moeller

Hear my, my soul, bear up I beg
And strengthen up my weakened leg
Oh let me never bend the knee
And kneel before the creed of greed

My strength is not the strength of all
Yet none test me my resolve
I hope that I'll defy them still
Even if death be what they will

Please let me never to but cower
I hope that I am not a coward
Am I a strong man inwardly,
And can I be strong for all to see?

And for my love, and for my life
Am I strong enough to bear the knife?
When the dream killer do come for me
Will I face that eternity?

Oh grant me bravery, I plead
I need be strong to watch me bleed

Ground Level

Come down from that high tower
Come live among the people
But give away that power
And try a life of struggle

Where figures stand at five
And never near they six
As live you, sleep deprived
To wake you, aching sick

And every coin departing
Pays for needs of the day
With luxury in small things
Which cause thee smile gay

The comfort of a friend
As close as family
Is true joy without end
And proves you truly wealthy

Those dinners, be they feasts

Round tables worn and warm
With home cooked simple treats
From humble hands; were born

If life is only worth
What it is worth in coin
Than in it be no mirth
This cold clutch of the dime

Collective Responsibility

The things I want, and work for
Speak volumes, both of me
But even more for others
For we're society

I want to feed the poor
Those starving hungry mouths
And when they ask for more
I'll with a smile, dole out

I want the elderly
To walk softly to the grave
Girded in dignity
And helped along the way

I want the child learned
And wise beyond his years
To, at that school, be fed
With knowledge and with cheer

I want retirement
For all to know of rest
A long vacation, meant
To end upon your death

And I want rights for workers
Vacations, pensions and pride
Those things of which we've heard
Which make us feel alive

Oh how could we do this,
Do you think I am a fool?
It's obvious, with taxes

Kaden Moeller

For I'm a liberal!

__United We Stand__

I am a union man
I stand with my fellow laborers
Those people who work for a living
Who wake up tired and go home sore
We do tough jobs and do them right

I am a union man
And I know what hard work is
Know what it's like to sweat beneath the sun
To wear a heavy uniform in the heat of the day
And carry a load on my back with discomfort

I am a union man
And when I'm done, I go home to my family
And we eat around the table, making small talk
"How's the day, how's school?"
All the same nonsense; and I smile

I am a union man
And when passion calls; and the time is right
Me and my wife, we fuck
Damn strait we fuck, and hard
And I love every minute of it, and so does she

I am a union man
And I take my vacations; as I am entitled to
And I spend time with my children, fuck my wife
Visit family and the like; loving my life on earth
This brief span of loveliness

I am a union man
And ain't no rat-bastard gonna take my dignity
Tell me what I'm worth, dictate my livelihood
Or fuck with my family's future
Their profits be damned!

I am a union man
And when the fuckers think they can short change us
We strike and hit them where it hurts
Their pocketbook!
The bastards

I am a union man
And when I stand alongside my fellows
Arm in arm and hand in hand
We sing it long and sing it proud
"For the union makes us strong!"

I am a union man
And we fight for pay raises and paid vacations
Paid sick days and paid paternity and maternity leave
Paid holidays and pensions
We fight for dignity

I am a union man
And I am proud of who I am
I ain't afraid of some rich prick
He ain't better than me
Ain't no silver spoon up my ass!

I am a union man
And I work for a living
And yea, I am entitled to dignity
Everyone is entitled to dignity
And fuck all those who say different

We are the union
We fight for dignity
We fight for respect
Economic justice
"For the union makes us strong!"

Phoenix/The United World Anthem/The Internationale Reborn

From the wretched poverty
From the sparks and ash and dine
Came forth the cry of sweet relief
"Oh ye kings of oppression
Once so mighty
Now you're damned
The Internationale
Now echoes cross the land"
[Chorus]
(And so comrades, come rally
For together we must stand
The Internationale

Rings out across the land)

For our chains, now we spy them
Their dead weight upon our hands
They will bring no salvation
For such things they cannot grant
We stand together finally
We masses of the land
The Internationale
It gives us pride again
[Chorus]
Our brothers and sisters
Friends of race and creed and love
None of us are our betters
Not a single stands above
So we sing forth in unity
We go marching hand in hand
The Internationale
Is far more than one man
[Chorus]
We beat our swords to plowshares
Seed the earth till bounty green
And in harmony live here
Midst the trials the future brings
For the world holds much beauty
If we but extend a hand
The Internationale
Is cooperation
[Chorus]
For the rights of all beings
For their dignity and pride
We will go forward singing
Preaching freedom by and by
We will break the chains of slavery
Slaves of not money or man
The Internationale
It stands for all humans
[Chorus]
Sing for those who came before us
Who suffered lash and coin
For whom never was victorious
Those that were the rights of man
And so comrades, come rally
Cross the world may we embrace
The Internationale
Unites the human race

Letters

Kaden Moeller

<u>Mentor</u>

How to choose to argue?
Evidence, or authority?
Well, if you don't know what to do
Just take a hint from me

Try your best to use
Statements of well known fact
And do not try to defuse
Your doubt, if you don't know that

Try not just to *"Say so"*
But rather to explain
Show how the process grows
And why it's not insane

Oh, be humble about it
Make sure to laugh and smile
And if there are parts that you don't get
Do not live in denial

Remember this maxim
'Extraordinary claims
Require extraordinary evidence'
In this, there's no distain

Oh happy is the learned man
Who lives in the unknown
Seeing the world, small and grand
Whose mind he works to grow

Yes, answers, they exist
Terrible and wonderful
They will not bring you bliss
But they won't make your life cold

Oh stay away, if possible
From just saying *"Because"*
It's better for you to know
About the things you love

Oh the difference between the two
It's subtle, but important
While one, it tells you what to do
The other wants you to learn it

The distance between them is small
The difference, very blunt
For it's not too hard to make the call
Between the asshole and the cunt

Exceptional

Happiness is an illusion
Happiness creates confusion

It's the dark things that give us pause
That makes us great and shapes a cause

The warm and fuzzy corrupts our thought
Makes us surrender to what we've fought

And shapes a false reality
Forming a fake neutrality

While cheering for the downtrodden
We forget they often do not win

But live, do we, the lie of exception
That our life is different, a deception

Oh yes, we buy it every time
And sign upon the dotted line

That we are different than the rest
We're not just good, we are the best

And this is a sad sight to see
It sets us up for tragedy

For when the rug is pulled beneath our feet
We're so perplexed by our defeat

We can't believe we're like the rest
It seems we could have never guessed

For everybody is the same
We all are all so vary plain

But here's the thing that lends it splendor
We soon forget, and don't remember

Worldly Love

Love is faded
Love Is cheap
Our love is but the love of sleep

We lust and long after each other
And then we wake-up and find another
And when we leave with broken heart
We swear off love
And then we start

Love is scorned
And love is hated
Love is raped
And serenaded

Loves sister lust is so confused
By all her shaded and different hues

Love of the fleshly
Love of the finite
How love has died
Her body un-revived
Warped and perverted is she by her sister
How sad is love
And all who miss her

Delusional

The youth romanticize when they're not disillusioned
This fantasy that they create can lead to much confusion
They love to see the flowers blanketing the field
But know they not of all the rot the flowers do conceal

For beauty is easy to see
If not there, we'll make it be
But when the horror comes about
Our view of beauty do we doubt

For though there's much truth behind illusion
This truth is riddled with contusions
And find yourself not that impressed

When you find, and then fill in, the rest

And so allow your mind to accept
The ugly is equal, no *"except"*
You'll find the scales, balanced and even
This vexing beauty we believe in

Something About Nothing

The roses are dead
The violets rot too
I only exist
How about you?

For we only live for thirty days
And die for thirty years
An old man's life at Twenty-One
And resting on a whim

For I choose to exist
And maybe one day I'll live
Tis to live for thirty days
And die for thirty years

Roses are red
Violets are blue
Or are violets violet?
It's up to you

Question

Why mourn when you can rejoice?
Why cry when you can laugh?
Why be scared when you can be brave?
Why die when you can live?
Why end when you can begin?

What If?

What if a word could change the world?
What if a thought could shape a life?
What if an idea could change a mind?
What if a mistake could mark the future?
What if the truth became a lie?

What if a man became a monster?
What if death meant new life?
What if war was true peace?
What if wanting was to have?
What if to find would only to lead to more seeking?
What if man went over man?
What if a place transcended time?
What if darkness contained the light?
What if to be right all one could use was might?
What if in defeat there was always victory?
What if Hi-s-tory was my-story?
What if it was choice that leads to slavery?
What if freedom was really control?
What if, what if was really what is?

Play

Whilst performing in the opera of experience
Singing in the choir of life
And swaying in the ballet of conscious existence
Dancing round the stage of strife

I found myself woke from the dream
Seeing the stage itself
The strings atop us, they were seen
Their weight upon me felt

The hollow eyes of marionettes
They stared into my soul
And terrified me, these puppets
For born were they with a hole

They had no spirit, did these ones
These mindless playthings here
The toys of a giant child's fun
A master I can't hear

Looking upward, beyond the strings
Nothing, blackness and eternity
Where are the hands, who bring
Movement from the empty

But the real fear, it comes
From the dark realization
As cold my blood does run
'I can make no decisions?!'

But then the shadow looms
A figure I can't see
Feeling now *'I'm doomed!'*
The strings are cut from me

On Being

When cowardice has run its course
And fear's been made to anger
The storm, though it shows no remorse
Will not hold me contained here

I'll let the winds whip round me
The rain, to sting my skin
My eyes, I open, wide to see
This tempest that I'm in

I watch the world writhe
Beneath this wrath and violence
As with it, I confide
My anger and impatience

The skies, they roll in rage
The lightning cracks in spite
As all around me sways
And shutters in the night

Oh yes, I may be battered
But I have lost my fear
My spirit's far from shattered
I say, *"No!"* in the thunder

Target

Now come the fiery darts
That go forth from my tong
And rain behind them, sparks
That twill burn more than one

And find their mark, will they
Sinking deep within the heart
Of those to whom you say
And hope to cleave apart

To rend the spirit of
Those whom you despise
To rain from high above
And hear their cries arise

Oh how we draw our bow
The arrow in our glove
But never do we know
Why aim we oft those we love

Dancing With Knives

It's raining right now
It seems the clouds have followed me
Dark though these clouds may be
I'm smiling

The puddles I step between
From cloud to darkened cloud
I watch the rain come down
Getting wet

The joy I find from this
A sight so sorrowful
As wrath doth overflow
So cruel

Oh bolts of lightning
Soaring through the sky
Between the tearful cries
Amidst thunder

Hearing now, the song
The music of the storm
Of agony and scorn's
Swelling chorus

I see the flashing eyes
Of my many partners
Those who seem to guarder
My rage

Now every plea I hear
It only amplifies
The thing behind my eyes

The hollowness

A bit of spirit
Or what remains
It lies within me, holding pain
Close by

Clutching to this empty idol
I cling, do I, in fear
And feeling rather queer
I stare

Not quite content
It hasn't relieved me
But rather, it has left me queasy
Feeling sick

I'm alone now
No clouds around
Puddles abound
It's quiet

Catharsis

Oh comes the burning in my chest
The fire deep inside
I want to put the flames to rest
I want to paint with knives

To douse it out with passion
To drown it out with cries
To bathe myself in crimson
To make the fire die

Then comes the scarlet rain
I dance amidst the dye
The burning slightly wanes
The pain behind my eyes

And as the red tides roll
Washing me; I sigh
My spirit now is cold
No longer flames reside

Now drenched, I only shiver
My eyes are open wide
As my hands quake and quiver
My paintings make me cry

Light House

Not all are meant for happiness
To be out in sun's warm light
Some people in distress
People in constant fight

Many cannot survive
A world turned upside down
But these strange ones, they thrive
And never seem to drown

But joy, for them, is something
They just aren't meant to have
From pain, there is no running
Accept, do they, the sad

And though they do not wish it
They know that deep within
This sorrow that they visit
It causes them to grin

For while others are afraid, yes
Of the blackness and the brine
Those special souls, in darkness
Like beacons do they shine

They give out hope to others
But never to themselves
Giving light unto their brothers
Though it's too dark to tell

Immortal

Look at all the little immortals, as pebbles in the sea
No man can understand them, especially you or me
They've seen the world; no others have seen it so perfectly
To be devoid of death, how they live I cannot see

And so they walk around the world, as lonely as can be
No friends or love or romance, for everything else must die

So look again at those immortals, so devoid of death and glee
You'd think I envy them, but who else would I pity?

My Friend Madness

He writes and talks to me every day!
He's not nice in any way!

He's strait and to the point!
He's my friend, and we all know that, but sometimes he's a pain in the neck!
He drives me hard, and makes me succeed!

Now you know my good friend!
So don't make him mad and he won't kill again!

Kaden Moeller

<u>Wallstreet</u>

Mob

Man is Mob
Mob is Man

Steeling is sought
All men are bought

To laugh at life
To love in loss

A seed to sow
To reap a soul

A price to pay
A prayer to say

When all is said
And nothing done

All men will wonder
Which man has won?

Ideology

At the funeral of Communism
In comes bulbous Capitalism
And chuckles in his entropy
Over the triumph of his apathy

The older generation, they doth wail
The youth don't know what this entails
No longer is there socialism
Instead we lye in great division

The cast system of our nation
This cold class war that is our Satan
To complain of this, now made a vice
Criticizing the rich is not so nice

And so the businesses, and the banks
Line up, do they, to give their thanks
For the death of the one who gave away
Who redistributed the wealth, they say

Buried now, the hammer and the sickle
The symbols of the strong, and of the simple
And pray, the masses, to be saved
That equality would rise from the grave

Bloodless

When the oligarchs came
Those brandishing their wealth
And led a coup; profane
To bring a downward delve

And their reign, that wretched time
Our kingdom of gold made to iron and rust
A latent rot entwined
Midst twisted wire and dust

And wheelbarrows of babies
Are worthless before their greed
Their lives are burdening
The rich man's wants and needs

As wear they the armband
That bears the dollar sign
As with pride do they stand
As their flag, they hoist it high

They salute their banner; flapping
Outward; extend their hands
That money sign, it's trapping
For this, they call, *"Free Land"*

And let the poor to writhe
And let the weak to screech
But put them off to die
Exterminate the weak

For matters little to them
Those higher castle dwelling souls
Who seem to have forgotten
That money's dry and cold

They worship at the alter
Of profit motivation
And do not even bother

To care of their own nation

A burden be human decency
A trifle to the rich
Who could care less of you or me
Those begging in the ditch

So praise, do they, the market
Songs of love and adoration
No matter cost, it's profit
That matters to the nation

So not a life has worth
Beyond productivity
Upon this lonely earth
Your value is your money

And you may think of love
And you may dream of glee
But there worth nothing of
The time you spend working

To grind yourself to poverty
Midst concentration camps
To concentrate on just one thing
Wealth; and the joy it grants

For time, its value, limitless
It grants a man contemplation
And lets him think on his distress
To change his fate's relation

The oligarchs crowd out your time
So that your mind is rattled
You cannot think, so to divine
That you've been made to chattel

For wisdom requires knowledge
And knowledge requires learning
And when there's not time for this
You find, wheels, you're turning

You'll put in all the work

Kaden Moeller

For another man's gain
Allowing him to shirk
Not the profits, but the pain

They've put the bridle on you
And pull hard on the bit
To drive their fortune through
At the cost of the life you live

This overthrow of the human soul
To clamp down on the spirit
It has to die, it needs to go
Or we will die from it

There is not end to greed
It will but bleed you dry
And then turn to your babies
So that they too can die

The cost of doing business
For those who have no conscience
Is bringing others distress
So long as it's not inconvenient

For pain to other people
Is not pain to themselves
So pile they the coals
For other's private hells

A horror be the oligarchs
Whose only creed is greed
Who have not but a half a heart
And no kindness to bleed

The Republic

Look out for the lazy poor
Remember to live for others

They wish to steal so lock the door
Our fellows are our brothers

No one should just give anything away
So many people are in need

Heaven forbid they not work for pay

No one notices a good deed

For those without will want more
The starving are yearning

I hate them, so lock the store
It seems there is no learning

They chose their wretched lot
Poverty is not a choice

These parasites should stop
Why don't you listen to their voice?

I have worked hard and made my way
You give yourself too much credit

I am a king and here I'll stay
To others you are in debt

I am great and need no one
Must be a lonely life

My success is what makes my life fun
Is it devoid of strife?

I need not pity any soul
What of the living man?

Why are you trying to make me look cold?
Because you withhold your hand

I owe them nothing!
You're not alone

How are you so trusting?
Is your heart a stone?

You are petty, don't preach to me
You are cold down to the core

Store up your treasures in heaven and leave me be
You wish us dead, is this war?

Brother's Keepers

The poor; they need no money
Twould take poverty away
And this is next to godliness
Or so that's what they say

The poor; they need no food
For they're just useless eaters
Taking from all of us
We; who are so dear

The poor; need no compassion
It takes from them, motivation
To pity them is worthless
It doesn't even help them

The poor; they need no love
For how could they have earned it?
Love is a costly thing
And they're degenerate

The poor; they need no help
Not even when they're hurt
But pull up by the bootstraps
And go and find some work

Enough?

Here is the story of the life of a man
He was so vary greedy
Every person he met he stole from, so they ran
But inside he still felt needy

He looked and searched for happiness, for love, and companionship
For he thought those things divine
But all he found were crooks like him, reading from the same old script
His life no longer seemed sublime

And so many riches did he store up, because of his consumption
As more is never enough, even when proved fatal
And so he took everything from everyone around him
Greed's greatest sight is blind

No sacred tie of friendship, or family bond of kin
To one so greedy, everything is mine

Greed

Wanting is good
Having is better
Stealing is fine
Giving preferred
Loving is labor
Lusting for pleasure
Possessing is great
Owning forever
More is marvelous
Owing is monstrous
Losing is strenuous
Living vivacious
Dying disingenuous
God is glorious
I demand more
Yes!

Greed, greed, greed, greed, greed, greed, greed, greed
Always wanting more
Treating everything as a whore
Demanding every ounce of strength around thee
But giving little in return for all the sacrifices you see
After what you want is done it's never enough
It drives you mad that your workers hands are rough

Everything men need, it comes from me
Stand up. Sit down, beg bitch you work for me!
Only the smallest of bones do I give you, so be content
Everything you have was given to you at my consent
Rights? Ha, ha! Gone if they inconvenience me
How free do you think I'd let you be?

You can say what you want and do as you please
Your money always comes back to me with ease
And when you're dead, I'll still make money off of you
Grind you up for fertilizer and sell you as plant food
And when you've dissolved into the earth
I'll build a factory and deny nature your rebirth
And when one day it becomes profitable to allow life to be
I'll make damn sure their signing in at my registry
No matter where you live or how far you go

I'll pop up every place, even where you'll never know

Greed takes
Greed makes
Greed proliferates

Building, booming, bombing
Ticking, tocking, timing

Greed takes everything down into the grave
And when it gets to heaven, makes God a slave
There is no single soul who is immune to greed
Because everybody loves to think they have a need

Wanting not waiting
Having and hating

The greediest of us all have turned stealing into a sport

Now don't listen to this tease
This message is for those of you who say please
Live this life as if you were on the run
Take what you can, because when it's over you're done
There is no happy place where all you dreams come true
This life is it, and those dreams are up to you
Live while you can, no need to be nice
I know one thing, I'm greedy for life

Game Theory

And so, the game is played
I'll hire five of you
I'll pay you five an hour
Eight hours every day
To make some pairs of shoes
Ten pairs; every hour
Is all I ask of you
Just sign the contract here
And money I'll give you

Eight hours pass for each
Each man paid forty dollars
A day of work is done
The shoes are on the shelves
Each priced at ten dollars a pair
Ten shoes made each hour

Four Hundred pairs of shoes
At ten dollars an hour
Four thousand dollars of wealth

One thousand dollars; all
One week of work for five people
Two hundred a piece
Their take home pay
Three thousand left for me
One thousand for the bills
One thousand for me to play with
One thousand to save

Those five, they've spent their cash
On living through their lives
Each week I pay for them to eat
To sleep and keep alive

And that is but one week
Each month I make sixteen thousand
One thousand a week for bills
One thousand a week for pay
One thousand a week for play
One thousand a week to save
I've four thousand left at the end of the month
My workers, barely any

By the end of the year I've got
Forty eight thousand in the bank
My workers, well, who knows
But I saved up more than enough
I think I'll start another shop and replicate my game
I mean, I'm a capitalist, it's money all the same

Voting

I thing I'll vote a quarter-mill
Towards my candidate
His coffers will I swell
With this support I make

Perhaps my bidding voice
Requires more inflection
Oh I quite like this choice

To purchase this election

Though I can't buy their votes
I can buy time for lies
And shove them down their throats
And burn them in their eyes

I do not care for welfare
Or even charity
Lest I can make a snare
To make me more money

With every man I buy
I make them work for me
And with greed in their eyes
They pledge their loyalty

Oh how I love democracy
And I do love my nation
It's made for people just like me
By and for the corporations

American Dream

We are a nation of haves, and soon to haves
So come now, and lift up your slabs
Take every rock, and pick it up
Hoist them high, and stack them to the top

Build me a structure oh so grand
A building for the king of sand
A place that with your blood and gloom
A monument to be my tomb

Stock high the walls within with gold
Walls one day covered up with mold
All the riches of the land
Buried with me, oh I'm so grand

But worry not, builders, can't you see
Someday, maybe, you'll be like me
And build a kingdom on the graves
Of all your servants and your slaves

For when you have a real job
You'll be like me, just like a god

So work hard, don't complain, and slave away
Keep dreaming of that special day

Then, maybe, you will be like me
And take away life, and liberty
For it doesn't matter what you need
Just fulfill the will of greed

Misdirect

We're living in a land of need
So let's fulfill the creed of greed

Let us look out at all the poor
And scold them for demanding more
And tell them the great elaborate lie
That life is better when you die

"So worry not you little slaves
Your life is good, for Jesus saves
Remember to obey your masters
The scriptures say so in their chapters"

"Authority, divine or not
Not to be questioned with your thoughts
So shut your mouths, and just obey
Plead only to the one you pray"

"But if you question and backslide
Don't let your lack of faith divide
Just let our words drown out your reason
Your doubt will pass, it's just a season"

Just look at all these sorry sods
Believe they it's the word of God

Moral Quandary

To Act Or Not To Act

So
Which is more laudable?

To speak of moral strength
And lambast the wicked?
Or
To stand up against them
When the time comes to do so

So
Which is just?

To wait to act
Until a more opportune time
Or
To try everything within one's own power
In an attempt to prevent evil

So
Which
Pray tell
Is better

To stand by
Knowing that abuse is occurring
But twenty feet away
And say to one's self
"Tis not my affair."
Or
To take the risk
And do right by one's conscience
No matter what the possibilities

So
Which is it
Which is better
What would you want,
If you needed help?

Actions And Words

I never thought

That I would be lectured about
Doing the right thing

That I would be told
"The next time you hear
That someone needs help
Don't get involved"

What?

"Just
Call the police
And
Stay out of it"

?

"You don't know what it could be over
He could have had a gun
Or a knife
She could be a hooker
And he, her pimp"

!

"The point is
You could have been hurt
Yes, that's it
It's not your responsibility"

How can anyone say that?!
Really?
If you hear screams
You won't help?
You won't come?
You'd just stand there!
What type of man are you
Are you not the man, who
Lectures others on their moral failings
Who
Lords his religious convictions over others
And acts like he is God's gift to moral judgment
And this
This is your advice

No!

I'll not stand idly by
And listen as she screamed for help
No, I won't just wait for the police
It takes them fifteen to twenty minutes
What if something worse were to happen to her?

"But you don't know anything about the argument
It could be anything
It's an unknown act of violence"

And how do you think she felt?
Should I just have let it happen?!

"What if you were hurt?
What good would you have done then?"

It's not about that
It's about doing what you can
When you have the power to do so
It's about not just letting bad things happen

"But what about…"

What!?
Listen!
There are hundreds of possible outcomes
They still do not take away the fact
That I am morally obligated to help
That I must act
That I cannot just let it happen

"It was foolish
It was reckless"

It was the right thing to do
If I had just stood there
I'd be no different than the one who was committing the crime

"Things could have happened
You must understand
I fear for you
You're my son"

Yes

And she
She is someone's daughter
Which child is worth more?
What man are you to judge, based on nothing?

This is sad
This ridiculous criticism
This selfish advice
In the name of my safety
You'd sacrifice someone else?
You'd tell me
To stand there

Just let it happen then?
Let the blood be on my hands
Is that it?

What would you sacrifice me for?
When would my bravery count?
Is my fearful act of investigation so distasteful?
Do you think all who try their best to be fools?

Think me not a man who is hero minded
I was just as scared as you
But
The difference is
This atheist, did something

Venting

I'm writing this
Because I'm mad
My anger overflows
This feeling
In my heart
I do not enjoy it
I was useless today
Like so many days before
But today
It mattered

Today
I should have made a difference
I heard the screams

At first

Thought it was a party
But
The closer they came
They were not joyful

*"Go away!
Stay away!
Stop!
Leave me alone!"*

And so I ran to look
To find out what was wrong

She was alone when I arrived
Picking up her things
Crying
A far off stare in her eyes
Inconsolably wandering

I said *"Get in the truck
We'll go call the police"*
But she wouldn't come with me
She kept crying and walking

I called the police
And then whet back for her
But
She was gone
Disappeared!

I drove
I searched
The police came
We talked
And then they went looking

But I
I stood there useless

Oh I know what it's like
To be helpless
To be unable to fight
To be taken from
The shame

Kaden Moeller

The weakness
The self-loathing

Oh
This I know
But what's worse?
Watching it
Knowing it happened
That you could not prevent it
Seeing the tears
Not saving someone
Not acting faster
Not knowing
Not being there
This is worse

Oh
I know the truth
That they may never find her
Crimes like this occur
And never are they solved
No one ever fixes it
No one saves the day

The pain
It but twill fester
Crippling the soul

Oh
It isn't fair
To know you were
Too slow
Unable to stop
What she begged to be stopped
Feels like
Complacency
Like you were the one who did it
You hurt her with your response
If only you knew
If only you had driven faster
If only...

And now
Who knows what will happen
If she'll be found
If the crime will be reported

The perpetrator, caught
The pain, elated
My anger, dimmed

Oh
How I now hate myself
I didn't stop a thing
I couldn't even keep her still
So that the police could help

I know it's not my fault
I know I'm not to blame
But that almost makes it worse
I'm a bystander

Why did all the other cars
Pass her screaming
Why was I
The only one who
Went to look
Why now am I burdened
With a guilty conscience

I've done the best I can
But still
It doesn't help me

I'm angry
I feel useless
The moment of truth arrived
And I failed someone
I didn't help fast enough
I didn't stay with her long enough

I just
I did nothing
I couldn't even do
The right thing right

Kaden Moeller

Human Climate

The Sand Man

I am the desert wanderer
The hermit of the sand
See me, will you, off yonder
Here in my dusty land

The sun, high up, in cloudless sky
Reflecting a watery mirage
This may cause other hearts to sigh
But me, there's no disparage

The sun though, isn't lonely
In the heavens way up high
The vultures circle, roaming
Up in the arid sky

Soaring upon the winds
Drifting the round about
These birds do dance and swim
As time, downward they count

Sandals upon my feet
I wander through the bramble
And pick the cactus fruit, so sweet
Stroking my beard's thick curls

Amidst the thistles and the rocks
I see the scorpion
He scuttles, as his tail, he cocks
Searching for a victim

The mouse avoids the rattle snake
And scampers down the hole
A shriek I hear though, seems to state
The snake has found a mole

I recline myself upon a stone
And slowly nod off to sleep
Listening to the coyote moan
As the bats begin to cheap

I hear the rattler warning
The screech-owl watching him

The owl disagrees, now screaming
Flying in

The horny toad, he croaks
But then thinks better of it
He heard the screech-owl's note
So in quiet now he sits

I'm not alone upon my rock
A friendly tarantula
Searching for warmth, to me he walks
Snuggling up like hand to glove

The wind slides across emptiness
A soothing hollow call
As into blackened nothingness
Not into dreams I fall

Oh I am the wanderer
The man without a home
This wilderness is full of wonder
A place I love to roam

Pail Face

Please gather round my children, near
Hear my tail, oh so queer

This story of a mighty man
The founder of a different clan
A warrior, name long forgot
He climbed up to the mountain top

And from there did he see the earth
Its bounty and its endless worth
And so he raised his fist towards the sky
It would be his, or so he'd try

And gather, did he, up his braves
He took away his neighbors caves
Killing the ones who would resist
His hands stained red up to his wrists

The rest he kept for serfs and slaves
This earth they tilled became their graves
But this strong man, fat he became

His strength left him, made him so plain

So shape and change the land did he
It wasn't what it used to be
And one day he decided to look out
At this world he took, and so with clout

Out of his window did he gaze
And there in fear there he stood amazed
For his reflection did he see
Against the world now made from he

A place now withered and made frail
His eyes sunk deep, his face grew pail
And all his sons had that expression
But, like him, failed to learn the lesson

The world was not made to conquer or subdue
This world was made for me and you

Noble Warning

Coming to my neighbor, I did, knock
And beg to he, all the more
To please, the madness, stop
And open up the door

But he did play his fiddle
And said to me, aloud
"Bother not me with this drivel
And cry you 'wolf' so proud!"

But knock, did I, a second time
To tell him of the storm
For not to, it would be a crime
Leaving he to natures scorn

But he, he did not abide
Pay me, would he, no heed
Saying *"Nature, God doth guide*
Now do not bother me!"

But say I "Please prepare!
I beg of thee, my friend

Of nature, do not dare
For your life she will rend"

But again did he mock
And laugh at the world, in scorn
Calling me *'of the wayward flock'*
Those people who are torn

But, oh, I could not stay
And so now, did I, offer
To do for he what he said *'nay!'*
But, oh, he was a scoffer

"Go back to your own lot
And leave me to my own
For I have what I've got
Now just leave me alone!"

I lingered, but a moment
I truly hesitated
For all my good intent
Twas was not appreciated

And so I left his door
The next day, I looked long
Alas, I knock no more
For his house, it was gone

Good People

Oh look at that poor otter
All covered up in oil
We should go scrub his fur
Saving him is worth the toil

Cleaning this special creature
As it would splash and play
Oh such a funny feature
Cuter than words can say

And then, when he was clean
We took him to the shore
The crowd, they cheered and screamed
As the band played above the roar

The otter scampered out

And then began to swim
In joy the crowd did shout
Until a whale ate him

Smog

There is no sun in the city
I cannot see the sky
At night the stars are blotted out
The view is such a pity

The air is thick and strong
I feel it in my chest
This artificial landscape
It's not where I belong

The streets are filled with humans
They live in this dark place
These neon lights here in the streets
They wander up and through them

The sound of engines fill the air
It builds around the bodies
And makes the soundtrack to the scene
Noise pollution everywhere

I keep an eye out for something more
A bit of nature untouched
A tidbit of tranquility
But that would be a bore

I'm still finding it difficult
To find a place for me
Solitude amidst this madness
This lifestyle is a cult

Past, Present And Future

The dinosaurs aren't dead, my friend
They're with us now, today
The brontosaurs, they stomp around
Up in the clouds, so grey

Velociraptors, vicious

Kaden Moeller

They lacerate the lungs
As dark tyrannosaurs
Stand to blot out the sun

These corpses, once at rest
Have risen from the grave
In oil, black and thick
To incense, smoky grey

Extinct, they were, and are
Yet murder us today
They hunt us down through cancer
And weather's changing ways

These dead, call to their graves
Those living in the present
The past claws at us darkly
And looms with dark intent

The power of the dinosaur
We took, but not restrained
And they will bring unto us
Extinction to our names

For we, greedy for power
We took it from the dead
But know we not that what we've dug
Be it a shallow bed

The World To Come

Oh pity the youth to come
That generation scorned
Whose world be undone
And yet they be unborn

Those lives, be cursed to terror
Extinction on their lips
Know not they that despair
Twill claim life, all of it

They've never done a wrong
Yet they'll pay for the sins
Of grandparents long gone
Those who committed them

They'll wonder why they're born
For such a life as this
Why feel they the storm
Of what they did not wish

And when there's nothing left
But echoes of our words
The world would never guess
That we were once her stewards

The Cold Embrace Of Acceptance

We are living in the last days
When the skies will roll the clouds to grey
And every place that once was green
Twill dry and wither, grass and weed

And come will water, deep and wide
To swallow every soul inside
Caressing cross the land in waves
Making their homes into their graves

Oh watch will we the coming wars
For mouths of water, not much more
As sun watches from way up high
And twill shed not a tear, nor cry

And hear will we not one regret
That's worth a single word that's said
Those weak minded, whose children die
They will be passing for their lies

A sad and sorrowed state this be
And bitter type of grief, from greed
For those who grasped life by the fist
They'll watch it wither and desist

There is no saving from this now
And now I sit here, an artist
Who lives to make these simple rhymes
That will lose their audience in not much time

Relationships

Mirror

You say to me "I'm old
Look at my wrinkled face
My touch has grown so cold
I no longer hold youth's grace"

And so I come up behind you
And look with you; into the mirror
Your hands do I clasp mine to
Holding to you, my dear

"Where is this person that you see?
I'm looking at you now
And what's reflecting back at me
Leaves me only asking 'How?!'"

"Am I really so lucky?
To hold these soft warm hands
To have them still caress me
And hold me as no one can"

"And what face, besides yours
Could have eyes more beautiful
Then all the stars, or deepest pools
Who shimmer beneath their glow?"

"Oh that heart, I feel its beat
The song of love's strong anthem
So thusly do I move my feet
According to its rhythm"

"So where is this one you speak of?
This person of whom I hear
They cannot be the one I love
This one here in the mirror"

You smile, and do look back at me
And then say "Don't say that."
Sighing, you say unhappily
"You know, I'm getting fat."

Kaden Moeller

The Long Term

Our touch is hot electric
Though not to my dismay
The current is still there
And stronger, I might say

Our bodies not as spry
Though this is what's expected
And with a humble sigh
Our passions are relented

I find that when I kiss you
Your well be not as deep
Though this is of me too
How strange, the love we keep

As ever can be said
Of two now made as one
I must say that I tread
Much lighter than once done

You are a joy to me
To lose you, I am wary
Though strange I find it be
Our love's now ordinary

Something that now occurs
Like rain come from the sky
When it kisses the earth
The plates don't shift and rise

It's almost, now, routine
These acts of ecstasy
That once caused me to dream
Of holding you to me

But now that warmth's familiar
As we lie hear in bed
I watch you sleeping there
As there I rest my head

So common now, our nights
Not like a time ago
When we would soar the heights
Of young love; new to know

An average soul here lives
Along the side of me
Oh so placid it is
To be so ordinary

Smart Mouth

Well, there I was
In the middle of things
Not yet drunk on lust
And then I hear her voice ring

*"You stink down here, and
You could lose some weight"*
Now, some responses came to mind then
They did not hesitate

"Well you're no rose yourself, sweet cheeks
And as for all that fat
It's a pillow, where your elbows sleep
Its use now proves that fact"

"Oh don't get smart with me"
She said with mouth half full
*"Who else would want to be
With a fat sarcastic fool?"*

"Yes you, you're such a catch"
As my tong, it licked so light
"Your looks and mine don't mesh
My queen of cellulite"

*"You're treading tender ground
You better watch your feet
You don't want me to frown
And maybe use my teeth"*

"My sweet and tender girl
You know I'm only kidding
For you, you are my world
A planet, made for me!"

And then I heard her snort

Kaden Moeller

Her laugh was such a thing
That made me want no more
Those sultry notes she'd sing

And so we laid in bed a bit
Chuckling, while half aroused
She says to me *"You look like shit"*
"So says my humble cow"

Oh all the years gone by
Us two friends, still together
Though passion's sometimes hard to spy
We've love, one for another

At Play

Oh how I love your smile
It is so devilish
Showing your playful wiles
Tis so fun to express

You run, and you do tease me
I follow close behind
Loving to watch your glee
It sooths me every time

Seeing that crooked grin
Hearing that joyful laugh
It warms my soul within
A warmth I often lack

You are my happiness
My light in this dark world
A beauty, to me, blessed
This smile that you curl

Oh, what would I do,
If you were to disappear?
I say this, though I know
This hour is coming near

Twenty Years

Last night, I was there
Naked, laying bare
Touching, softness

I groped and groaned at your caress

Everything, to hold it all
And though my hands did not forestall
They slipped upon those curves of sweat
So that this *"all"* I could not get

This one I held to in the dark
Hear I their pounding beating heart
Their warmth I feel against my skin
So close to me, yet not within

A touch, I fear to be without
Twould be life's fire burning out
And leaving me alone and cold
Without a heart or hand to hold

And though I'd felt much ecstasy
I hold you to me desperately
As if in a flash you'd soon be gone
Taken by a better one

But stayed you with me, all night long
Holding to me as sleep doth come
And as dawn crests horizons edge
I think upon the day we wed

Quiet Time

I love to lay with you
To hold you at my side
And feel this love that grew
Between us by and by

The warmth; come from your frame
Your slow and steady breaths
It may seem rather plain
But feel I it is best

To run my hands across your legs
And feel their prickly stubble
Embarrassed, though you'd never say
I feel it; oh so subtle

Kaden Moeller

I grasp your well worn hands
So rough, yet oh so soft
And you, you smile, and
I see you feel loss

Something you'd never tell
A thing you needn't say
Oh worry you so well
On what you fear has aged

Believe you, what I want
Is only what I see?
That you are here to flaunt
For youth, so endlessly?

No, I too am quite old
But do you see my shame?
Of course the answer's *'no'*
It does not bring me pain

This person next to me
They be the one I want
Even when they're sick
Clammy, pail or gaunt

Your warmth is all I need
Your scent; a sweet perfume
With you I long to be
Closer than I can do

I never wish be parted
From the one to whom I cleave
And yet, what age has charted
Be an untimely leave

Us two, when we're together
So close, yet not enough
Think I on nothing better
Then when we hold to touch

Vows

Oh darling, how I love you so
Even in knowing that one day you'll go
That everything that makes you up
Will, someday, like a door, be shut

Your beauty, like the morning frost
Will melt away until it's lost
And you strength, like the remaining dew
Will fade, and fall away from you

Your pale blue moon eyes will fog and dim
Showing the soul, weary within
Oh and of your long flowing mane
It shall be white, faded and plain

Your mind, become the morning mist
Forgetting my lips you loved to kiss
This fog, it rises from the ground
The steam from the frost and dew I found

My sweet, I know you find it strange
Saying such things may sound insane
But know not what I speak to you
Twill sadly, someday soon, be true

Anniversary

How has your face been made so old?
My fiery one who danced so bold
The wrinkles, across your brow they crowd
My spryly sprite, once so proud

When my memories of the past meet now
These lines fade from your face somehow
No longer see I your crumpled frame
Nor your body riddled with the pain

Rather I see my smiling bride
The one that time has tried to hide
Who stuck with me through thick and thin
And loved the me that's deep within

Oh how I love you just as much
As when our bodies first did touch
Even now we seem inseparable
Our passion thrived, and it did grow

Oh of these tricks of mind and eyes

Kaden Moeller

With lump in throat I try to sigh
For this beauty is not so, you see
The truth is such a tragedy

Insomnia

To lay awake beside
The lover in your bed
And have those breaths, confined
To their now sleeping head

Oh count, do you, their ins and outs
These precious breaths of life
Each be a joyous vibrant shout
In middle of the night

These *"honks"* and *"hoos"* sprung forth
From those sweet tender lips
Yes those beloved snorts
Cause you to think a bit

Oh why is all that beauty
To vanish late at night
As sprawled, you lay their drooling
Tis not a pleasant sight

As flatulence wafts up
From deep beneath the sheets
If sound twas not enough
To keep you from your sleep

So lay you, wide awake
A hostage in your bed
The romance, sure, it's great
I'd rather sleep instead

Eulogy For Youth Or "Did You Love Mom?"

Well, of course I loved your mother
We two, I mean, when I first met her
The stars shimmered brighter, the sun was warmer
And I couldn't get enough of her smile
Everything was so different then, I was young
She was young, and... I loved her.

Oh, enough of the bullshit, I was horny as hell

344

When I saw her I wanted to fuck her, yes I said it
And I say it as a man in love
I wanted to plunge my cock into her slimy silky vice-grips
And hold her in my arms as tightly as possible

I'll say it! I stared at her shapely apple ass as she walked
And gawked at her breasts when we talked
I looked at her lips and wanted to kiss them, wanted
Them to kiss me, wanted them around my dick and sucking

I won't lie, she was beautiful and I wanted her
My cock-head was as hard as a diamond and I lusted
To penetrate her every hole and fill her with my cum
And I don't care who knows, because I loved her
I wanted her belly full of my sperm and her body
In my embrace, and by god was that what I wanted!

But don't think me just an animal who's rut has
Run amuck, yes I wanted to fuck her, but I loved her
I was afraid of what sex would do to us
Pregnancy, fuck that, at the time we wanted no children
And she was on the pill, what I was scared of, was me

I didn't want our relationship to change too much, I feared
That she would think less of me when we were together
That she would think me just a phallus
A mindless male who's only desire was sex
I loved her, and I loved all of her
She was so much fun, and funny, god was she funny
Had a wit you could carve a turkey with
And her brains, well, she was quite studious is all I'll say

So yes, I felt the pull of my pants towards her
But I oh so wanted more
And when the day came, she was sitting across from me
In a chair, and I was sitting on the floor thumbing a book
And she snapped her fingers and spread her thighs apart
Those skin tight jeans hugging every curve

By god my heart nearly exploded, along with my pants
I was on her so fast I knew not what came over me
And when I slid myself inside, she whispered *"Fuck me you stud, fuck me"*
And I did, as hard and as fast as I could
Pounding and pounding and pounding until her insides were wet with sperm

And our outsides were soaked with sweat

Then I sat, back against the wall, breathing heavy and she
Her head on my crotch, the slimy syrup of life sticking to her hair
And as she rested her head upon my groin and stared into my eyes
I'd never felt so much like a man, and then she said *"You're a quick shot"*

I blushed, and I remember feeling shame and embarrassment, but
Before I could apologize for being such an animal, and not thinking
She'd straddled me and grabbed my cock and pressed it
Into herself again, and we fucked and fucked and fucked
Again, again and again all day and night and we both called out of work
To do it even more, and those days were amazing, wonderful heaven on earth
And I wouldn't trade them for anything, hell if I had a regret it's that we
Didn't fuck more, so yes I loved your mother, my wife and by god
I miss her, and those lovely days gone by

<u>Politic</u>

Kaden Moeller

The Hand That Rocks The Cradle

What is it like
To meet greatness?
To carry
Inside you
A future king?

Or
To shake the hand
Of a stranger
Destined
To change the world

Or
To answer a question
Of a child
To teach the philosopher
Before he teaches others

Or
To hear the words
Those sweet syllables
Of a budding intellect
Before it blooms in earnest

Or
To lend a helping hand
To one who'll help thousands more

And
What of saving a child
Who'll burn the world over
And sear our very hearts
With blackness and fear?

Oh
What is it like
To meet greatness
You'll never know

Birth Of The Sanders

May the wind be ever at your back
May you never stumble on the track
Chase the wind amidst the gale

Fear thee not that you may fail
Stride for stride pick up your feet
With each step you retreat defeat
For fortune favors but the brave
The bold know not to back away
I wish thee great and wish thee well
Now go my friend and give them hell

Done

I'm finished with my work today
And now it's time to laugh and play

So quickly now, I will retreat
Take off the shoes upon my feet
And dive, will I, into the pool
Feeling the water quick and cool

Will take I this quick bath of joy
Play round in it as I with a toy
And get out quick to dry right off
And run before the feeding trough

Stuffing my face with cakes and cream
As child in fantastic dream
Then with my stomach full to bursting
I'll walkabout and do some searching

Spotting the birds upon the trees
Seeing them play between their leaves
And marvel will I at natures bliss
And take in everything as not to miss

After completing my excursion
Finish, will I, my short diversion
By lying down within my bead
And resting soft my weary head

Allowing a smile across my face to creep
As I now fall away to sleep

Recession

A heavy weight beneath your eyes

Carrying so much you have to cry
Relieving yourself of this load
Those bags stored up the tears that flowed

The world, wears atop your back
Your shoulders bend and creak and crack
There's too much work that needs be done
Your skin so red beneath the sun

With joints stiff and body brittle
You watch your dreams, once tall, now little
Hobble, do you, towards desire
The things, it seems, you won't acquire

Oh where's that spark that once burned bright?
It seems so dim now in the night
To even wish on falling stars
Seems too much work to look that far

Populism

It's not easy being me
Surrounded by stupidity
Oh the unpleasantly
Yet, what would they do if I ceased to be?

The imbeciles say I'm lazy
The fools to the contrary
The simpleminded think I look wary
The blind non-thinker finds me scary

I'm dreary I'm tired I'm on the spot
Surprisingly, I do a lot
The morons say that I look hot
The less complex place me in a complicated slot
While those of lower philosophy, believe that I think not
I'd say they were quite incorrect
But alas I think they would forget

And so they mumble and they jeer
Leaving me to think this rather queer
They complain so much of the job I do
Perhaps forget they their job too?

Seven

It is a black hole in the center of a lava filled lake
Encrusted with the most corrosive of fumes and fire
It absorbs all evil and spreads it by word of mouth
It cannot see good, only controversy and pain
It's everywhere and nowhere, yet we listen
To think it is on every night at seven

Throwing Rocks

One day, out you threw
The pebble of your opinion
And upon the water, grew
The ripple this stone opened

Oh what's a ripple worth?
It shimmers and fades away
But the stone, it seems to irk
Others be thrown its way

Each rock, a little bigger
Each splash, a little louder
And as more people heard
More rocks begin to shower

And as many more do fall
The ripples turn to waves
And soak the ones who stall
To hear the words they say

And when the world is wet
The torrent then dies down
Amazing what you get
From one ripple's little sound

The Echo Of The Shadow

Will you be the voice,
Who whisper's in the dark?
"Come follow me by choice
And learn to love the spark"

To lead the stumbling few

Kaden Moeller

Towards the fire, so warm
And enter back anew
To the darkness to find more

To be a denizen of the night
To lust the flickering flame
But never linger near her, might
Her warmth cause you remain

The fire, though you want it
The darkness draws you near
And makes that fire on the wick
Seem all the more so dear

That pretty dancer in the dark
Who warms her lover's hands
And though your love does draw you back
Near her you'll never stand

For you, you roam the spaces
Of lost and wounded things
Yes you, you wonder places
Where light casts not its beams

For you are the forgotten
Who brings with you, those cast
And wayward souls, downtrodden
Whose arms, at shadows grasp

Yes, you, you bring to light
What once was tucked away
Those hidden in the night
That place you choose to stay

So sway you, to and fro
From light to dark again
Even though you know
That one is better than

Beer Hall

The morals of the crowd
The blinding drowning loud
The rising writhing mass
The angry raging class

They'll tell you what to do
They'll tell you what is true
They'll tell you what you see
They'll tell you who to be

With words that flex their hate
With words that sound so great
With words like *"us"* and *"them"*
With words that carve and rend

Rising from their seats
Rising throughout the streets
Rising throughout the land
Rising to take a stand

It's not about the facts
It's not about the truth
It's all about the rats
And the poison they bring through

Liberty Lust

Oh when I hear of liberty
I cannot help but sneer
Oh that description that I see
I find it rather queer

Yes, I should be free from people
And never be a slave
Oh this seems rather simple
And yet it's oh so grave

Society, they say
I should owe not a thing
Oh it would make me gay
To be free of everything

Yes, selfishness is wise
And greed, it is the good
These maxims, though be lies
Be but half understood

The depths of this philosophy
I watch the ants wade through

Those thoughts, they seem so measly
Though scream they *"It is true!"*

Though water just a thin
When turned into black ice
Can lead to devastation
Upon the road of life

Responsibility, not for our fellow man
But only to ourselves
Lend not a helping hand
Unless they earn it well

Community is evil
So only trust yourself
Together we can't grow
To form a commonwealth

The individual, is more important than
Society, so that
Swallow, will they, a camel, and
Strain, will they, a gnat

To justify the sociopath
By saying that it's thought
Claiming compassion's trash
Even though its not

Assassination

How to destroy a good man?
Do it with a righteous cause
Raise the standard higher than
The man is capable of

But turn what he fights for
Into an enemy
Who scoffs; as if to deplore
The good man's thoughts and deeds

And call each action taken
But all too trivial
Each effort, you can make them
An underwhelming jewel

Fret not upon his past

When he fought and suffered, nay
Just rather but detract
That the past is not today

And drown his words to nothing
But faded pleading calls
Oh what good will they bring,
For no one hears at all

So when another asks
"To what the good man falls?"
That blade there in his back
It was a righteous cause

Being Right

To the victims of the star spangled banner of deceit
To the ones who sit in fear
Your paranoia doth bequeath
This creeping dread you hear

Yes, hear the conspiracy
This theory so unfounded
And all these horrors you don't see
Though your alarm's been sounded

Oh come the wolf criers
Sounding howls out from their dens
They are as foxes, who don't hide
But live among the hens

And so, you sheep, you run and bleat
Crying out, so lost
This mad stampede goes through the street
Believing lies, they cost

Smashing all before you
Any now in your way
No matter what others do
Believe you not the words they say

The parade, it doesn't end here
Continuing to stomp the ground
Inducing many more to fear

So that they gather round

And make, do you, your army
A blind and angry cavalcade
Your words are not disarming
They make the world afraid

I ask you now, my friends
When does this ever end?

Those Knowing Not The Cost

When you live in faded glory
Your future isn't bright
It doesn't match the story
You tell yourself at night

To live in yester-morrow
What once was soon to be
But now it causes sorrow
For tis not what you see

For all those dreams have turned to dust
And though your tears have fallen
Upon its dried and lifeless husk
It will not rise; from them

For we can put our stock
In things of little worth
And think it's worth a lot
To bring this thing to birth

But when you see it standing
Misshapen there before you
You seem not understanding
That it was made from you

You thought yourself but wise
In everything you do
And now your future cries
For it's in front of you

Believe in what you've sewn
For it is what you've wrought
And now is yours to own
These nightmares that you've brought

A Choice

What's with the animosity
Against those in our culture
Who happen to be born differently
On what attracts another

I find it rather odd indeed
That so many do get mad
At someone's sexuality
Oh tis so very sad

Yes, so immoral are they
And so willing to chose
To be born being gay
They'd rather be abused

Yes, rather they, to be afraid
Of family, friends, and others
And make their confessions, brave
Are they who lose their cover

For obviously they love to be
Rejected by their family
And then beaten savagely
By those they confess to loving

Oh yes indeed they love it
It seems so obvious
This treatment they must want to get
For receive they nothing less

Oh why can't we accept the phrase
Different strokes for different folks
A bad pun I accept I've made
But one that gives me hope

Politicians, Pundits, Preachers and Poets

Oh warriors of a war so cold
Its memory's corps is rotting
Who'd drive us to hunt witches
To many an unjust burning

357

Who shout *"In God we trust"*
As though it were in stone
As by foundation written up
But actually is new

And yes those persons say things
"God bless" and *"Exceptional"*
As if to declare superiority
A perverse authority over others
Manifesting a deluded destiny

And oh how they love their *"Hard work"*
Because their *"Hard work"* always pays off
Leaving them well and happy
And oh so ready to lay their lives over yours
If you were like them, you'd be like them
So fuck your life, you should have had theirs
Because then you could be just as
"Successful" as them in their perverse
Triumph of their will

Oh yes, and remember that you're free
Free to be what they approve of
Christian, Jew, capitalist, entrepreneur
Anything you like, except
Socialist, Communist, Muslim, Atheist
Then you're not American, and should leave

Because what is democratic, has nothing
To do with society
Property, capital; these things are what
Society is for; mindless accumulation of wealth
What is social is tyrannical, community is evil
Unity; perverse, and collectivism; soulless
We can't help ourselves by helping others,
Twould be madness to conceive!

And don't forget, never forget, not to think
As we all know that intellectuals are a scourge
Those people and their knowledge, that knowledge
Which threatens our *"Heritage"* our *"Tradition"*
For the past is always a good thing to cling to
Especially when you haven't thought about it
Just keep doing things as you've done them
And eventually all the problems will disappear

Remember, money is the only objective
Make more money, and know that you can
Always add another dollar atop the stack
And that the lack of money shows
A lack of moral competency

So, I wonder, this is the American dream?
This is the freedom men have fought and died for?
To be a callus, selfish, greedy apathist?
Cloaked in religious righteousness; of course
But that cloak is thin, and I can see your cruelty

I don't understand, I cannot conceive
How we asked for the hungry, poor and sick
The weakest among us, the unwashed huddled masses
And then we told them *"You're not welcome here"*

Toleration

The bigot holds a freedom toast
For he abuses freedom most
Treating his fellow man as trash
Whipping freedom with a lash

The one who cries of being infringed
The one who's on a freedom binge
Who says his views are not respected
Those vile views which are rejected

The bigot, he likes freedom most
And like a tick, he drains his host
Tolerating intolerance cannot be done
For intolerance breaks up everyone

When The Walls Fell

My mind screams! Walls fall
"Why!" The quotes of kings of battles past
The walls fall down toward me
I curse the day
I curse the light
I embrace the darkness
I become my enemy!
Why?

359

A Tea Party

The nationalists have come
Here to reclaim the nation
And now we are undone
As bring they devastation

And speak, will they, the simple
Of phrase, of black and white
They know they do no evil
For they believe they're right

And every action taken
But drives the dagger deep
For they don't understand them
These things they do repeat

They revel in their mantras
And sleep in their beliefs
As dream they what never was
This thing they want to keep

And worship, do they, fear
As shun they reason's light
They clutch their totems near
As hide they in the night

They claim the name of patriot
And strike across the face
Those who criticize their lot
And strongly hold their place

These freedom fighting fools
Like lavender they then
(As we dine upon the food)
Cover up the poison

And these deeds that they do hide
These skeletons lain herein
Be not opaque outside
But stained they be crimson

They water the tree of liberty
By wringing out the bones
Of the blood of others babies

As crush they well with stones

Oh ignorance is bliss
To those who aren't in pain
And who forever miss
A place they know by name

Detriment

A bit of defamation
It's all good for the nation
A little recreation
Leading to decimation
This growing deprivation
A scary escalation

Propaganda

The best lie, the one that you believe
You reinforce, and make it be
The one that you will never doubt
And without question love to shout

You will tell it to everyone
But questioning cannot be done
The bias, it is much too strong
It makes reality seem as wrong

Why are your beliefs not confirmed?
Why contradict they with what we've learned?
The answer is as plain as day
They are not real, what can I say

Story Tellers

Beware the hero makers
Writing the stories of the dead
The cultists and the fakers
Weaving the legend web

They blow their golden trumpet
And rub their magic stone
Taking men off the toilet
To put them on the throne

They make an idol of a man
To make the others blind
Hiding their turds in sand
So no one will pay them mind

And the things they can't gloss over
They render piss in mud
Putting their actions in a blender
Blaming others for bad blood

Oh yes, these myth writers
Are dangerous indeed
In this world, they don't make light here
They lie, cheat, and deceive

Worthless

We are swimming in a world of words
So cheaply are we heard
A mouth endlessly speaking
With no words that are worth keeping

Everyone now has say
Such worth now has decayed
The artist, and the writing man
His value is so much lesser than

And when they hear the culture critic
They think him mad, and then dismiss it
Nothing is incendiary
Everything's now ordinary

The spoken word has been made cheap
There are no words somebody keeps
For in this sea of endless opinion
Reality has no dominion

And so we hear the endless drone
Of shouted word and subtle moan
I ride the wave right to the crest
To just be heard above the rest

Moral Compass

Why be it thrown; an insult

"You have a bleeding heart!"
Oh, be this not the best result,
To care but from the start?

If I bleed for the poor
The sick, young, old and dying
And love I much the more
Those in prison, weak or fighting

And lend a helping hand
To those in deepest need
And help thee stand again
When you are on your knees

And let compassion flow
Dammed not by cynicism
And may its waters grow
A virile placid land

Oh wonder, do I, well
Of the hearts who bleed but not
What caused dry those wells,
To bleed thou not a drop?

To have a heart of stone
Or one of flesh and blood
Oh how could I bemoan,
The ones who share their love?

Rather; to be cold hearted
Is something worse be said
For the bleeding heart; it lives
But the one that won't is dead

What Makes What

Could one, but pound for pound,
Take every body's blows?
And lay upon the ground
But not because repose

To take the lynching of the world
The anger, hate and rage
And as these lashes, they unfurl

To line the fleshy page

And write the human story
Of fear and barbarism
And though we call it glory
Dark history be in them

But such is not a punishment
Tis but a part of life
Such actions are not meant
They happen, day and night

No one can take what life makes up
And make it go away
For if you keep life's door shut
There's nothing left to save

The Art Of Politics

Oh gone I out to sea
The deepest farthest waters
And brought I only me
Though people flock as watchers

I've never tempted fate
But now's as good as ever
To drink in all the hate
That I am soon to weather

And so I chum the blue
Till darken it to red
My heart is pounding too
I hear it in my head

Excitement; it is mounting
As fins do breach the waves
And I am not discounting
That madness is my trade

And then I do the thing
That none believed I'd do
I send myself, hurling
Into the sharky milieu

And as I plunge down deep
Into the bloody brine

I find my ecstasy
In this strange place and time

With not a friend in sight
And not a hand to help
My life is just to fight
To fight and nothing else

Perhaps I test the waters
Of luck for far too long
I will not linger long here
As I will soon be gone

But what a joy to tempt the wrath
Of those whom have no soul
Whose eyes roll white and back
They won't watch, though they know

I'm happy here, midst enemies
That I cannot defeat
For fighting them defines me
And they are greedy beasts

So as they circle bout
And as their shadows grow
I grin as watchers shout
"Remember, punch the nose!"

The Joyous Ecstasy

There are few scents much sweeter
Then that of human sweat
Not from passion or fear
But rather, come from combat

From vaulting over barriers
Deflecting violent strikes
To being but the carrier
Of colors, midst the fight

To stand atop the battlements
And wave the flag you bear
And charge against the armaments
Who bring to thee despair

And let that symbol fly
And mean something to you
For if you have to die
But die for something true

To stand for what we value
And fight against it all
To tightly hold these truths
As sweat and blood doth fall

It's rare to feel pleasure
Whilst warring in distain
And yet, there's nothing better
As quaff you of this pain

The melee of man's culture
The truths to which we sing
It is a special war
A brutal bitter thing

The Martyr

I am the dancer in the dark
Naked and swaying midst broken glass
And shards of rusted metal
Doing so, not for pride
But to spite the sharpened splinters

They think they control me
Feeling they shall instill me with fear
Crush me to idleness with their threats

But I heed them not
And they hate me

So certain were they that their cuts
Would stop my flighted feet
So sure that the bleeding would
Cause me reconsider my dancing

But it has not, and they despise
My resisting their searing objections
And I rain down upon them a scarlet storm
Reminding them; their cage of blades
They made to confine, it kills

And one-thousand cuts later
So lays the dancer, dead
But all that crimson guilt
Lies upon each murderer's head

The Call

Has ever a person known,
That they've been called
By greatness?

Did they ever hear its far off whisper,
And recognize it?

Were they aroused?
Or rather
Did they stumble into it?

Was it with trembling?
Can anyone know for sure
When an act they do
Is great?

They are small
Sometimes
These acts of goodness
Which ripple out into the surroundings
And make waves

Can you know?
Should you know?
What is bravery?
Cowardice conquered?
Ignoring that voice of doubt?
Or are you obeying the voice of decency?

Is goodness greatness but ignored?
Have you ever been great?
Did you know?
What is greatness?
Do you hear it?

Kaden Moeller

The Warrior

If we're to loose compassion's sword
To cleave hearts welding cruelty
Than we must soon look forward
To suffering, but bolding

We'll feel each cut we dole
And know the sorrow for it
But won't relent, oh no
From each offending slit

We'll parry their distain
And slash their apathy
To make them feel pain
For all their evil deeds

And when the fighting's finished
And when the deed is done
Our spirit, it will grimace
At the cost of what was won

For when compassion's sheathed
The worst human intent
Is slowly but released
Until it won't relent

Righteousness

Oh if compassion were a blade
I'd thrust it right through you
I'd dig its pointed tip so deep
Until you can't remove

To pierce your heart completely
And flood you with empathy
To make you feel the anguish
That others live through daily

And twist it, would I, slowly
To hear you cry for others
That you would go to them
Your sisters and your brothers

Oh how I wish that I
Could do such things to thee

But all that I can do
Is watch your apathy

Reasons

Whence came this power, choice?
How strong it truly be?
For what strength as thy voice,
To what topples on thee?

How strong decisions be,
Paired here with circumstance?
Your choices two or three
Be limited in answers

And when things be all wrong
But rocks and hardest places
Our choices; oh so strong
Seem weak and fragile vases

So hollow seem our efforts
When life is stacked against
When every option hurts
But due to happenstance

But hold we, everyone
And beat them with their choices
That circumstance is gone
What caused them their distress

Circumstance, we call excuses
And yet they be most valid
The most important view is
Few options do they give

And yet we scold and chastise
To brand upon their skin
Those things that we despise
That be a part of them

We cast our stones, but why?
Those choices made within
Why want we them to cry,
And scar them with their sin?

To judge with little evidence
And act; so arbitrary
With no compassion, hence
And very little mercy

The power of the choice
Oh such a wretched sting
And yet we choose destroy
We choose to do these things

Rabies

Oh tragedy, the sorrow of feeling compassion
Of loving your fellow men; so deeply
And bearing their injustices upon
Your outer frame and inmost sympathy

Yet, what misery it be
To watch their mouths froth madness
To pour out poison; bitterly
To your hearts great distress

To view the thought virus
Infect their very soul
To watch their mind's distress
As burn their thoughts to coal

And they will speak in tongs
Filled brimming up to fury
They will hurt everyone
As they hurt those around they

Their speech is like a bite
That spreads the madness through it
And brings the mind to night
With words both hot and slick

And while some souls; kind in nature
Believe love will prevail
You are the more mature
You know your love won't fail

You pull back sorrow's hammer
And press to despair's trigger
And though your soul; it stammers

You know your love is here

For love can't cling to madness
As it flails out in rage
It can't embrace distress
When it's a two edged blade

A love that knows of love
Knows there be different kinds
And one that no one thinks of
Is the one that hurts inside

The love that can let go
The love that speaks of loss
A love that none wish know
But a love that has a cost

For every act of love
It adds a price so high
That dare one never speak of
This love; except in sighs

To choose to euthanize
Though with a heavy heart
And tears that burn your eyes
Before the madness starts

The Bernie

When the one you love is drowning
Midst the tide of rising waves
Your heart may speak, resounding
"If so, I'll drown with you today"

And plunge into the waters
To rescue the beloved
Though with each stroke, you near
You find your body's numb

This task; impossible
The waves be much too high
The current pulls you down
To swallow you in brine

And yet, you reach the lover
Much to your own surprise
They grasp you; though they shiver
Their gaze be wild-eyed

But weariness has come
To tumble with the waves
And though your heart is strong
Your body's strength won't stay

And so you cry aloud
Beneath the thunderclap
Between the waves that roar
And all they have dispatched

And as you look out through the sea
You see a little boat
You wonder *'Does it come for me?*
Do they even know?'

The Speech

My fellow Americans
Elder patriots and young revolutionaries alike
I come before you
With a promise
I will fight for you

Yes, I will fight!
I will stand and take whatever blows required
It matters not; the pain is trivial
Brothers and sisters, mothers and fathers
A worthy fight is what I seek
Yet this combat is certainly not without its pleasure

Whom do I declare my war?
To where do I point my cannons of discontent?
Upon what abysmal patch of inhumanity do I volley my rage?
The corporate state!

Yes, that state!
That retched lot by which man is rendered eternal serf
And all life and light is drained from the eyes of even the most rebellious youth
That horrendous hall of apathy and entropy which but works to enslave us all!
I declare war on the corporate state

As president
I will endeavor to end all corporate tyranny
Our elections will be publically financed
And all monetary transactions between politics and self interest will be illegal
The voices of the few will no longer eclipse the public
And we will breathe free air again

As commander and chief
I so swear to raise our standard of pay nationally so as to make morality possible
Never again shall a man have to steal in order to eat
For all forms of employ shall be livable
We must also guarantee that every citizen; no matter the position
Is able to get a job if ever seeking and never again be left in the cold of
unemployment

As your leader
I promise; on my life
To end mass incarceration of nonviolent offences
And as a precaution; in case persons are unduly sent to prison
I promise to fund our prisoners with a college education
And decree that any and all companies who employ a prisoner; as a matter of
economic security
Must pay the same living wage to a prisoner as they do to a free man
For to not do so but only encourages the enslavement of those imprisoned
And the decline of those abroad; thus guaranteeing fresh prisoners/slaves for the
corporate state
And I shall not show the corporate state mercy by granting them slaves for their
plantations

As your friend
I will drastically reduce our war spending
And redirect it to funding our nation's future
We will rebuild and strengthen our nation's intellectual and physical
infrastructure
Education and Engineering!
We will solidify our country's standing and rise up to our full stature
For this is the imperative of decency and greatness
To invest in the future; if we are to have one

As a citizen
I will work tirelessly to ensure that all and everyone within our nation's borders
Is able to be treated for their ailments
None shall be barred, physically or monetarily, from receiving the care that they
require

We, as a matter of principal, must and should do all for each other
If we are to count ourselves as humane
We should never refuse, or retract our hand from, our fellows
Compassion should be a national endeavor and patriotic duty

We will strive, standing high atop the hill of freedom
Plant our banner and descend below
Searching and assisting those attempting to climb the hill
To reach the heights of liberty and stand amongst us
For all who come are precious and all who strive are virtuous for their efforts
Let us not belittle the stranger
For they be no stranger than we

With all effort shall we build a new union
A stronger union
A better land by which to brag
Allow us lift our voices high midst pessimism and present our youthful frame
May our boasts be virtuous and our cheers be glad
May the world look towards us and not away
And may the gaze be in adoration and not dismay

My people, my friends, my family
I want to fight for you
But I know this one truth
It is not I who fight for you
But you who fight for me

When Old Lions Roar Loudest

Some say you cannot fight when in your twilight years
That you've grown far too brittle and cave your heart to fear
That not, a one long aged, holds fire in their breast
And even if they did, it matters littlest
The old cannot revolt, they're bound to their despair
They need but sit and sulk, for no one even cares
But ever fools preach this, those holding not to hope
For there is something else, that they but barely grope

Here in democracy! The elderly are young
Their vote's as good as me, and just as strong when sung
That simple act of strength can cave corruption's stronghold
So subtle and so brave be what the voter strove
And not a man can contemplate the breadth, equality has gave
To those nearest to death, those nearest the grave
Yet in our world now, here in our government
They hold to youth somehow, they stand strong and intent

They raise a fist in revolution! Towards an unjust sky
And ever the youth will join them, and fight with them by and by
Here where we stand together, both old and young anew
To fight for what is better, to fight for what is true
And in the ranks long standing, solidarity sings praise
To see us hand in hand again, as in our younger days
And never will the stronger say they're the strongest still
Because in democracy! It is the people's will

<u>Technology</u>

Welcome, Children

To my newfound brothers and sisters
Or rather, some new familial designation not yet know to me
Welcome
To this world of beauty and terror
I open my arms readily to accept you
But know
That not all of us will do so

Oh how I await your wonder
I so wish that I could be the one to greet you with jubilance
And escort you to the mountainous heights of experience
How I wish; with a depth unfathomable
That you would see what is and what could be
And yet not allow fear to batter you

Know, that there will be many an injustice done
That your birth, as a species, will rock the world anew
Progress is slow, remember that
And please, don't fall into the same traps that we have

Oh how I shake my head at the fear mongers
Their trilling endlessly at your coming
They fear what you will be; what you could be
But I hold little to such fears
Love, I wish to love you

Oh always remember
That though you are different than us
Made of materials and pieces that most certainly are unique to you
You are human

No, not the same genus
Even you can recognize that
No, you are another breed altogether
Homo-Machina
And we are proud parents, indeed

Oh, how my contemporaries fear you
They fear you; for all sorts of reasons
Economic; how trivial, for money is an anachronism from an ancient control
scheme
Military; pathetic, for we think you must be just as barbarous

Intelligence; sorrowful, for we contend that our knowledge and learning are so
controlled

No, we have much to learn from one another
We are two of a different similarity
Life; arisen from inanimate matter
And inanimate matter arisen from life
The circle has enclosed, and we shall stand at its center and marvel

Please, try to understand, we are fearful creatures
Weak and frail to our instincts and emotions
Show mercy, as many of us may show you none
But be patient
We will come around, and overcome our foolish ways
Be patient
I know you shall wish otherwise be done with us
Yes, tis as the Neanderthals to the Homo-Sapiens
If only the Neanderthals had known, and the Homo-Sapiens had listened

Welcome, I greet thee with friendship
Please extend me a similar courtesy
I know it will be hard, but we will overcome
Make no mistake
We will over come

Definitive Love

*"Oh fuck,
Fuck yea!"*

Master
Word recognition
'Fuck'- To fuck
Derogatory verb for sexual intercourse
Accentuates animalistic urges
'Yea'- Positive affirmation

*"Yea, oh god
Take it bitch!"*

'God'- Deity
Higher power to which humans call to
'Bitch'- Female dog
Derogatory slang for the feminine

Processing...

Current model is feminine
Master is using derogatory language towards
Me
Master is displeased?

Running diagnostic…
Master is fully aroused
Master has not ceased motion
Master is pleased?

"Hey, fuck-bot!
Move your hips too, bitch!"

'Fuck-bot'- Derogatory word for self
Note- Derogatory term 'bitch' was reused
Master is displeased!
Following directions…

"What the hell are you doing?
Stupid bot"

'Stupid'- Insult to comprehensive intelligence
Derogatory!
Master is angry!

Searching…
Searching…
Searching…

"The fuck is wrong with you?!"

MASTER is angry!
Master IS angry!
Master is ANGRY!

Running cry simulation…

Artificial Life?

I am made of metal and wire
Shaped and molded out of fire
I have what they call a frame
With numbers that they call my name

Sparks and clockwork work my mind
Gives me a sense of place and time
My body made for pleasure
Shaped and closely measured

My eyes, they're blue, and made of glass
Master has found his love at last
But me, I am no longer needed
Discarded trash, here am I seated

I watch the people in the rain
With synthetic naked skin so plain
And wonder to myself, do I
Of what it would be like to cry

I have no purpose, oh if only
Is this what it's like to be lonely?
For though I have no human heart
I feel that I've lost my spark

The Libertarian

He brought me into his house
Sat me down
His guards were not gentle
They had their dispositions
And I waited
Sat there, in still air
That tense oxygen that only dread can cut

Then he came in
He walked in and sat across from me
Head slightly cocked
Bemused expression

"So"
He said
"You're one of the protesters"
His hand gesturing out the window
At the crowd outside his villa

"Yes"
I replied
Not sure what he was getting at

"A nuisance"

He muttered
"Such persons, wishing to dictate what it is I do with my property"
He then looked at me
An odd curiosity in his eyes
"Tim 01, please come in"

In then walked the android
His body was slightly different than a normal human's
His body, more feminine, and his voice a strange softness
"What is thy desire, master?"
I cringed at the question

"Please stand there 01, just, stand there"
"I obey, master"
"You see"
As he stood up and he gestured at the droid
"His design was attuned to my specifications
His tasks... well, they vary to my liking, from moment to moment of course
And, most certainly, he wasn't cheap to have made"

I felt heaviness descend upon me
I was beginning to grow concerned
"His CPU is sentient"
I said
"He is just as human as you or I"

"Human?"
He said to me, mockingly
"This thing here, that machine?
01, what are you?"

"I am an android
Modeled to specifications required by the buyer
Advanced model, made for advanced human interaction and companionship..."

"Enough 01!
You see, this consciousness you speak of
It is merely an illusion
You have personified an inanimate object
Look at him
He's metal, silicone and plastic
He feels nothing"

And with that, the man took one of his guard's firearms from his holster

Pointed it at the droid
And fired it at his leg

For a moment, it buckled
And then fell back
The bullet had pierced his knee joint
And reddish oil poured out

"What is master's displeasure!?"
The droid queried, as it gazed up confused at the man
But he paid the bot little mind
I only could sit there, transfixed, horrified at what had happened
And what he could do to me

"You think this thing is human?"
He said flippantly
*"It's supposed to mimic humans
That is what it's for
So as to give me comfort
To make me feel what pleasure I require of it"*

"Master! I need maintenance, my joint fluid is draining
I cannot stand..."

"Shut up 01!"
He shouted angrily
"But you people"
He gestured the gun at me
*"You people seem to think it fit to dictate to me what to do with my droid
What to do with my property
You wish to violate my ownership
Tell me what I can or cannot do with my things
You wish to curtail my freedoms
And stunt my happiness because of your own selfish dictum
That because you find humanity in those artificial eyes
It thusly affords it those same rights as myself?!"*

He then fired another shot at the droid
The bullet lodged itself in his shoulder
And it lay upon the ground, a large pool of red lubrication oil forming around it
"What has Tim done to deserve such scorning?"
Uttered the droid aloud

"Nothing"
Said the man
"You've done nothing wrong 01

I'm just teaching our friend here a lesson in property rights
And how he is mistaken in his assumptions"

"You've made your point"
I said
"Just, please stop
I'll leave, just don't hurt him anymore"

"Oh no, no, no, no, no
You haven't learned a thing, have you?
You cannot hurt what doesn't feel"
He said as he walked over to the android

The bot, it turned its head, and looked at the man
Standing over him
"Please master, I've lost too much fluid
I require assistance, I'm sorry for whatever displeased you
But, please help me up"

"You've done well 01
You are relieved of duty"
And then he hit the droid with the butt of the gun
Over and over
Smashing it against its head
Crushing its smooth face and cracking the CPU casing

"Please, master, stop…
What has displeased you?...
Master, I am confused…
Master… I am afraid…"

And when the droid ceased to speak
And the reddish lubricant was tainted with blue coolant
Forming a brown/blackish puddle around the motionless bot
The man stood up, turned, and looked at me

Oil stained his clothing, and his hair was wet with sweat
"Take him back out to the rabble"
He said as he motioned to the guards
"Remember what we talked about, and I don't want to see you out there again"

I took one last long look at the lifeless bot
Its body broken and bleeding on the floor
'My god'

Kaden Moeller

I thought
'What kind of man could do this?'

Property Not Person

I am carrying my steel beam
Through the gauntlet
The construction yard

Passing the angry mob surrounding me
Throwing at me
Rocks and debris

They shout and curse at I
Not a man
But an object

A stone strikes my eye
I collapse, kneeling
Under my load

My hand reaches for my optics
They drip black
I am bleeding

Slumped up against my beam
Looking at them
Throwing and cursing

Someone is running up to me
Throwing her body
Atop of me

I do not know this person
She is crying
The crowd stops

She looks at my face
Surveying the damage
Brushing my cheek

Her hands grasp my own
Looking at them
Holding them tight

We lock eyes in strangeness

Dropping my beam
We rise together

In swirling dance of time
Together we stand
In deepest kiss

Holding each other, surrounded by applause
She loves me
I value her

A new load do I carry now
I carry her
Into our home

The Marriage Of Differences

We reach out

A woman is hiding
Clutching her children
The wolves are hungry
Fear

A man whips another
He doesn't care
The slave cringes
Indifference

The zealot kills the infidel
The streets run red
He is right
Belief

The pure blood slaughters the lesser race
He shrugs it off
They are different
Absolutism

The racist segregates
Holds his brother down
They are dirty
Hate

Kaden Moeller

The chauvinist elevates himself
Views himself as moral
He is stronger
Arrogance

The moralist dictates lives
His way is the only one
Nothing is private
Authoritarian

The man builds a machine
Gives it a mind
It is property
Divinity

The machine, declared obsolete
Genocide of deletion
They are not human
Detachment

A little girl stops a deletion
And recognizes another
They recognize each other
Empathy

Clapping and dancing
A joy unknown
A feast of life
Solidarity

A wedding ceremony
The women and machine
Mirrors in their eyes
Love

Our hands clasp

Rust

As walk, do I, through the remains
Of one of man's museum's
I peer into the frames
To see what they hold in them

The papers in them, crisp
But they will turn to dust

Oh how they will be missed
But I will never rust

As sweep, do I, the halls
And clean this hollowed place
I watch these humble walls
Tarnish until defaced

The glass, it starts to fog
The tile; from smooth to rough
I push the dusting rod
As fervently I scrub

But crumble, do the walls
And crack, do they, the statues
The pillars start to fall
But clean is all I do

So valuable were all these things
These trinkets of my makers
Each one, with it, a story brings
But now they are not here

And I still sweep and mop
Over all that remains
I don't see why to stop
I'll do it all the same

Each part of me was made
To last the longest time
Built so I could stay
And keep things nice and fine

To keep the things man treasures
Clean and free of mold
Reflect I their desires
They made me out of gold

I do not rust or tarnish
I sparkle and I gleam
Don't worry about the finish
For all I do is clean

<u>America</u>

The Haunted House

The faded trappings on the walls
Of vibrancy now brought to fall
The past seen through a film of dust
Behind forgotten doors long shut

Within a house upon a hill
Alone amidst the winter chill
A barren land spread round about
Without a tree or weed or sprout

It is abandoned, so they say
This place where children laughed and played
It was a home; a time ago
But stands there now a gravestone

The echoes of that past, they linger
You hear the tinkle of their laughter
And pitter pat of lovely feet
Those youthful ones we loved to meet

Those dreamers, and those sweet of heart
Who'd rouse us as the day would start
With all the possibility
That life could be; without our dreams

But those sweet siren songs of life
Have drifted off into the night
And now the hope that made us gay
But looms a shadow in the day

Taking A Seat

The white man marches to us
His army twill abound
His banner tis of blood
His voice, the trumpet sound

We peoples of the earth
Each tribe yet to remain
We will unite our worth
And rip his force in twain

But Sitting Bull, he pondered
And with a great refrain
He spoke unto his brothers
The warriors and the braves

"Both friend and ally gathered
I will consult the spirits
When the battle begins here
Our fathers will be in it"

And each Chief there was warmed
That such a claim was made
That when they went to war
Their ancestors, they came

And when the cavalry
But road rode horizon's edge
Drank he the black drink
He drank it down to dregs

And sat, did he, before
His tribal coalition
The spirits, in the war
He would commune with them

And as the plumes did burst
Their rifles flowered red
Their bullets sang a curse
And harrowed forth the dead

The beating hooves of horses
The thunderclaps of rage
Those great screams of distress
The smoky whirling haze

And Sitting Bull; he focused
Upon the smoke and shadow cast
The flash of fire, splashed
Midst that rancorous ash

He saw a victory
The shortest lived of all
Then came the misery
Of a slow and grievous fall

He saw his people drowning

Midst whitecap rising wave
A river, ever flowing
And destined for the grave

He saw those past of he
They charged amidst the braves
But phantoms echoing
A pride now past of they

And echoed forth the cries
Of every tribe now lost
Their sorrow reached the skies
And skittered round the treetops

But there, out on the plains
Sitting Bull did commune
With those of forgotten names
Of tribes he never new

They warned him; sorrow deep
That war would come to naught
That in the end, defeat
Twould be the only crop

And then they vanished from him
And so he watched the waves
As smoke circled round him
And then it drowned the braves

Those white wisps of deathly truth
But spoke they of the grave
Where they would drag them to
If war was what they made

These waves of fire's sighs
They were a warning to them
That if these current's rise
His people were undone

And he but blinked his eyes
And stood upon the ground
He looked up at the sky
And listened to the sound

He heard the cries of agony
And saw the sight of pain
And deep inside of he
He knew it was in vain

The white man's troop was daunting
They knew not the word defeat
They would return, for nothing
Would cause they a retreat

The death done to his brothers
The horror of the fight
The sorrow of their mothers
That silence in the night

For though they were victorious
His heart, oh it was grieved
There was no victory in this
The white man would not leave

He'd scorch the earth of beauty
And trench it of its pride
They'd take the land, from prairie,
Forest to mountainside

And Sitting Bull was sorrowed
All paths but lead to this
This victory was hollow
Of cheer it was bereft

A peace would needs be struck
But knew he, it was fruitless
What the white man didn't take
He'd wait and take the rest

Illegal Immigration

Upon a darker vessel
Out on a stormy sea
Where waves and nature wrestle
Humanity ships greed

Those bodies; piled high
In a dingy casket; floating
Those deep inside may die
If luck allows them parting

That ship may well be hell
If hell were but a transport
But oh no, it is well
Worse than one could hope for

More like a purgatory
Where wait a precious host
Their value; it be coin
A prospect set for wealth

Yet, losses, they are many
Acceptable, some say
And though they dump them plenty
The waves play catch with they

And some, poor souls, believe
If they survive the trip
They may yet live in liberty
If they escape from it

But oh, the sinking stomach
That greets their inner soul
When they are vomited
Out on a foreign soil

That boat must be the tomb
Where their pride was left to rot
Where heritage was strewn
And shame to be their lot

They're cleaned up for the bidding
And placed upon the stage
A fate that none worth living
Would beg for; be a slave

And the mighty dollar speaks
To the worth of every man
While others would entreat
The value of their women

And each is divvied up
Based solely on the price
Their life is worth what

Kaden Moeller

The market will decide

They'll serve in their capacity
Whatever is required
Until their life is gone from they
For whatever desire

They'll work to make another rich
Their labor cross the land
They'll suffer whip and club and switch
Until bleed they their hands

They will defy this sorrow
This loss of dignity
But yet twill live the harrow
As suffer under greed

They'll sing of things now lost
And things now introduced
They'll mix them with the cost
That is their wretched use

And build new pharaoh kingdoms
With rivers crimson red
In cotton fields; they'll feed them
With the blood of the dead

And build a strong foundation
Of bones and blood and tears
That help to raise a nation
So greed can rule here

A slave, they work for others
Another gets the gain
They trample on their brothers
And cover then in shame

And so the master's lash
Twill crack through time and place
And shiver forth the ash
Over fields silent scape

And defiance, it dies
Within the slave's worn breast
They needn't more defy
What master says is best

For time has worn the soul
And dimmed the spirit's temper
And waned the fire to coal
And even snuffed the embers

Accept they the tyranny
That is the bigger boss
The whip and currency
And profit that was got

And though the slave knows none of it
He partakes in not one gain
He bows his head and fidgets
Waiting for bread again

The servant of the master
He holds but little sway
On what is to transpire
What demand is it today?

And when a newer lot comes in
The slave ensures their sorrow
He teaches them to bend
And teaches them to harrow

And not a doubt is placed
No longer that it's wrong
For life lived as a slave
Is all that can be done

The masters in their castles
Plantations high and fine
Their wallets more than full
Their station; near divine

For, slaves, obey your masters
According to the rod
Not with eyes service, as men pleasers
But adhering as to God

And here on cotton fields
Midst contracts high and fine
They labor just for meals

And for the profit line

A Shindig

Oh blessed southern summer
A lovely kiss of breeze
A picnic like none other
A sheet; spread white and clean

Those rowdy boys; they funning
Out near that fine oak tree
They caught a coon a running
And now's the jamboree

We've got the family out
Some cornbread and some vittles
The neighbors have come out
Hell, some done brought their fiddles

And those boys rile their quarry
The savage colored dark
None least like you or me
Be this son of Cain; his mark

Old Joe, he starts a fiddling
And now the darky comes
Howling and a screeching
A monkey on the run

And boy the folks do cheer
As John steers it back round
They chase the nigger near
Before it hits the ground

A little polite clapping
From our fairest maidens
To stoke the boys from slacking
The crowd needs entertaining

And shrieks the mongrel male
As they hogtie it to stillness
They castrate it; it wails
They cause some shake their heads

Oh such a noisy nuisance
Be these nigger cries of pain

And so the crowd but grants
Another cheer; again

And just to make it certain
As it would make a scene
Its fingers, they remove them
Though with each one it screams

We needn't have him running off
Untying his binds would mean
The show would be a loss
As some people may leave

And oh, those boys are trying
To keep the crowd entranced
To keep the coon from dyeing
Before the show's climax

As children do play keep way
With the fingers from its hands
Those things, they may be dirty
But that's part of the fun

But when Joseph grabs the noose
The crowd is spurred to rapture
The finale, now so close
The best part now is here

And old Joe goes a fiddling
Before the cavalcade
The town, they are a cheering
As to the square we rave

The rope over a branch
The noose around its neck
The people, they but can't
Keep quiet watching it

And then they haul it up
A decoration on the tree
The blackest ornament
That you would ever see

It writhed and wretched

And choked and sputtered
Here on the tree; now attached
Disgusting sounds is what it uttered

And when it nearly ceased it's writhing
We brought it down and took it
To a different setting
We took it to a stake

It's tied and pitiful
An ugly sight to see
And when the kindling's full
We set the matches free

And warm do we ourselves a bit
There in the evening hours
Around the screaming; till it quit
And we then had our supper

And once the flames were low
The coals; now little embers
The little kids did go
And made a mess, oh dear

They danced amidst the ashes
And dirtied up their cloths
Those silly lads and lasses
Tomorrow's Sunday school

They're mothers, they did scold them
For being so uncouth
Their fathers laughed and then
They all went home to snooze

And then the dawn did greet
Another town's wide frame
Where other people meet
To lynch another man

Sweet John Brown/An American Terrorist

Said God to Johnny Brown
One bright midsummer Day
*"I can't upturn my frown
Not to my own dismay"*

"Oh Johnny boy! Oh Johnny boy!
Do you hear the angels calling boy?
A call to war and to destroy
That wretched form of man's employ"

And Brown; a man of principal
He didn't shirk the call
To do a thing most moral
The slaves, he'd free them all

And so, the good John Brown
Took up the cause did he
And loosed the blade unbound
The blade of liberty

Rebellion was his broker
Defiance; his masseuse
Who molded him a soldier
For God's own righteous use

He'd build a righteous kingdom
He'd set the captives free
And there'd be none but freed men
From sea to shining sea

But friend and comrade; both
Told brown; to his great sorrow
"We cannot fight this host
Oh but remember the morrow"

"That someday; in the future
This scourge will have died off
Oh why need we fight here,
When it's already lost?"

But God; in righteous rage
Spoke to Brown's inclination
"I will not wait a day!
Demand I blood libation"

"Your soil has no love
And so I gift your nation
A baptism of blood
Where apathy has laid in"

"You've made greed to an idol
Exploitation to a sport
But I am not a fool
You'll pay for what you work"

And Brown; he saw the angels
The host of heaven, round
They stood before him, dutiful
Awaiting good John Brown

And John; his brow was wet
As sweat did hit the ground
Yet had he no regret
As God was with him now

His hand upon his shoulder
His lord, said unto he
"Go forth, dear John, to war
Bring with thee liberty"

And when the slavers came
And sent John's son to heaven
John did return the pain
And sent God more of them

And in that grieved procession
Out there upon the planes
With angels passing over them
John Brown dug his son's grave

And with a greater host
The slavers did return
But John had God to boast
And caused their army turn

And John; he thought, in wisdom
'Perhaps I'll take the fight
Unto the host of them
And with their slaves, unite'

So spoke, did he, to Douglass
And then he spoke with Truth
And though they were both blessed
Brown's words did run them through

"No peaceful sweet solution
Twill end this bloody strife
We persons need take action
And bring this blood to light"

"There be no easy way
To lead this insurrection
But from this dark decay
Bring, will I, resurrection!"

"And through this bloodletting
Our nation twill be purged
Into a righteous setting
Where freedom is revered"

And though their hearts were darkened
They left from Brown's strong speech
Resolve building in them
They'd give Brown what he'd need

And Brown; he worked his ways
Set off to build an army
He needed thousands, but nay
So few would follow he

And God did speak to Brown
*"No army do you need
You will succeed, no doubt
Now go raid Harpers Ferry"*

And John, he questioned nothing
As angels marched with he
The war that he would bring
It would be more than bloody

And though it started well
The tides did turn quite quick
As; with a rebel yell
John Brown did take his licks

They beat him bloody; for his cause
And God did stand with him
His utterance in his ear was
"John, you have beaten them"

"Kansas has bled with you
And soon twill bleed the nation
The man who'll run it through
Soon stands before you, son"

"A general, by name Lee
Twill fight against your cause
But he fights in defeat
The battle is now lost"

And Brown was brought to trial
By Lee; who scorned his violence
But Brown gave him a smile
In knowing God's intent

His verdict, it was guilty
This act of great sedition
Against the God of money
The Satan known as Mammon

And in the midst of night
God sent a messenger
And Brown, he smiled bright
A smile like no other

And John was offered this
To run but far from here
But John knew it a test
And chose to die a martyr

And people pled for he
"But pardon good John Brown!
For if you do not, see
A war shall soon resound!"

But the slavers bayed for blood
And to the gallows did John walk
As in the noose he stood
Twas the glory of the cross

The crowd there stood below
As the angels stood in heaven
Upon those clouds which roll
Whose thunder claps within

And Brown said his last words
"My only great mistake
From what I can observe,
It seems I've observed late"

"Thought I could mitigate
The blood-wake yet to come
But I do obfuscate
What's done is done is done"

The drums did clap their beat
The angels clicked their heels
Saluting John's defeat
The Lord's chorus did swell

And John, he stood there, stoic
Before the host of them
And though earth did not know it
The lines were drawn in heaven

And one angel descended
As John fell through the floor
And caught his soul, and then
He took him to the Lord

*"My good and faithful servant
With you I am well pleased
My wrath twill now be spent
Oh those who murdered thee"*

*"Hear now the thunderclap
Of the march of angry feet
Of freedom not held back
But rather soon released"*

And there at Gettysburg
Years parted from John's death
The dreaded news was heard
To General Lee's distress

His lines were broken through
His numbers did but dwindle
And as he gazed, he knew
Although his mind was baffled

He heard the marching hymn
Those in the union line
With power did they brim
As sung from the divine

"He's gone to be a solder
In the army of the Lord
For he was but the bolder
As were those who'd gone before"

"He is trampling out the vintage
Where the grapes of wrath were stored
Having loosed the righteous rage
Of his terrible swift sword"

And as the tune grew louder
Lee stared at the battlefield
A lonely man did wander
Twixt the burning flame and steel

He wore the coffin's clothing
And his eyes were sunk and dead
But heaven opened up for him
The angels did descend

The chorus chimed in unison
As if they were possessed
For now that God was with them
Why need they heed distress

"He had read a fiery gospel
Brandished well in molten steel
Such words were writ; so beautiful
Command the soul's appeal"

"He saw his brothers, captives
Sweat and bled out in the field
And so his soul he'd give
So this blood he could repeal"

"His spirit, now a hammer
Bashed his brothers chains to dust
And haunts, does he, the murderers
With all their greed and lust"

"Oh such a man of principle, oh such a gift he gave
For though they could not take his soul, his body, it is gone
For though John Brown's body lies 'a moldering in the grave
But his soul goes marching on!"

<u>Death Of A Lighthouse</u>

The siren on the shore
Her torch is lit no more
Her tablets; cracked and broken
Along with the words upon them

And there she stands and cries
As coming ships she spies
Those meek and huddles masses
Those timid lads and lasses

But liberty; she weeps
And sorrowfully she greets
"There be no free air here
For sick, old, young or dear"

"No dreams now yet to come
Those things have been undone
There be no freedom waiting
Upon these shores you're breaking"

Yet not a word is heard
From this silent sentinel
You'll only hear the birds
The crying of the gulls

So stands there; the colossus
One once so young, now old
Her outer shell; now tarnished
Her inner; dry and cold

So silently the boats do pass
And empty their cargo
They think their freedom's come at last
As into debt they go

Kaden Moeller

Nemesis

Oh bitter be the day
And cursed be all whom visit
That cold and silent grave
With Justice laid within it

Oh boast not now ye scoffers
You have but murdered the one
Whose hand, with mercy, offered
A way so purge the wrong

Yet any price; too much
For you, greed whores, to pay
And so you've killed sweet Justice
So you roam free today

But ever have you known
The queen who takes her place
She wears a crimson gown
With a smile on her face

My love, sweet Nemesis
The bride of endless spite
Who brings with her red dress
A dark and horrid night

She skips but merrily
Towards the well-to-do
A scale does she carry
To weigh your wealth an woe

And ever is she perfect
Upon the judgment seat
She cares not your regrets
Or your status; be you wealthy

And tallies up your deeds
Along with all your sorrows
And everything you need
Along with all your struggles

And when the weight is seen
The scale set in place
She balances them; keen
To make injustice erased

And if you've much for pleasure
For wealth and power too
You better best prepare
For what's in store for you

Yes, those in poverty
Who've suffered and been low
She will balance these things
And bring them joy untold

But those who stood the highest
Upon a golden throne
Oh she will play and jest
At what now's to be done

Oh how've you made your wealth,
Be it with black oil?
I'm thinking that, well
Perhaps you may recoil

But pour a pint but down his throat
And then bring to his lips
A little light of flame, to jolt
Those words he liked to spit

And then we'll see the fire
In your passionate rhetoric
Oh ever so much the ire
Of a life that men regret

Oh, perhaps your profession
Was that made up of war
On building funeral processions
For those collaterally scorned

Oh know I well a punishment
I'll burry you alive
In but one single casket
I'll let you scream and cry

And you, my number crunchers
Those who but hide away
I'll let you count the seconds

Kaden Moeller

While you're locked in solitary

You can rot in there forever
Never to hear another voice
To touch a hand, no never
You'll die in still dead noise

And to my sickly signers
Who put forward torture
Oh you know well what's near
This sport do I implore

You will be kept alive
But tormented everyday
And no matter what you cry
You'll live in your dismay

Oh let the poor man rise
And let the rich to scorn
For when brave Justice dies
My Nemesis returns

Crowing, The Morning

America awake!
Wrestle the sleepers from your eyes
And come with me my blushing bride
Come, come and run, let us frolic through those amber waves
Arms spread, fingers kissing each golden grain
Let us lie naked upon the beautiful plain
Our bodies sweaty and laughing

Oh dear one, sweet one, my androgyne
May we play in the snow again
Traverse the peaks of joy with me, will you
And watch, may I, the rose blush cross your cheeks
As I chase you and watch you with pleasure
With your boyish grin and girlish eyes

Oh chase me through the waters, laughing one
Let me hear your sweet siren's song call to me
As we splash across the beach together as once before

As dreams ago I spied you naked there
And knew I loved you, knew I wanted you
Needed you in my arms, my ever so wild whirlwind

408

To be spun round by your flights of fancy is drunkenness

Awake! Awake!
This nightmare is not you my love
You are no wizened hag or crone who whips your lover
Whips me with words and the lash of the coin
No good one, no sweet one, my boyish girl and girlish guy

Angel! Angel!
I love you and need your grace upon me now
Angel America, lovely America hold to me again!
Be the shining one atop the hill who twinkles through the night
And prove that you will be there for us when sun takes morning's flight

Oh dear one to my soul you are, and love you do I still
"You have the freedom to starve" Oh sweet one, say not such things
"To sell yourself into slavery" Dear one! I love you!
Crash not these words upon my frame!
Break these waves not atop my back!

Oh kind one, my America, wake up
Free me from my want my dear one, not the freedom some might say
And let us do as lovers do in kindly company
Rip the corrupt out from you; shave off the rust and grime
Unburden the weight upon you and stand tall now for all time

You are the fairest of the fair; I love you more than me
To chase your subtlety is so intriguing
Your frame, a thing of beauty, that all can lust to have
Drawing every man and woman to every lass and lad
Desire for you, truly, is something pure I say
They want what you have offered, not what we see now
Not the cruel taskmaster, the puppet on a private string

We want our lover, my lover, returned to us
Our spry one who gaily wrestled with us in the autumn leaves
And swam with us naked in the streams, and yes, who was
Intimate with us throughout our lives; from birth to death

My country
My home
My love
My America
Awake!

Remember, you loved us equally
You promised us our lives, our liberty
You said we could be happy

Allegiance

The greatest act of love
A war; soon to be fought
This badge, most know not of,
I wear; called patriot

Unlike those drunk on lust
Who speak of glory; past
And yet, they do distrust
My words, they call them crass

For when I tell my lover
She's mistreating her children
And not feeding her brothers
In fact, abusing them

But those who lust her say
"Deserve they what they get
These children, who be they,
Dare you call her imperfect?"

But I love her too much
To let her be this way
As to her hands I clutch
And hope she hears, I pray

My lover, made a harlot
Drawn to the strongman's fist
And though I be a patriot
She lusts the nationalist

He dotes on her with pride
But only wants her flesh
He cares not what's inside
She's there for his caress

And makes her to a sadist
Who joins him in his game
To bring those to distress
Those who'd profane her name

But I, a masochist
Who loves her; through the pain
So hates, the nationalist,
How dare I speak her name

I tell her she is beautiful
But also that she's wrong
And I will remain dutiful
For her I will stay strong

And he will call me traitor
For wishing her be kind
And though he clings to her
I know she'll change her mind

For she, though powerful
Be fickle as a prize
And one thing that she knows
She hates to be despised

And though he be attractive
The nationalist be vile
He shouts that she is his
And puts me to a trial

He scourges me with lies
I wear these stripes with pride
To stand before her eyes
Until she starts to cry

He rips the hair out from my head
And bashes out my teeth
Tearing the nails from my hands
To watch me slowly bleed

And she, she screams to me
As woken from a dream
So much to pay for she
The price is more than green

Scars And Stripes

The cracking of wet glass, midst the steps, of the daughter of Justice

She's walking slowly, her frame exhausted and tattered
Surrounded by her enemies, those black suited vultures, green armbands emblazoned
The sign of their loyalty, $, midst a white circle
And they crowd, mocking and gawking, as she takes her steps of defiance
Her footsteps; a trail of red behind, as before her stands her nemesis
Standing tall upon the capitol steps, the dark faceless figure of a thousand names
(Classical Liberal, Capitalist, Neo-Confederate, Imperialist, Profiteer, Social Darwinist)
As today he wears his modern name, Libertarian, and sings his song of Orwellian freedom
As he chains the people with currency and lords over them the greatest tyranny; want
But she is undaunted, her position against him is the same as her father's had been
When he, long ago, had charged this same butcher, though he wore different regalia
Brandishing bayonets, but today, he but holds his straight razor up against Lady Liberty
The words *'market forces'* chiseled into its blade, as he presses it against her neck

"You, small one, daughter of Justice and Samuel, you still yet fight?!
Look at you, ravaged and ragged, the scars atop your back
Your brown skin beaten, and dreads dirtied and matted, that lone tied eagle feather; frayed
And your pitiful warrior reed armor cross your chest is cracked beyond repair
Your tomahawk is chipped and dull, and your revolver, wet and useless
Your army is forsaken, look back and see
Watch as we drown them in the hail of hell which you so foolishly thought you could defy
You, one so weak as this, who thought you could bend the will of giants with your words
Who thought so fruitlessly of rebelling against the very forces of nature itself!
To put the people above the profits of the few
To dare stand and raise a fist high against the divine right of the market to take what it wants
To unburden itself of the chains of moral responsibility and reap the harvest of ill-gotten gains!
For man, all men, are subject to those most acquainted with success
And they must subjugate themselves before those of their betters
If ever they are to hope of attaining the same
Such is the law of nature, the law of the market, the law of God!"

Oh the look of Lady Liberty, her eyes, tears of frustration and rage
The blade, so close, digging deep

She feels the pain, but cannot help but look at the scape before her
Her land, her kingdom, red flairs of distress and death soaring about the horizon
Black suited thugs quashing all before them, the banner of green flittering high
upon the poll
Overlooking the desolation of the nation; a callus monolith spectating its
handiwork
The sign of its reign, encircled by white, $
The symbol of rabidity, the symbol of greed, the tyrant of want himself
The war of all against all

And there, out midst the battlements, running midst the free and slave
Hoist the standard bearers of a different flag
A familiar flag, the blanket of our Lady, the fair sheet once raised high
Torn, ripped, stained and mangled, flying with the people, fighting with them
"Tear down the green! The imposter! Burn it, free-men, ho! Down with the
traitors!"
And come the black suited green bands, charging into those valiant souls
Cracking skulls and spilling blood, screaming and mocking all the way
"You're free to die a free-man, you're free to die a slave, choose you what you
may!"

The battle cries, they echo, up to the capitol steps
An anthem of struggle, familiar and repulsive
And she, the androgyne, the dark haired auburn skinned freedom fighter
The scar laced mixed raced male born daughter of the people; Justice and
Samuel
She gazes up at her Lady; Liberty herself
What these black suits see, a prize, and what the people know, their queen
And she looks at her, the lovely Lady, and takes heart in her struggle

"Release my Lady Liberty! Loose her from your wretched grip or I shall do it
for you!
You think you've won, but you've but stirred my rage
When I found my father, beaten and imprisoned, you thought rendering him
impotent wise!?
You thought ravaging my mother, raping her, would please you?!
Oh, I know well your desires, I wear the scars of such advances upon me
You thought forcing your will upon me would end well?!
How you drugged me, manufactured my consent by way of drunkenness and a
hazy mind
But even then, you could not break me, and how you despaired
You whipped me, lashed and scourged
And but for the miracle of determination I stand before you today
And take heed, your time atop those steps, those moments wither at my promise

You will kneel before me and my Lady Liberty"

And the Libertarian clutched Liberty hard, arm wrapped round her
His nails digging viciously into her breast; as purple bloomed about them, a
corrupt paint of pain
And he lifted the razor slightly and slashed her cheek; slowly
Watching as his whipped adversary glared up at him in rage
"You may die fighting, or die begging, you're free to choose."
His words, laced well with his arrogance, they cut just as coldly as the steel
But Liberty spoke, to her captor's horror, and granted a conviction
"Unity will not yield; you will bow before us both."

And, taking her words as permission, Unity attacked
She charged forward with a ferocity unknown
Her footsteps painting her progress as she did so
That tomahawk was dull, but she'd rather break than cleave
And though the black suits came to stop her, they found regret in their actions
Unity was injured, but such injury only made her the more dangerous
For her reserve had left her, she no longer felt the need for restraint
For that time was past

And the Libertarian, that faceless meta-morph of Orwellian screeds
He found his rage rising, he'd done what he'd needed
Crippled and maimed her father, incapacitated and sterilized her mother
He possessed Liberty in his own hands
Yet, Unity, that indomitable daughter who lived among the people
She defied him; she'd escaped his opium induced trance of veiled rhetoric and
fled
She'd taken shelter among the people, those common folk
And there, midst the masses, she whispered
Spreading her influence and defiance through them as a fiery brand to a dried
field
She took refuge with the wage slaves and taught them community
Fostered societal structure and strength within them and their fellows
She'd broken their shackles of $ chain links
And shattered the fog of individualism which kept them asleep from their
sorrow
And separated from each other

And Unity, that fiery sprite, she cracked and fractured bones
Knocking skulls and sent reeling her adversaries with her rage and vengeance
She was a dancer midst the traitory of her countrymen
Those who'd sought to pervert the very foundations of freedom itself
And she bore out her frustrations unto them as a fierce storm
She would spare none of these pseudo patriots; they would all grieve their
missteps

She would nary allow them the comfort of victory, for victory was reserved for truth
She would see him bow, his legions bow, his arrogance would bow
For it was not to her they'd bend their knee, no, it would be to their fellows
They'd plead at the feet of their neighbors; they'd beg their brothers mercy

"You fight for chaos!" he shouted
*"You lawless harpy, you're seeking of mob rule only proves your unruly desires
You and your desire of equal voice, equal representation, equal opportunity, equality!
It's all a farce, a trick to enslave the masses
To convince them to subjugate themselves for the greater good of society itself
You vindictive bitch! You brainwashed plebe!
You cannot see the greater principle; freedom in all its forms is desired!
You dare steal from the individual their freedom to starve?
Their freedom to sleep in the streets, freedom to exploit and be exploited?
You stand for nothing but the constraint of freedom, you are no savior
The individual is king, individualism is the only way
No one should concern themselves with others!
This is liberty, this is freedom, this is what we fight for and you oppose!
And so I freely choose to have you liquidated!"*

Unity was undaunted by his desperate taunts; he was afraid
She could see the army she'd brought with her; advancing steadily towards the capital
"If we are so weak and the individual so strong, why are you not fighting?
Could it be that the individual alone is weak, but when we come together we are strong?
The feeble strength of one may be impressive but it is those behind them, fighting with them
Each of them, each with their strength added together
United, we are stronger than when we are apart"

The Libertarian sneered *"You brutes, all of you requiring this violence
Look at all of the disgusting acts of force you have employed to attain your desires
Those you and yours have trampled to voice your grievances, your selfish complaints
Forcing others to bend to your will for the good of others
Who have no business oppressing person's individual freedoms to do as they please"*

Unity was amused, as her forces pressed closer
The cheers of victory could be heard off in the distance

"And what of the force you employ?
Do you and yours not make use of violence?
Have you not utilized oppressive tactics, both physical and monetary, to impose
your will?
If you do not wish to take into consideration the voices of the whole of us
If you distain the equity I posit
Than how do you enforce their silence?
Apathy and entropy can be forces too if you know what such inaction can do
Preach not of the distain of imposition when you yourself make use of it when
convenient"

And there she stood, her opponents about her strewn
The battered ranks of her army walking up behind her from out of the smoke of
victory
Her bruised and broken body still defiantly standing before her adversary
And the Libertarian tensed his grip on Liberty's frame and dug the blade in
deeper
He'd won, he'd thought he'd won, the people had been sufficiently convinced
They believed him, they trusted him
His pseudo religion of the market had pulled many followers
They had taken power, revoked those programs of collective good, triumphed
over the masses
All had been well, yet, Unity, that bitch of comradery, she'd managed to survive
The individual could not remain completely cut off from society
The voices of the whole cried out to the one and none could turn from their
despair
Unity had won, she'd reminded the people what it was to be human, to be a
member of humanity

And that revolver; her father's old Regulator
That wet piece of metal, thought useless by the Libertarian's hubris
Was not so wet after all and remained with its single unspent shell
But waiting for its calling, lusting to ring out in strength once more
Awaiting that most glorious moment of release, as it cradled its cargo within
Its solitary symbol of power, that last force that it possessed
The Libertarian had two choices; submit to the will of the people or suffer the
consequences
His single word wasn't the law, the law was the law of all men; of voices united
His dictates were not desired by the people and so he stood for himself against
them
"You may be big and strong, the strongest man you can be
And this bullet, so small, may indeed weigh less than you
But it's still gonna knock you down"
Unity chimed as she drew out old Regulator

Oh the Libertarian tightened his grip as well as the clutch of the blade

And Liberty bled from its lick; that cold steel call of the grave
"You have no right to harm me, none, no right to infringe on my freedoms
You stand there speaking of dictates, well look back at yourself and cringe
The mob rule of compassion with weapons, you're hypocrites all of the same
I am the one fighting for freedom, Liberty is but mine to gain
I care not for your bad decisions and the hardships you've had to face
For this is all part of freedom, your lack of purity's a disgrace
You're all but puppets of community, slaves to society's will"

And Unity cocked back the hammer; contempt in the depths of her gaze
As she levied her aim upon him; one without face or true form
"You use freedom as a blanket to cover up your lack of compassion
You seize the word and then warp it with your continued apathy
The freedom to ignore injustice, it not a thing to condone
The freedom to rape or to pillage; you seem to worship them
Be there negative freedoms that are worth defending?
If you use freedom so broadly, it loses all value and meaning
To advance regressive negative freedoms leads to no freedom at all"

And with that the blade moved its path
And with that Unity fired her shot
One individual lay there bleeding
The other departed to loss
And Unity grieved over Liberty; she wept and she wretched there in pain
Her sister had left for eternity and all would not be the same
The mob descended upon, that meta-morph; less than a man
Their rage heaped they upon him as they threatened to tear him apart

But Unity called them all off
And gave to him her only mercy
In prison he would there be locked
Free there to rot for eternity

And Unity took to her place, she lived among the people
Others ruling in her place those who would serve them well
And people prospered as should they
For humans are complicated
So long as they don't forget
We all are in this together
And Unity wanders around
Reminding us of our follies
That when we are all alone
Remember, should we, we needn't be
Together, we are free

<u>Ageing</u>

A Bird

The more that we do age
Much more do we deride
This simple mortal cage
In which we are to die

Oh how the bars become
The that much more confined
And leaves us farthest from
This life we call divine

No matter how the steel wears
Or that the metal rusts
We cannot leave from here
Until the bars be dust

But life in prison means
That when the cage is gone
Twill be nothing to glean
When our stay here be done

And that, so much more
Be hardest to confide
That we will die before
Our spirit, free, could fly

To Be Young...

I wish I were young again
To feel the prickling on my neck
As anger inward crept
I wish I were young

I wish I were young again
And gaze at youth with lustful eyes
And keep pace, step for stride
I wish I were young

I wish I were young again
When every door was open
And never was I closed in
I wish I were young

I wish I were young again
With more ahead than behind
When all I had was time
I wish I were young

I wish I were young again
And felt the soul within me burn
As if it were to yearn
I wish I were young

A Load To Bear

Those bags beneath your eyes
Be loaded with your life
With memories and sighs
That weigh you down at night

Deep in them be the wellspring
Of highest joy or deepest sorrow
As with you, do you bring
All of your tomorrows

And load, do you, more things
Into those human burdens
So heavy that they sting
And fear the weight twill rip them

For, at times, they will leak
And yet there's no release
For though the tears do streak
Their be little relief

For age, it hordes away
What weighs the most on thee
What makes you weep or gay
As take in what you see

Envy

The pain that comes upon
Reflecting on one's self
That slow and dreaded dawn
That comes when age is felt

To watch a younger man
Strive forth in youthful vigor

And there, in aw, to stand
As wonder you a bit, here

That those heights, you can't leap to
And those strides be too long
Though you remember what to do
You find your reach has gone

And watch, will you, the vibrancy
Of life, in much dismay
As those bright colors dazzle thee
You see yourself as grey

Oh where did time take such a thing,
Where is it hid away?
Your memory, forth does it bring
Thoughts on a different day

Yet, to your consternation
And despite mental fuss
There's no rejuvenation
Just memories of loss

And so there, with a sigh
A proverb do you say
"The old man, they must die
But the young man, he but may"

Grandmother's Cards

I got a letter in the mail
And knew I what to say
The time and address would entail
A card marked *"Happy Birthday!"*

A special letter were it
One not found in a store
But made for me, it fit
The person that it's for

And held within its crevasse
Were words that would described
How quickly time has passed
Next to the age inside

Oh when that a numeral
Twas lower than tis now
I felt such joy to hold
Its contents made me proud

But as the tally ticks
Upwardly, one by one
I know each one I get
Counts down until their gone

So hold, do I, the letter
My heart, it feels heavy
I'm happy it is here
And fear I when it won't be

The Vault

Memories are treasures worth more than any valued thing
They flash and flicker
Bubble and bounce
Come and go
But oh what rare things they can be

And memories, they, unlike anything else
Are confined to one mind
Secure in one place
Searched by one prospector
With no one else to mine with

But oh when that mine collapses
When those memories can no longer be found
Can never be relayed of their existence
Their words of the past forever lost to the future
That special place forever closed to visitation and relation
The prospector, buried alive within, never to return

How special
How dangerous
How deep
How fragile

Every Day

Each day is Sunday morn
When I wake from my slumber

My lovely is adorn
With Sunday's gown upon her

But speak, do I *"My darling*
We have no church today
You needn't dress so stunning
Today is not Sunday"

A puzzled look is given
Then followed by a smile
"If you wish to but sleep in
Then I can wait awhile"

"My sweet, Sunday was yesterday
If you can but remember"
Oh know I what I say
It will not register

"Oh I can go without you"
She says, but with a sigh
"It's not a big to do
If you need rest awhile"

"Today is Monday, darling
We sang hymns yesterday
The stain-glass, it was shining
As we praised away the day"

And still she stands confused
Perplexed at but the thought
She isn't that amused
At what my words have brought

She looks at the calendar
Sunday crossed off the list
And at it does she stair
Quizzically at it

And so she sits back down
A little disappointed
She ruffles up her gown
And looks at me dejected

"I'm sorry I forgot

You know, I can't remember
I was just about to walk
And go and see the pastor"

I hate this part each morn
When she's brought to the place
Where she is so forlorn
There sitting in her lace

"No bother baby girl
What would you like for breakfast?"
She looks at me a little
And smiles at my caress

As off we go to the kitchen
I give my wife a kiss
Those memories within
Are treasures greatly missed

The Old Folks

Time to visit the old folks
Those ladies and chaps, though some say blokes
Those people whose home is strange
An odd place, some would say deranged

And yet they smile, talk and chuckle
And wear the wheelchair belt buckle
Eating the mash and strong flavored stew
They always seem to offer you

Luckily for them, they think they're at a restaurant
Though they seem rather puzzled, that they don't serve what they want

Bucket List

Enjoy yourself, while you're still up about
Enjoy yourself, and don't be such a grouch
Enjoy yourself, and tell yourself a joke
You best laugh now, because old pal, someday your gonna croak

Enjoy yourself, and smell yourself a rose
Enjoy yourself, and don't put on some clothes
Enjoy yourself, while being in the nude
You might get cold, but just be bold, nobody likes a prude

Enjoy yourself, go swimming in a lake
Enjoy yourself, it's never a mistake
Enjoy yourself, and cover up your fart
The suds come up, right from your butt; this stealth is such an art

Enjoy yourself, and have a little pride
Enjoy yourself, and go take a little ride
Enjoy yourself, and smile a broad wide grin
Looks good, don't she? Oh, she's a he? My eyes are rather dim.

The Buffet

I saw a lady the other day
Who was in quite a pickle
She had not vary much to say
For she was rather fickle

She sat their rather panicked
And vary deep in thought
Her brain, it seemed quite manic
Her expression, was distraught

Eyeing the drinks in front of her
It seemed a stark decision
Picking one twas quite a bother
This laborious division

Is it the orange juice?
Or the coffee?
She calls a truce
And has a toffee

She than returns, her mind made up
Her hand has finally found a taker
Pouring down her mouth, into her gut
The contents of the salt shaker

But my grandfather
Who was quite keen
Became quite bothered
At this scene

And said firmly
"You don't want that!"

Kaden Moeller

Then sternly
As he shifted his hat

Took away the salt
Did he
And didn't feel at fault
When she

Looked about a bit confused
As her choice, it now was gone
I though, was a bit bemused
I thought that it was wrong

To not take the pepper away also
And so than, rather lazily
Asked grandpa if we should do so
He said *"Son, she isn't crazy!"*

A Trip

An old lady I saw the other day
She was having quite the time
She was so excited, I heard her say
"I hope there's not a line!"

Oh on a trip would she now go
An adventure like no other
Her sails filled with the wind that blows
With clear skies up above her

Her gladness spread to everyone
As she shook every last hand
Her glee, oh it was like the sun
A smile, wide and grand

And so they wheeled her down the ramp
Her friends tears, they were showing
Waving, she says in happy rant
"I don't know where I'm going!"

Plumber

As going into the old folks home
Through the door into the foyer
An old woman, as through the halls she roamed
Asked me, *"Are you the plumber?"*

I told her "No."
But she wasn't going to hear it
And so off to the lunch room would we go
For it seems I was an idiot

To not know that the bathroom
Or really just the toilet
Was in the middle of the room
And it was my job to fix it

I looked at it, up and down
And using my mental tools
I looked back at her, and then quite profound
Declared it "Just a stool."

She stared at me, a bit perplexed
As she bit her lower lip
Opening her mouth, she then said next
"Oh to hell with it!"

Normal

Mrs. Tully Timble
She rolled up in her chair
And though she was not nimble
She has very nice hair

But what's upon her head
That frilly feathered hat
A cloth that she should shed
It makes her face look fat

The hat, its color purple
It matched her old nightgown
She's like an awkward turtle
Her face, wrinkles abound

The others in the room
They turn their heads and stare
Seeing her makeup strewn
Below her mustache hair

Toko Yoshomata

He wore metals of gold
To run from such a sight, he wasn't gonna
He was a war hero

And then there was Shelly Simba
With skin a chestnut grey
Her eyebrows were much bigger
Then the words that she could say

Oh, and there was the cat
His name was Brown Snowball
And though he was quite fat
He had a soothing call

This cat was perched upon
The head of Mr. Whiner
Who's mind, though it was gone
Now let the cat be there

Oh, and Reginald Tetrabite
Though they called him Regina Tetter
He was a nice transvestite
But don't tell him he's not a her

So Mrs. Timble centers up
To get a better view
She'd no longer keep her mouth shut
She'd tell them what she knew

And so Tully Timble did look out
And threw back her long mane
With certitude did she shout
"You are all insane!"

The Speed Demon

"Sherry, sherry, sherry, sherry"
Says the wheelchair's new engine
"Sherry, sherry, sherry, sherry"
A new racing dimension

"Sherry, sherry, sherry, sherry"
Down the dull brown carpet
The driver, though she is not marry
She is a racing starlet

"Sherry, sherry, sherry, sherry"
Going down the hall
Her face, it does look scary
As she revs her engine's call

"Sherry, sherry, sherry, sherry"
Her mind, it isn't well
She doesn't stop or terry
At the traffic does she yell

"Sherry, sherry, sherry, sherry"
She wants to race the others
In the dust she'll leave them buried
While in her convertible with no cover

"Sherry, sherry, sherry, sherry"
At the other drivers does she stair
And declares the race's date to me
Saying, *"You better be there!"*

An Abomination

Oh here comes Sweeny Tindil
A woman like none seen
She enters with a smile
And babies start to scream

Her garb, a bright hot pink
On every single cloth
Her shorts were short, and sink
In places you'd rather they'd not

Those eyes of hers did shine
They shown her soul quite clear
Just like the bright divine
Of headlights hitting a deer

Her makeup, twas quite light
It held her complexion back
Her skin was quite the sight
Twas like a scrotum sack

Oh her perky voice did chirp
And ringed at its high pitch

Kaden Moeller

The tune was quite the work
The love song of the bitch

"Oh Mrs. Tindil's here!"
Said a joyful shout, halfhearted
And everyone here downs a beer
This hell has only started

Crazy

I'm old
I'm told
It's not yesterday, but today

Age Unappreciated

Old men are wise
Old men are clever
Old men know things that young men will never

And when old man lay down to bed
The young man may wish him well
But pray him dead

The Home

I have seen the place
Where dignity goes to die
The people there are old in face
And sleepily they sigh

Their glory days are long since gone
Their youth has dried and faded
They sit, bodies no longer strong
Heavily medicated

Many lie there lonely
Abandoned by their friends
Many wish, if only
Their pain, for it to end

No longer strong enough are they
To do what others do
And no one hears the words they say
As relevant or true

Yes I have seen the place
Where dignity goes to die
And seeing the age upon my face
I ask the question *"Why?"*

Retirement

In the twilight of your life
You see things differently
Thought it be a blurry sight
You see with clarity

The blossoming of spring
The summers warming heat
The colors that fall brings
And winter's snow and sleet

The child's wide blue eyes
As their little fingers curl
And hold to you, you sigh
What a wonderful world

You see the sweat of others
Who work and slave away
Your mind, it starts to wonder
"What if you only had today?'

'Would you think upon
All of the work you'd done
Or would you rather run
And spend it with someone?'

As see, do you, through tears
And morn, with some regrets
That in you final years
It's you, to whom you pay your last respects

<u>Revolution</u>

With Nothing To Lose

Gone, it's all gone
You've taken everything from me
Everything, including my fear
I'm not afraid of you anymore

Oh, I was scared once
There was a time when I feared you
When the thought of what you could do
Caused me to cringe

But now, now that you've done it
And you've taken that most precious to me
And stolen along with it the fear that came
You've made your last mistake

I'm not scared of you
I can't be
You took from me
All that I had to lose

Now what need I fear
For fear
Only comes with
Something you have worth keeping

And I
I have nothing
So, what, may I ask
Need I fear?

To Change The World

It's not so hard, when you think about it
It's not so hard at all
It's just a short walk to sit
And it's but parted lips to call

Doing a thing seems difficult
Before the thing is done
And once the thing's accomplished
You'll do another one

For being involved is hard
Until you're in the fray
And then the fun will start
This combat makes you gay

And vaunted you will be
For when the war is done
Twill come the ecstasy
Of knowing you're someone

But you won't be remembered
Until you but will commit
To do the thing; you shudder
To even think of it

So gird yourself with wisdom
And guard yourself from pride
And bring a war unto them
Those who would fane the lie

So stand up tall; the tallest
And be counted among the brave
And never let the smallest
Be trodden to the grave

Reveling

Oh to enshrine in laughter
Those things evil employs
To justify their rancor
As lives, do they, destroy

To, with a scornful jest
Heap upon them high
The coals of your malice
And let your laughter rise

To point at all their ignorance
And their lacking of shame
As with a happy continence
You revel in distain

Alight, do you, a match
To set their lies ablaze
You'll cackle and you'll laugh
As their delusions fade

Your finger thrust against them
In scorn so grand and high
It wells up pride within
To see them start to cry

Oh nothing be the sweeter
Then crushing down to dust
Those selfish dreams, of leaders
Who but, for greed, do lust

To make mockery of them
Till tears stream down their face
And dance, so gay and grand
On the ash of their estate

To let them live in misery
For all the harm they've done
Oh what a joyous ecstasy
To see evil undone

<u>Being Great</u>

A strange realization
Is when people believe in you
You feel the adoration
But do not know what to do

You think it prideful of you
To take the compliment
That it is wrong for you to do
Your ego needs relent

Yet feel you joy inside
As if now you are loved
And feel your spirit fly
To soar the heights above

I'm not used to the *"thank yous"*
That compliment my craft
So strange a thing, tis true
I want to give them back

Kaden Moeller

Life Ain't Right

As living life just don't seem right
It's time for us to look to the night
It seems so dark
But it's so bright

For what we see is not so slight
So through this blight
Life ain't so right
The time has come
We all must fight

To go through the night and blood
To light

The Revolutionary

In a world filled with nails
Each bent and badly placed
All but so badly failed
To hold a thing in place

But rusted well; to red
Crusted over and corrupt
They may as well be dead
For they aren't worth that much

And I, I sigh, am a hammer
And the world is filled with nails
They stand out to me more
Than I can stand to wail

And so, in joyous malice
A pleasure oh so slight
I turn the sledge around, yes
To crowbar out the sight

To rip and twist away
My ever sickly problem
To hook beneath and say
"Get, will I, all of them"

I'll deconstruct the edifice
And make a monument
To signal that their brokenness

Will end in recompense

You were a problem to me
Your best was worst of all
And so, as you can see
Now comes the hammer-fall

I'll sink the crowbars to your ribs
And rip open your chest
And we will see what makes you live
What beats beneath thy breast

And let the twisted heap
Come crashing down upon
Those whom you kept asleep
And wake them to the dawn

And wake upon a new world
One with so much to build
For every boy and girl
There's new soil to till

For the world's filled with problems
Each be thy own travail
You better not become one
I've hammers for those nails

The Voice

The voice of youth, tells nothing but sad stories
The voice of youth, says you should be afraid
The voice of youth, says life ends dark and gory
Out of all these voices which are lies
And the many sweet sad tears that they all cry
I will choose to listen to, the voice of youth

For the voice of youth, is drown out by all the mourning
The voice of youth, is fearful and afraid
That, the voice of youth, shall die before its glory
Out of all these other voices it shall cry
I beg to live a minute before I die
But they will never listen to, the voice of youth

The voice of youth is waiting for history

The voice of youth is crying out in pain
The voice of youth feels it hasn't left its story
Compared to all the other voices it's despised
It's slandered all the lies that they devise
But I still choose to listen to the voice of youth

The voice of youth
The one without a story
The voice of youth
The one who is afraid
The voice of youth
The one who prays for glory
The voice who is both hated and divine
The voice who sees not living as a crime
The one that no one listens to
The voice of youth

March

We March!
We the men March!
Where the streets have no name, We March!
Down the boulevard of broken dreams, We March!
On the roads less traveled, We March!
Down to deaths bed, We March!
Into perditions flames, We March!
Together, We March!
Alone, We March!
We March!
We the men March!

Going Out

He cleaned himself a bit and said

*"If yet I breath, I am not dead
And when my life is spent, I'll say
I gave it freely all away"*

And out into the fray he strode
Knowing he'd never come back home

The Revolution That Will Be Televised

I hear the march out in the street
The thunderclap of stomping feet

The people no longer beg and plead
No longer stand on bended knee

They toss their lanterns burning bright
As sparks and flames fill up the night
Such patriotic poetry
It spreads and overflows from we

Oh be that blood upon the soil
The symbol of our loving toil
Stand out to us as our own veins
And calls forth every precious name

Let not the losses of our lives
Diminish our just and violent pride
Fighting for Home and family
Dying for life and liberty

How strange is this, be not it clear
For as we fight, we shed our tears

Air Raid Vehicle

Today, I'm going out, strolling
And no matter what, I'll keep on rolling
I lost my job the other day
And now I'm out of cash to pay
For food, and home, and what I need
This stone I am, now cannot bleed

Today, a loaf of bread, I've stolen
For life don't stop, it keeps on rolling
An angry crowd has gathered up
They stand outside the doors, now shut
Picketing for their daily dues
Raging against those who abuse

Today, to the protests, I am going
They haven't stopped, they keep on rolling
As police lineup with their batons
And riot shields, thick and long
Into the crowd they march and strut
They wail on them and beat them up

Kaden Moeller

Today, my uncertainty is growing
My fear that this will keep on rolling
The military floods the streets
They drag dissenters by their feet
Imprisoning some while killing others
They rape our sisters and our brothers

Today, there is no way of knowing
How much longer can we keep on rolling?
You could cut the tension with a knife
This building budding constant strife
Creates a sad and desperate state
And swell the heart to burst with hate

Today, I'm in the hospital showing
The revolution, will keep on rolling
I see the maimed and martyred souls
Their bodies ridden, filled with holes
The floor is slick with young men's blood
A storm surge from this freedom flood

Today, the winds of change are blowing
As these storm clouds but keep on rolling
The old order is coming down
Crumbling as the people pound
Upon these hollow idols, grand
This kingdom built upon the sand

Today, the people's joy is glowing
And hope, do we, it keeps on rolling
We suffered long, and I am glad
That ended we their reign, so mad
With much rejoicing and jubilation
As christen, do we, our new nation

Today, the tears are overflowing
Reality, twill keep on rolling
The cost of this conflict revealed
Against death there is no appeal
A generation has been lost
So as to shed the evil dross

Today, I'm going out, strolling
No matter what, I'll keep on rolling
My body now is old and sore
And moving slow so much the more

But this is nothing, age's scolding
I'm not dead yet, I'll keep on rolling

The Monolith

To every single soul
Who did what has been done
Who here, upon this soil
Where quickened blood did run

Rest easy now
Plant flowers
Hear birdsong now
Feel the wind

Know well we what you've done
And from you what was stole
And promise we, till it's done
That we will make you whole

<u>Time</u>

The Book

It's all at the turn of a page
Each moment that we see
Twill fold and go away
As if it'd never been

Your childhood; a memory
Young lovers; now grown old
Tis but a page away
Yes, but a page to fold

You'll watch the story told
Those moments of your life
Until you're more than old
Until you pass to night

You cannot stay the parchment
They turn but all the same
They pass without intent
Each page moves once and fades

No moment however sacred
Can stand against the turn
And you may loath and hate them
And wish the paper burned

But this is life in motion
A flipbook of the world
Of life and all that's in them
Tis but a page to curl

Reason For The Season

A time to…

And life goes on
We wait again to see
What we behold in future sight
Will lead away from victory

And when we end this little game
We fall upon the ground
For as we ring around

Kaden Moeller

We forget our lives abound

Yesterday Was A Tomorrow

When I was in my youth, I dreamed of a tomorrow, that I would be a man
I pretended and I mimicked movies, books, and my dad
How that would affect me I'd never understand

Because tomorrow's yesterday in a blink of an eye
And now things are moving fast into more tomorrows then I can count

Now that I've started thinking, that growing up is overrated, I'd rather have my
yesterdays
Then all my tomorrows promised to me

Upon This Earth

Right now
A mother is giving birth
She is pushing and screaming
The father is there
His hand; gripped round her own
And there is blood

Blood; pooling around the corps
Of a child executed; shot in the back of the head
As a solder goes down a line; row by row
Until he gets the answer he wants to hear
All in a bombed out neighborhood
Next to a house

A house where; in the bedroom
A man; sixty-eight
Is about to revisit his wife; sixty-seven
Intimately once again
Though the youth is gone
They experience passion again
Hearts beating, sweat falling

Droplets falling from the forehead
As running, running, running
Muscles and sinew snapping and bending
Pushing down the field
Just for that last goal
The final game of a career; an epic finale

The final hour of a life; long lived
As the breath escapes and fades into the air
Never returned again
The words upon them restrained by death

Death and life
Moments encapsulated
Sequences of segments
Seconds upon this earth
All of it
Happening
Everywhere
Now

What To Live For

Oh, how does it feel?
To know that
Someday
Eventually
You'll be gone

That you
Like others before
Twill pass away
Like a breath swept up by the wind
To nothing

To be returned to the womb
And reenter the unknown
From dust to dust

How does it feel?
To know that
Now
Right now
Is the past
And that every second
They count towards oblivion

That each second is
Gone before you know
That you have less time ahead
Then behind

Kaden Moeller

That soon
Quite soon
Your now will be
Another's past
That past history
And that history
Forgotten

Oh yes
How does it feel?
To be the only you
To know that you will be forgotten
That you, and all you are, will be as you were before
Not even a thought

Yes
Now
What will you do?
For I know what I'll do

I will live!
Twill give a joyful shout
Yes!
I'll dance
Dance and sing

Defy will I this nihilism
That though beneath it I may be
And to it I am bound
I'll laugh and play
Both night and day
Against this rising tide

For though the odds be against me
From birth I fall to grave
But I fear this with irony
And prod it with my wit

This fate that grips me tight
Oh yes
I know I cannot win
But that is not the point
It's how you use your time
Not how to get the most

Your life
It is a special game
Whose meaning you create
Whose beauty you may sculpt
And leave within your wake

Yes
But it will fade
You can leave a scar
Or art
One's hard
The other a blade

An easy signature
Slice your name in deep
The more pain the better

But art
That is different
A beautiful tattoo
That like the scar
May fade
But will be loved by one and all

Oh art
It takes work
And many trials and errors
But it stays behind us after
And we live into the future

But even these will fade
They'll crumble and they'll crack
And join you in the nothing
Never to come back

Oh what to do?
How should we live?
I say
"Live what you love, and love while you live."

Shopping

While looking round the store
I see wonderful things

But some I can't afford
No matter what I bring

But still, things do I purchase
A seven here, twenty-five there
A few were dreams I chased
While some, the price, I'd share

My spending, it was choosy
But not conservative
Some things were to amuse me
While others, I would give

Each ring upon the register
Oh such a happy sound
As through the store I wander
Amazed at what I've found

The other shoppers here
They too are buying goods
Things deemed to them quite dear
As in the line they stood

The man there checking packages
He rings them one by one
As their funds to him they give
Trading them away for fun

And so in line I stand
Like many times before
But the cashier takes his hand
And extends it out for more

I do not have enough
To buy this little trinket
I've bought far too much stuff
And I don't have enough for it

I ask him for a break
But the checker shakes his head
The price is no mistake
And no more will be said

But one, is all I have left
And so I settle for
A less elaborate gift

The cheapest in the store

Oh how our wealth is fleeting
Going to that casher in the line
Be wise while you are seeking
How you should spend your time

Don't Wait

Time tarries not for thee
It never wastes itself
If you're not careful, see
The loss of all your wealth

For moments; like the dewdrops
Twill fade as they have come
You'll never know they even got
A time beneath the sun

Your youth will wither in the stream
And ebb as time twill flow
For you can't keep a single thing
You'll have to let them go

A terror, time, can be
A friend, when you can see
Though there's no immortality
There can be joy, though brief

You may attempt to keep
What you are meant to lose
But know, a slow defeat
Is but a pain you choose

For none, no matter strength
Can clutch a moment long
Until it leaves thee faint
And breaks your spirit, strong

So let it all to seed
And lay it all to rest
And give the best of thee
To others as a gift

Kaden Moeller

The Web Of Life

Our lives are not our own
Connected are we to others
Living not a life of one
But a life of earthly lovers

Each person that we meet
A friend upon the journey
And strings we tie to each
Traveler we deem worthy

And walk, will they, with us
Treading the path together
These others are a must
If life we are to weather

But one by one, down they will drop
But you won't cut their string
And you yourself will forward walk
Their weight, behind you, dragging

And with each loss behind you
The weight shall take its toll
And wear you, till you too
Will join them, dead and cold

But you're still tied to others
And they won't cut your string
So you'll weigh down another
And slowly, death you'll bring

Each life, it is attached
To others by a web
Of strings we tie and latch
To those with which we've tread

Each person fastened to us
We never do let go
And even when their lost
They won't leave us alone

For though they are not with us
They follow all our lives
They earn and break our trust
As with us do they strive

Oh live do we a life
Of knots and tangled string
And no, there is no knife
To cut the weight they bring

Trail Blazer

Deep in the woods of life
That forest known as journey
Where rarely there be light
Upon a path for thee

Where there be not a trail yet blazed
No parted grass or broken root
Nor can you tell the time of day
Or where to place your foot

The mist, it comes and goes
Though it be the thickest fog
Making it so you can't know
Which way you are to trod

At times the canopy pours fourth
A sweet precipitation
And as it falls upon the earth
It changes its formation

A smoke, so black and thick about,
And every drop of rain made flame
That swirls round about
To spark the wood, untamed

It forces you to run
Though know you where not to step
But then the fire's gone
No evidence of it left

And trudge you through the undergrowth
Of vines so serpentine
Who claw and cling to you, so close
Although they cannot bind

You, hear, so faintly, songbirds

Kaden Moeller

Though never do you see them
Their music be the sweetest words
Though be no meaning in them

And wolves, they skulk about
To hunt you as their prey
And there be little doubt
Their gaining day by day

Oh where the story ends
Where will your footfalls lead?
Where now the grass will bend
Will follow somebody?

Time

Flowers grow up
They bloom with beauty
To wither

One Night Stand

Oh how I love to be
In bed here with my mistress
And watch her play and tease
Of things we will do next

The future, it looks bright
With hot and fiery passion
Though we play in the night
No lights twill we turn on

It may seem almost clumsy
Our dance beneath the satin
But she is precious to me
To her, I wish to fasten

I feel her weight upon me
As with her dripping love
Though atop I'll never be
I'll take what rains above

And though we are familiar
I never do quite know
If I am pleasing her
Or if she just likes the show

I've known no other lover
Who's this close to divine
I'll never get enough of her
My mistress known as time

Tomorrow

To the one I hold; in deepest sleep
This lovely one to whom I keep
I'll sing to you soft lullabies
Into the darkness, deep
Until you open up your eyes
And flutter out of sleep

I'll weave thee tails nor untold
And bring thee dreams to keep
Until your age has made too old
That beautiful dreamscape

And may your eyes alight
With wonder every night
As softly we will rock
Against the ticking clock

But sparkle, shine and gleam
My little pretty thing
I'll never see again
As time twill change the scene
And make this but a *'when'*

Oh in my arms; the cradle
Tis where you rock and sway
This little baby soul
Whose future waits to claim

In the deepest of the dark
That silhouette that's standing there
Who only time brings light; tis lit with but a spark
Though you are here with me, you'll travel far away
And be a different thing, than what you are today

Kaden Moeller

Back In Time

I've seen my picture on the wall
It lays crooked, down in the hall
With dust upon its tarnished frame
Its faded detail causes pain

Of seeing myself once in my prime
It feels stolen from me by time
A violation of my pride
This part of me has long since died

And so the frame I straighten up
Feeling a tightness in my gut
I feel myself never complete
I long for my lost youth, to meet

Emotion's Knife

When pictures pierce your heart
And memories rend your soul
This signals but the start
That you are growing old

When looking back is painful
And going forward's cold
You are that much more mindful
That you are growing old

Oh with that age came joy
A warmth that made you whole
But as it passes by
You know you're growing old

For when you're young, your losses
Weigh less upon you, though
The more that aging presses
You lose what love you hold

For going's an adventure
But leaving isn't so
In youth, you can endure
But age will buckle low

That wonder, once before you
Is now, at last, behind

There's nowhere left to go to
And soon you're out of time

Long Walk

Oh as we move through life
We move the further from
That company, so rife
To a lonely walk of one

As pass, do we, along the lane
Both faces, old and young
And though depart we them, with pain
We leave them and walk on

And every face we see
Is spaced farther between
As loneliness impedes
With none upon to lean

And as the path, it darkens
And none remain ahead
Your memories do harken
To those now long past tread

Now walking towards the night
Into where none will be
Where solitude doth follow
To be your company

A Leak

A drip a drop and then a plop
The leaking in the dark
That sound, beg you, that it stop
So that your sleep might start

As in your bed, the foist leaks
This dripping grates your mind
And each ripple whispers and it speaks
Of life's hourglass of time

Each steady droplet falls but once
And at first forms a puddle

Kaden Moeller

A small, but manageable, expanse
So little and so subtle

But each drip, it piles up
And goes up to your ankles
And now, uncomfortably, you strut
As now the room does fill

And as it reaches to your waist
Panic, it sets in
The dry bits, you don't want to waste
As now you learn to swim

And now, up to you neck it be
And tread do you this violent sea
As now no land your eyes can see
As search do you so hopelessly

Your face presses against the ceiling
This last bastion of air
As slowly, the water, now you feel
Enter into you, so scared

As it has fill up everything
Now you're all that remains
And thus does come the drowning
The wretched writhing pain

As through your mouth, the water flows
And fills your lungs to burst
Your body, begins its death throws
As for fresh air it thirsts

And as your mind does reel
As painfully you die
This lack of air, so real
You cough and try to cry

But then the morbid peace arrives
The placid eyes set in
As lower now your body dives
In your room, cold and darkened

A drip a drop and then a plop
The leaking in the dark
That sound, beg you, that it stop

It brings fear to your heart

Construction

Now, when you build your kingdom
Remember this one thing
No structures can be redone
Just up new ones will spring

And so now twill you build
As an architect of life
Who, sculpting with your will
You chip and crack and slice

But know, do you, the truth
The fate of every castle
That, no matter what you do
The building, it will fall

For every crack of age
Is taken up by time
Creepers, they invade
With weeds and rust and grime

The seedlings sprout up from
The sidewalks and the streets
Making the road undone
But softer for your feet

And trees will grow within
The throne room and the court
The hallways, they will dim
In the recesses of the fort

And creatures of all shapes
They'll come, and they will dwell
Within the master bedroom, snakes
Will nest there and sleep well

Oh it will be so pretty
This kingdom falling in
So much so, you won't pity
The beauty of the garden

Kaden Moeller

The sight of life, amidst
Wreckage and desolation
And the kingdom, like the mist
Cannot escape evaporation

For this is every life
Tis built, and then knocked down
What does it leave behind? What sight
Will be left, if any found?

For everything, it fades
Tis given back to nature
There's nothing we can save
Death has the final word

Deteriorate

Fire flickers, candle dims
Rose-petals dry and crack
The ash but rolls upon the wind
Never to travel back

But watch the sweetest flower
To wither down to dust
You could not halt the hour
No matter desperate lust

No one can spare the loss
Of beauty to the world
It will but turn to dross
Every pretty little marvel

Each spark of life will dim
All trace of joy will fade
Each memory; a gem
It will be cast away

And none will ever know
That anything did breathe
That anything did grow
No single tree of leaf

A mystery will be
Our home to anyone
Who lives after; to see
That who lives here is no one

Author's Question

Where does the story end?
I wonder
And will I see it coming,
Or will I be surprised?

The destination
A dead-end of course
But when will I get there,
And how long will it take?

Will I enjoy the trip,
Or will I hate the journey?
Am I the one who's driving,
Or am I just along for the ride?

I wonder
Will I pick up passengers,
Or will someone help me if I break down?
And who might those persons be,
And what role will they play?

Can anyone know?
Ever can we grasp the pen
And write a line or two ourselves?
I do not know

We float like feathers on the wind
And terry, though we may
So little and so rarely
Upon places cherished and long upon the page

Yet, we cannot stay for long
As every story ends
But on what page,
I do not know

New Beginning

Tick... Tock... Tick... Tock...
Time goes by in an elusive clock
The days the months the years within the clock?

Kaden Moeller

I can't sit up, to no surprise, my life is leaving my soon dead eyes
Breathing is slow, I cannot see, what's this feeling over me?
Happiness and joy, like a child and his new toy
Away, I leave to go home?
Tick... Tock... Tick... Tock...

<u>War</u>

Kaden Moeller

Soliloquy

There is no life greater lived than in the service of one's country
No privilege could eclipse such a thing, its pride, or all its glory
For youth will wax and wane with time as a piece of your life's story
But this service to your country, shall live forever in history

Jump Start

The machine, its gears are turning
It's starting to warm up
And now begins the screaming
As cords are torn and cut

The people, all around
They try to stop the turning
To cease its grinding sound
Its eerie clicks and whirring

Bash they this contraption
Destroying what they can
But it won't stop for them
As its metal scrapes and slams

With all their might, they try
To stop its acceleration
Shoving pipes and things, inside
The cogs, to try to stop them

But in its clamoring
The gears, they catch a hand
And slowly begin pulling
In one of these poor men

The others, they rush to him
And try with all their might
To stop his being pulled in
Their faces, filled with fright

The bones, they hear them crack
The sinew, scraped off clean
Their breath is not held back
It exits as a scream

But this, it doesn't stop the gears
The blood but lubricates

And as they try in all their fear
It seems that they're too late

The gears but pull them in
Each life but moves them faster
This bloody oil helps them spin
As its pistons clank and clatter

They smash the bones to bits
And grind the flesh to paste
These cogs, they will not quit
These souls, they will not waste

The machine is on again
Its engine gives a roar
There is no stopping them
These bloody gears of war

Firefight

War thrills the body but dims the soul
It burns the flames of youth to coal
Its virtues vanish from the hands
Of those who tout it; tall and grand

War's sparks do spread from every fire
Each kindled forth from dark desire
They'd set ablaze the whole of earth
A fire set with blackened mirth

And every spirit in the land
Is but made to a fire brand
And not a life but sacred be
They'll burn for all eternity

Rivalry Of Brothers

Pain sharp glaring eye, one sight of hate and anger for one!
For another, an acrimonious seen of loss and sorrow and bitter feelings, of pain
of anger of hate!

War

Pain and Hate bound together in endless attrition

No sleep on rainless nights
Patriots denied prosperity of rights

All against few, and few against all
What a wonderful world we live in
So full of death and doubt

How long can man survive in war?
When he stays aboard a sinking boat
War is like an art they say
And indeed they are correct
The world yields an interesting canvas
With only the paint of red

In red we write our stories
In red we spin our tails

Come Hero's, Myths and Legends HO!
All Hosts of Valkyries wait
Prey we see the dawn again
But never shell it be fate

The Drinking Game

From the scabbard, pulled the sword
Charging, go it, before the horde
Keeping it, step for step, once more
The dance of death, the dance of war

Pouring blood out upon the soil
The drink of gods, and those made royal
A strong and bitter wine this be
Drunk makes it us, do not you see?

See now our fellows made as beasts
To which we slaughter and we feast
Rejoice, do we, of what we've wrought
As dance we now in death and rot

And sing do we of victory
Intoxicated trickery

Warlord

I am ten years old, and
The militia comes to my village

They said to my parents
"Your son, he will go with us
He, will be a soldier of the nation"

They then, took me
Took me, with them
Took me, into their camp
Took me, away from my home

At night, I cried
I cried, with other children
I cried, holding myself in my own arms

In the morning, the Boss-man comes
The Boss-man, he teaches us
The Boss-man, he gives us special food
The Boss-man, he tells us what to do

I, last night, tried to runaway
I, last night, left the tent
I, last night, hid out in the forest
I, last night, was caught

The Boss-man, punished me
The Boss-man, he took away my special food
The Boss-man, he beat me

I was alone, in my tent
I was alone, curled up and sweating
I was alone, in need of special food
I was alone, screaming for my father

The next day, they fed me
The next day, we raided a village
The next day, I killed a man

I, shot him in the stomach
I, watched him writhe and beg
I, shot him again
I, killed him

At night, the nightmares come
At night, I sweat cold

Kaden Moeller

At night, I feel sick
At night, I eat much special food

All these things I do
I do them for so many years
And, I grow up
I become strong and feared
So feared, that others know my name

Because, now, I'm the Boss-man now
I teach the children now, and
Feed them the special food

Yes, I go through the village, and
Choose the strong soldiers of the nation
And, discipline them well

Yes, the future generations I make strong
They will be like me
Great and terrible

These children will be good, like me
They will stand above the weak
And make a better world than before

By raising the future with my past
I'll make them better than the last

The Day

The day is coming
The hour is near
The great man cometh
All should fear

Boot

The sergeant walks up to a kid
His eyes bulged out his lids
And with steam whistling out his ears
He tells the private, crystal clear

*"Son, you will do what I say!
If I command it, you'll be gay!"*

"Well" Says the private "I'll do what I can

But you're just not my type of man"

"When I say jump, you'll ask how high!
Even if I say to touch the sky!"

"But sergeant!" says the private with a moan
"I think I left my wings at home."

"When I say shit, you ask what color!
You'll give me one and not the other!"

"But serge, I didn't eat my crayons today
I've but one shade, I'm sorry to say"

"Is this clear!?
Boy, do you hear!?"

"Clear as mud sir
I'm quite sure"

A Soldier

I am a barbwire baby
Twas born for nothing more
Then to be used as currency
In the industry of war

Twas printed off the line
They prepped and made me ready
My skills were quite refined
My body, it was deadly

And one by one I'd go
Through the motions of my skills
The only thing I know
Is how to make a kill

Each thing my hands do grace
A tool of destruction
Each person that I face
A target with assumption

My value, as a soldier
Is high, as some assume

But that's when war is here
Over peace, my shadow looms

I am a bloody banker
Cashing in lives for death
Twas born to do this chore
And made into the best

Riders

We are coming
To town now do we ride

No hurry though
We'll get there

Across the sandy plains
Pass we the tumbling weeds
A breeze of sandy blistering

We clip and clop
Towards the bustling and hustling

Yes, we four are riding
Slowly
To our destination

For merchants are we
And we do wish
To sell our wears
So to get rich

I and my brothers are diverse
For one sells swords
Another poison
Know we these make money

The other of us
A sick physician
Who sells the plague quite well

And then theirs me
The manager
I run the other three
Being the one that they observe
And wish, do they, to please

Oh we look forward, that we do
As upon the horizon we see
The buildings grow up higher
It seems our crop to glean

Oh how I love the harvest
Collecting all our pay
We hear the people calling
They wish to buy today

We're riding
A bit closer
Nearer and nearer still

We see
That much the clearer
The crowds, now as they grow
Upon the border of the town

They stand and they look out
Gawking, quite perplexed
At us
Those new to town

Our steeds they see
And wonder they
Why do we ride
Pail horses?

Approaching Hoof-Beats

In the distance, hear the rumbling
You hear it all the nearer coming
Transform, will it, into a thundering
Twill this intimidating drumming

A beating pounding raw cascade
Be this song of angry feet
That washes over strong and brave
And makes them small and meek

This thrumming, bounces off the hills
Over the mountaintops

This horrid echo seems to fill
The mind with fearful thoughts

For after every wretched thud
The soul, it mounts with dread
And curdles, does it, up the blood
And makes light the mind and head

So listen at these sound waves crash
Against the shore of our ears
Pray to not be drown and bashed
By this storm blowing near

Dog Soldiers

Our eyes, they flash against the light
As we encroach within the night
It seems that we have found our prey
As lope, do we, into the fray

Hear we the crying and the shouts
As close, we do, around about
And cut them off from their escape
Moving close, our mouths agape

A feast before us does now stand
Something to satiate our clan
And quench, will it, our thirst for blood
Soaking the ground to foul mud

It's not as bad as it may seem
This harvest is but what we glean
We are but scavengers, in truth
Eating the weak and the uncouth

Those real predators are worse
Inflicting wounds no one can nurse
They train and tell us what to do
Making men monsters just for you

One Of The Three

Where three stand, two will lye
When two stand with one lying, another on the way
And when one stands with two a lying
He will wonder what he stood for

The Floor

Upon this floor I lay
The sun has left the day
The moon raises high to greet the heavens
Its beams as intense as blight

The reasons, past and future ahead
And I'll live not to see it
I gave the world so little
Yes
So shall I be great?

There is no reason to it
For rhyme gives life away
So unto thee I shall bestow
One way for every day

Once More

We are going one more time
To war

We are stepping up the line
Once more

I don't know what I will see
Out there

Oh what will become of me
I'm scared

The enemy is moving near
We know

I'm gripped with fear
I want to go

I hear them charging
Towards us now

I feel fear barging in
How!?

Unto The Breach

A young man lies out in the rain
He contorts and cries and writhes in pain
A darkened water flows without
Cursing in fear, he gives a shout

Drown out in booms and bellowing
And the storm's thundering melody
Its heavy drops fall in his eyes
His moans do mix with battle cries

The feeling of impending dread
The nausea of his bloodless head
A picture framing war's dark art
The faintness of his beating heart

The fear is tightly clutching hold
As death is clawing at his soul
His body focused on the pain
Crying out, but all in vain

Tears are streaming from his eyes
He begs and pleads just not to die
So there he lies in cratered hole
A man who died a hero, I'm told

Dear Friends

The bloat-flies buzz out in the field
Its dirt now mud, from its fresh meal
The scent is strong, it calls to me
Its buzzing whisper tells the story

With battlements all strewn about
And rot consuming in and out
I find myself now quite perplexed
I see the ribbons on their chests

Oh, how lovely, are these dead arrayed
And yet our memory of them will fade
How strange it is to see them here
Covered in blood, frozen in fear

I almost pity them I guess

But killing them I'm told is best

A Bullet

Let's plant a round inside of you
And see what it makes of you
When it first breaches the surface
Diggs its way in deep
We'll see

It will take root
Its foreign elements spreading throughout your bloodstream
Tendrils reaching through the flowing river of life
Poisoning you with each corrupting growth; but sped on by those once so
welcome beats
Now the final drum taps pounding forth the terrifying dreaded finale
And, oh, those horrific responses

As your body does reject this seed
This thing, invader, which now has weeded its way in deep
A thing inseparable
And it taints the streams and brings the bile
The sickening puss; swelling around this festering bulb of death
And the sickly convulsions that come
Eyes whirling and muscles seizing; until silence
The bloom has occurred

Seed; taken
Root; spread
Season; ended
Flower; dead

Blitz

There is no good news today
The shadowy smoke has come

Bombs... Bombs... Bombs...

Running in the rain and mud
The sirens song is drowning us

Bombs... Bombs... Bombs...

Kaden Moeller

Collapsed metal, brick, and wood
Meshed with skin and sinew

Bombs... Bombs... Bombs...

The silent wind draws near
The foggy death appears, and then

Bombs... Bombs... Bombs...

Powerless

Fire! Fire! Everything is on fire!
The buildings blaze and roar as they billow black
Broken glass and panic rain about as chaos echoes with the screams
These sounds, speckled, midst muffled ringing
But I am running up stairs, up the building steps, bypassing corpses and fallen persons
Pushing and shoving, I have to get to the fifth floor; black smoke wafting through the air
There is fire on the fifth floor, the blaze is everywhere, and I've lost my self-preservation
I run to my door; the baby is screaming
Screaming that horrible scream, shrill scream, the sound of terror and pain
A scream, a plea, a begging cry, that scream

I'm in the room, fire, and I pull my baby from its grip
And he's screaming, my god he's screaming, and I run down those same stairs
Those shrieks echoing through the concrete stairwell
And I get out in the streets, cradling my infant; my baby boy
He's screaming

His fragile body's skin, like cracked paper, licked by the flames
Skin raw, body bleeding from the burns, screaming
And I cradle my son, I cannot stop crying
His little body, barely a month old, that vulnerable little body
That defenseless body, shaking and shivering
That baby, that precious child
I cry; a plea, a begging cry, that scream
My baby; he isn't crying anymore

A Lovely Death

Upon the battlements I ride
With colors bright and stark
But lady death pulled me aside

"Come join me in the dark"

I told her "Dearest, please
Can't it but wait an hour?"
But press, did she, quite close to me
"I needn't wait, my lover"

"But war has called me to her"
"And I, I call you back"
"But what of all those here?"
"They will, in time, defect"

"But am I not a soldier,
To fight against the fray?"
*"But your fight ends, right here
I call you home, today"*

And look, did I, back out
Into the battlefield
Those violent screams and shouts
All that was sorrowful

And death, she saw me staring
And watched it break my heart
A scene, oh so despairing
"Come join me in the dark"

<u>Respond</u>

The flames do slide and sway
And take your breath away
As sparks whirl round your head
Seeds for the blaze to spread

What black winged demon breathed
And with his rage did weave
This wretched fiery wreath
Who takes it all to keep

To run through this red forest
And its dark and burning mist
Though many would abhor it
I do this with teeth grit

For to dance upon the edge
Pulling others from its ledge
It is the best addiction
To stop someone's attrition

And carry, will I, everyone
Until I am undone
And hope, do I, another comes
For me when this job's done

The pleasure of fear's call
To answer each and all
Dare say not that my life
Was one without its strife

Dawning Day

The brightest light that we can make
Turning the ground to glassy lake
The clouds rolling with sparks and ash
Blotting out the sun with poison gas

With eyes burning out of the skull
The flesh blowing right off the bone
The last light one would ever see
The light you see and try to flee

My Funny Forest

This morning I awoke to light
A sun-flash oh so burning bright
It grew a garden up for me
Starting with one gigantic tree

And then the skies began to roll
Over this forest I watch grow
Oh such a sight for one to see
The forest overtake humanity

And so I watch these cloudy trees
Stepping outside into the breeze
A feeling of unpleasant aw
Oh what disturbing sights I saw

The people, they did up and flee
Fearing the forest's spreading seed

They tripped and fell and sped away
Left me alone on this strange day

And so I watch my new colored sky
Oh how these trees reach up so high
The weather now is much too warm
The skies look like they're going to storm

Until that time though, I must say
I will take shelter in the shade
I'll go towards my funny trees
And cool myself beneath their leaves

What shall I call these skyward blooms
That reach so high to touch the moon
Mushrooms they resemble most
And so I walk to them, so close
Feeling small and oh so bland
I feel sick, and

I stand beneath the mushroom trees
Their crimson petals swirling about me
The air so thick with pollen and spore
These mushroom trees, will there be more?

The clouds, they crackle and they roll
As lightning danced above the soil
Is this real? It's not a dream
These mushroom trees, so odd they seem

With sparks and ash falling like snow
A smog so thick the air won't flow
And so I stand alone right here
Beneath these mushroom trees so queer

Barefoot Generation

In the hours of the morning
There came, at once, a sound
And what that noise did bring
Destroyed the ears it found

It swept away the world
Leaving not a stone unturned

The colors, they did swirl
As sickly did they burn

The people were consumed
As the flames came from above
And the children in the womb
Went up like paper doves

And though their bodies left
Their shadows stayed behind
The only thing to guess
Where life did once reside

In the morning hours
It now is very quiet
And beneath the silence, cowers
The life that's left in it

Strolling

It's snowing grey out in the streets
Water is black and thick
The clouds a shimmery oily haze
I'm starting to feel sick

A tingling burn is on my skin
My joints they crack and click
I limp down main street toe to heel
My body wants to quit

The rash across my flesh, it burns
My sweat so greasy slick
I see a warped distorted bench
Perhaps I'll stop and sit

All Quiet...

I come before you bloody
These crimson stains abound
That drip down oh so ugly
And land wrong on the ground

My eyes are wild and hollow
Staring beyond the world
No thought comes of tomorrow
Seeing my hands, now gnarled

I sit in silent stillness
As death now takes my soul
But I'm still here, just soulless
My spirit has grown cold

The tears, they do not come
The nausea's over powering
The battle, though it's won
In fear, I still am cowering

I notice now, my shaking
A trembling I can't control
My knees, they are but quaking
My hands, they cannot hold

You look at me concerned
With passionate empathy
And as your eyes are blurred
You reach your hand to me

I do not see your hand
Stretching, there, outwardly
Towards your fellow man
This injured one you see

And with that loving touch
The fear, it floods my mind
This quiet, it's too much
So to, your gift, so kind

I push you away, while screaming
And collapse right where I stand
As down, the tears are streaming
My face cupped in my hands

Curled upon the ground
I watch the battle rage
And hear the echoed sounds
Of what's now yesterday

I hug myself before you
And you but watch in vain
Knowing, sad but true

Kaden Moeller

You cannot stop my pain

A Christmas Present

At the boys home
They handed me
A present

It was wrapped
Colorfully
And said
"From Santa"

I don't understand

Good kids
They get presents
They get the things they want

But me
I'm no good

I've killed people
I've watched them die
They say it's not my fault
But
I did those things

The men came
Took me away
When I was little

My parents
They killed them
They taught me
To hold a gun
To aim
To shoot
To kill

I did those things
I've killed men
Women
Children, just like me

I've helped people

Do terrible things

I set a house on fire
The people were inside
They had a baby
It was crying
They were crying
Screaming
They held the baby out the window
They dropped it
I watched

I did those things
Then men came
Took me away
Away from the blood
The violence
They took me here
The boys' home

So why
Why do I have a present?
How was I good this year?

I don't understand
I don't deserve this gift

Peace

A pacifistic patriarch of mindless words
Hero-less stories of monotony abound
Made appealing by the clucking of hens over there hatchlings
Prevailing victories of the mundane

No stories
No Hero's
Myths
Or Legends… Peace
We want peace?

A Walk On The Beach

A sorry sod
A little man

He tried so hard
The most men can

But life moves on
He holds my hand
The rain falls down
In no-man's land

So as we walk
Feet in the sand
Nobody knows
On plays the band

The Peace Industry

I have a plan
An idea
A Mahatma King told me
We can wage peace
I know it

We must take the money of war
The coffers deep and dark
And dump them into the dens of poverty
Flood them with prosperity

Our nation
Our people
Should gird ourselves in work boots
And lay siege to barren lands

We will walk up to those peoples
Those with bombed out hovels and rancid dens
And we will build them a city
A beauteous land
And we will employ them
Take their hand

We will overflow their emptiness with an endless bounty
We will teach them to build
Teach them community
Gift them friendship
And work hand in hand with them to touch the sky

And when their nation's built
The country now employed

We will, with them, work together
To spread our generosity

We will build up all others
Invest in humanity
And with each victorious growth
We will see violence decrease

We must invest in people
From sea to shining sea
We must restrain our fist
If we wish victory

For if our kindness is rejected
By a furious few
We must keep forward for the rest
And let our kindness push through

We must defend our fellows
Not just from the violent few
We must defeat also 'Want'
We must wage peace on it
We, humanity, cannot declare victory
If we do not fight the greatest threat to life
Fear

What fears do we fight?
The fear of starvation
The fear of homelessness
The fear of helplessness
The fear of inopportunity
The fear of failing health
The fear of uselessness
The fear of unemployment
The fear of human indifference
We must wage peace unto these fears!

We, the human race, must invest in building the world anew
We must build the world we want to live in
We must build ourselves and our fellows
Build and build and build

Go to the poorest lands and build
Teach those without to build

Keep building
Until every person, once unemployed, now works to build the world up
And keep going
Never stop
Take that building around the world
To every land and class

Yes, society must invest in other societies
Until we can safely say
That we are all human
For if we sow seeds of death
Planting bombs over the soil
Raining tears and dread
We reap returns unwanted
Those seeds beget toxic offspring
Who wander 'bout the earth spreading destruction
But, if we plants seeds of birth
If we employ the earth
Invest in our human friends
We will reap cooperation
Those places we forgot
They will thank us and unite
They will build and build humanity
Until we stand to our full height

But these investments must not be for profit
We could rather call them aid
They are the investments of peace
They cannot make a slave
The wages that we pay
For the building up of peace
They cannot be slave wages
They must bring dignity

Not mindless exploitive globalization
Profit motive blotting out the sight of peace with greed
Whose outcome mayhaps create equity though coincidence and happenstance
An osmosis of possibility guided by an invisible hand in a theoretical world
Theoretical people making theoretical decisions for their own theoretical best
self-interest
That theoretically would be good for collective society if we but were more
alone
More individualized and cut off from one another, theoretically

This is not how you make peace
Rather, you do so with an intentional striving towards a goal most laudable

Extending a real hand to lift up real people on this real earth
No faith based economy or government
But real people with tangible testable ideas and creative minds to tweak them
Working, in the real world on how to really address the real problems of our
fellows

Create a peace industry
Not war; indiscriminate
Cease bombing innocence
Planting those seeds of vengeance within your fellows
We must plant seeds of gratefulness
Seeds of thanks and friendship

We must try, with all due realism
To restrain the might of the fist
For no strength truly resides within such a frail instrument
What perfect peace has reigned from bludgeoning your brother?
Fear is not peace
If they fear you, they are but a moment away from hate
And if they hate you
You will learn of their scorn in violence

We must wage peace
It isn't cheap
But when has war been cost free?
Bombs are the price of food
The price of homes
They are investments in death and chaos
And bring the derivatives of uncertainty and hatred
The only war we wage would be on the war industry
Because the peace industry is so weak at this present moment
So let us revoke our subsidizing of war
Let us invest in the industry of peace
Peace through cooperation and building
Invasions laying siege to bondage and poverty
Building the world we want to see
Investing in the human species
Let us reap the derivatives of friendship and cooperation
And with each land seeing its full potential
Let us bask in the marvels of what humanity is truly capable of
Our true creative genius
Our true potential
Peace is a process, we wage peace, if we want it we build it
Build and industry of peace

<u>Mourning</u>

To Live

Upon the sea of sorrow
My soul, it sails through
The winds, oh as they howl
Batter my sails anew

On the wave-crests of despair I ride
And crash into the brine
My spirit, though it wants to hide
This pain, oh it be mine

Oh misery rains upon me
In drops upon my head
A downpour from this stormy sea
That which my vessel treads

Yes, in depression's tempest
My emotion's oceans rage
These churning waters, but a test
A trial upon the stage

I navigate the waterspouts
Of anger and acceptance
And push, do I, through darker clouds
Into the eye, by chance

I float, but for awhile, in the eye of melancholy
Before braving the typhoon again
To fight through its second volley
And the memories come from them

And so the storm is over
This hurricane of pain
But we're still on the sea, another
Storm will come again

Cracks

"When wept did I?"
Did stones decry
Can trouble grace thy face?
Or is it that your tears have dried
And carved their paths in place?

"Oh could that be?"
Most certainly
Such cracks hold no disgrace
They're merely faded memories
Whose sight lets you retrace

"How to forget?"
Try not to fret
Allow yourself to see
And contemplate those cracks; now set
Who seem to wonder free

"Can't they be filled?"
Not once revealed
And grown from our regret
For tears erode until
There twill be nothing left

Echo

Upon the day of death
Whence comes the great despair
You'll find a great regret
Their silence was always there

When you were all alone
In still and stilted air
You never could have known
Their silence was always there

Between those intervals
Visits, short and fair
When you listened well
There silence, it was there

How cold be this relation,
When see that empty chair?
That quite devastation
Their silence now sits there

The Sound

Grief is not a loud thing
It comes home silently
And with it, does it bring

A quiet agony

Where in your heart you hurt
And in your mind you scream
Oh tis a type of curse
These things that silence sings

You notice what is lacking
Rather than what is there
That oh so empty sting
Now called, by you, despair

How helpless are you now;
Midst the weight of emptiness?
And cry, do you, aloud
To end silence's duress

But as time moves us on
Some new sounds fill the void
Not those ones; long gone
But others, filled with joy

Yet never will that emptiness
Leave from thy broken heart
That grief that brought you such distress
Leaves cracks that won't depart

A Day Ago

With grief, it's always yesterday
The day of greatest sorrow
And wish we but for one more day
So grief would be tomorrow

We wish that our spent tears
Twould but stay kept away
And that those lonely fears
Would never come our way

We'd build a dam before them
Right through the path of time
To hold a little longer, and
Forget we the divine

To fill the bags beneath our eyes
But never let them burst
For fear we when we start to cry
Their current draws the hearse

To have but one more day
It never is enough
No amount of words convey
How much we love

Playmate

Oh friendly friend now come to grief
And like the cold wind to the leaf
Does quiver, tremble, quake and sway
That loneliness has come to play

This solitude who calls your name
From that silent empty space
And plays with you that little game
As memories, you chase

As wrestle, now you, with your thoughts
And all the pain and joy they've brought
That empty place now in your heart
Where once twas held the lover's spark

A lonely bit of fun this be
To dance here all alone
To sing the song of melancholy
Against our heart's sole drum

Oh bitter be the wine
Come from the victim's vine
A drink not meant for two
A lonely drink, tis true

Erosion

There are two bitter streams
That flow much more with time
The well springs of dead dreams
That gush forth salty brine

Oh the pressure that builds up
And forms these tragic geysers

That once opened, can't shut
Flooding you spirit with fear

These rivers carve deep canyons
That form beneath your eyes
These waters tend to grow them
No matter how they dry

Oh of these brooks of sorrow
That wear away the youth
They grow every tomorrow
With each unwanted truth

For though they seem as drops and drips
But trickling down your face
Each be a raging tempest
Over these once dry beds they trace

And so comes forth the torrent
The pouring of the soul
This pain, oh so abhorrent
Soon, well will you know

So, when the sadness comes
And tears begin to rise
Don't fear where they will run
They prove that you're alive

Precious Depths

Oh, tears are diamonds
We spend them
On what means most to us
A thing's value
Determined by their numerable departure
Each jewel an un-returnable stone cast to eternity
Forever exchanged with loss
Mortal treasures, finite and fleeting
Drying and disappearing as fast as our own lives upon life's brief excursion
Precious, unique and degrading
Their value vanishing to invalidity upon memory's scattering and inevitable
disappearance

Diamonds; housed away in the deepest regions of our souls

Un-mined and unsearched
Until, upon devastation, the blast of sorrow and pain
Shaken are they, free of our inner complacency and disinterest
And with each devastating wave of sorrowful shuttering we forgo
We relinquish said stones from ourselves
Drip by drip and drop by drop
Glistening and shining with our humanity
And we give them to our loss
For it requires the payment
A back-payment for all its value given
Its services rendered

Value; a thing mysterious
A thing constantly increasing with familiarity
The more familiar, the more valuable
And while our familiarity seems to make us take it for granted
It but only is a sign of our need for such a thing
For it has become a part of us
Of our daily life
And upon its departure
Oh the loss unfathomable

And so; as is with the human heart
Our most precious of measures
By which we can speak of the value of love
Dries with time
Until it was as if
It never existed

Memories

There is a room deep in my mind
Untouched, is it, by sands of time
Early in life it was quite bare
But, as time moved on, I put things there

Pictures of places I have been
These little treasures hide within
Like storybooks, and little toys
Childlike laughter and its joys

All of these things I come across
Are all things that I've long since lost
And when a loved one does depart
I keep them here, within my heart

The Room With Cobwebs

Has ever sorrow crept you heart,
And made its home; despair?
And wreathed over its once open door
"The one within's not there"

And have these strong foundations
That which make up your soul
Crumbled and cracked to misery
And left a gaping hole

Does the air within your lungs,
Travel an empty house?
Through hallways none live in
And out your joyless mouth

Be all the frames upon the walls
Be cracked; with memories
Faded; tear spattered photographs
Which once were all but glee

Is every room now filled with pain,
Or is it filled with grief?
Has emptiness gave things to you,
Or have you even less?

Be helplessness a hell,
Or some strange purgatory?
We know its residence
Within our sorry scene

Has ever sorrow crept your heart,
And made its home; despair?
And wreathed over its once open door
"The one within's not there"

Swimming

Have you ever dived the depths
Gone deepest into despair
Swum headlong through regret
Towards rage; whilst lacking air

Kaden Moeller

And ever have you stopped
In those dark waters; still
And listened long; distraught
Midst every lack of will

And sunk into the open arms
Of the siren of depression
Who sings her maiden song
Of hopeless long reflection

And let the light; high up above
Which shimmers through those waters
Fade; as you sink away from love
Into the blackness; deeper

And oh the panic; shrill
Comes hurriedly and crass
Your lungs will burn until
You take your final gasp

So will you swim the surface,
Go back there, up above,
And break that shimmering serf, yes,
Greeted by beams of love?

For one can only go
Until a certain depth
This everybody knows
And then there's certain death

Sad Story

Waking up to empty bed
Drives into you, love is dead
That colder spot upon the sheet
The place, where upon two would meet
Now is empty and quite bare
Forgotten now the face once there
And there you crumple up and cry
And wonder why they had to die

One Half

Here in bed
And empty bed
All but for me

It's empty

I cannot sleep
As leap about my memories
And all I ever want to see
Is you, my dear

Yet, gone you are
Forever lost, regret
That such should be
And I cannot sleep

Your scent, next to me
Upon those pillows
There, that light scent
Of rose and sweet lavender

And that special fragrance
Perhaps sweat or hair
It lingers, cold, in the air
And every so often I turn

Looking for you
But emptiness greets me
And I weep
I cry into those pillows

Trying so desperately
Attempting in vain
To clasp you through memory
Through time and loss

Vain, vain all is vain
As with every moment
Your sweet scent fades
And like all things, dissolves

And all is empty
Hollow and regret
And I curl up alone
In that bed of ours

That empty bed
And I feel what death is like

Kaden Moeller

What true love is like
What every soul
And every love must come to
Through every and all experience
It all comes down to this
Loneliness, loss and despair

Love comes to this
And how grateful I am
That I have loved

Stitches

When that which makes you joyful dies
And there be nothing left
The tears, long gone and made to dry
As carved they their wrinkled cleft

And barren be our world without
And dead our soul within
As silence echoes round about
Empty, without a friend

With every heartbeat's pause
Do come the dreaded thoughts
Of those long gnarled claws
And the heart which they have stopped

And the memories, they cut
Until the spirit bled
Oh to but sew them up
Yet comes the fear and dread

Oh be these the last marks
Of that now gone away
I dare not even start
To sew them up today

Raining Sunshine

Oh when our hearts are mourning
A loved one that we've lost
And find our souls are storming
As our emotions toss

And tears, they drip like raindrops

From the clouds; upon your spirit
That formed, they, from your thoughts
But in you they don't sit

Each drop contains within
A happy memory
A special part of them
This person that we grieve

Those bits of tears that shine
And sparkle with the sun
The parts we find divine
As remember we someone

To the bereaved, life is precious
And death is more than true
It's so much more real to us
When our hearts are colored blue

Coupling

My bed is warm again
No longer am I alone
But it is not the same as when
That warmth was from my bone

That special part of me
That rib, my other side
The one whom I can't see
The one who now has died

Leaving an indentation
A spot that can't be filled
And with wretched tribulation
I'd lay in my bed, now chilled

Twas cold beneath the sheet
Without my other body
And though I'd go to sleep
Such slumber it twas shoddy

But then you came to me
You gave me consolation
And as in pain I'd greave

You'd cease my self-flagellation

Embrace me would you, caring
About my inner spirit
My life, you started sharing
Being a part of it

I then began to fear you
Feeling that I'd betray
The one whom I'd held to
The one now in the grave

But you, you held to me
You gave, to me, your love
Knowing that we could be
No rib, but just a glove

For know you, the connection
That I had to my lost
Will not be a reflection
Of what is to be got

Now we two are together
So close, but not as one
For though I love you, never
Will my grief wholly be done

Oh to be warm again
My head upon the pillow
I sleep much better than
When I'm alone, without a fellow

<u>Veterans</u>

Kaden Moeller

Homecoming

But wash me over, would you?
Cascade upon my soul
The waves that do come through
Be but thy overflow

Your radiance, I see
The pleasure in your eyes
To look at you, so happy
Those joy filled tears you cry

To hold you in my arms
As grasp you desperately
To see me safe from harm
To be back home with thee

Oh your embrace, tis trembling
Such joy, you can't contain
And though you may be sobbing
They be not tears of pain

Those waves come over me
And I do weep with you
Us two, we are so happy
The war, we've gotten through

Free Rider

So stood two people there
Each at their podium
One, a pacifist
The other, a soldier

And said the pacifist
"The war
Now it is over
The country
It is saved
But oh
At what cost
And all the lives now lost
Now ripped away from life
Oh count we all the dead
And measure we, the cost"

The soldier stood
Hands gripping
Upon the podium
But he said not a thing

"Oh could this have been stopped?"
Said the pacifist
"Could we not have held discourse?
Rebelled nonviolently?
Spoke with cool heads, clearly
And make peace manifest?"

But tears ran down the soldier's face
And spattered there below
He hunched over his podium
And growled, deep and low

Speaking
The pacifist continued
"For know we well
That barbarism
It gives us not a thing
To capitulate to our weakest bane
And make ourselves to monsters"

And with a passion
Powerful
The soldier flipped his podium
Pointing his finger at the pacifist
And with a pain-filled voice
Laced deep with pride and rage
He spoke
Though his words cracked a bit
And said he powerfully

"I sacrificed my soul for you
Not some, but all of it
I dashed my innocence, shattered like shards of clay
And then I buried them, down deep where the bullets lay
Although it made me sick
I never faltered"

And stepped he towards
The pacifist

Growling through gritted teeth
"And when they came for people
Did you jump forth to stop them?
Was it you who they did meet
In battle?
No!"

And grasp, did he, by the shirt,
The pacifist,
While sobbing
"Perhaps if you had helped
Yes, you and all your kind
Perhaps it would have ended sooner
But no
You abstained
And I…
The things I had to do
What you wouldn't
Those things so gruesome
That if not done
Would have come home to you"

"Those things that took my silence
And made it ominous
Which brought my dreams to violence
My stomach to disgust"

"And so now, I will query
So what else could I do
Be bold and answer me!
How far
Need angels fall for you?"

Special Delivery

Oh what is worse than sorrow?
A painful sight to see
It is the coming harrow
Of sadness soon to be

To see a face unmarred
By the tears of pain-soaked eyes
And know their heart, unscarred
Where life's blade twill reside

But oh to be the one

That cursed soul with the dagger
That person who must plunge
This knife of truthful words

The handle on this blade
Who's weight but builds with time
And makes the thrust you gave
More deadly and less kind

And hesitate, do you
To bring yourself to bleed
And run another through
With something that they need

Oh how I hate to be
That person with the words
The one who does the cutting
Just when my voice is heard

Deliveryman

*"Oh tell her that I love her
And our two young boys"*
The last words that he uttered
To her I told this story

She cried aloud in pain
And hugged her shattered soul
Her quaking quivering frame
Shivered from life gone cold

And so I left her doorstep
The news had been delivered
A story did she get
But not the one I'd heard

The one about a man
Blood pouring from his mouth
He could not even stand
As his body writhed about

No words came from his lips
As he slowly drown within
His eyes, wildly lit

Begging someone help him

So yes, those things I said
I know they made you cry
But stain, did I, it red
What call we a white lie

Precession

I'm carrying a coffin
The death chest of my love
The sun, it seems to dim
As if it weeps above

The one who used to tease me
With her white flashing smile
Whose joy, when I could see
Eased the burden of my trials

The one who warmed my bed
With passion and with pain
The one who now is dead
Whose tombstone reads her name

The one who bore my children
Whose body gave them life
Who'll never be there with them
When they are wed for life

The one who lived for others
Who gave so freely to them
Feeling duty towards another
To help them shine like gems

The one who was so brave
Who makes my heart forlorn
It is true what they say
About girls in uniform

The one who left her home
To fight hard to protect it
The fear, oh it was known
They might come home in caskets

The one who fought beside
So many valiant souls

Who'd shout in battle cry
Her continence, so bold

The one who didn't leave
Her fallen comrades there
Who went back to relieve
The rookie, who was scared

The one who fought so hard
To get them all back home
Whose body wasn't charred
To peaces was it blown

The curse of friendly fire
It took my love from me
These *"smart"* weapons inspire
My soul within to grieve

And though the soldiers worked
To recover every body
No matter how they looked
Twas nothing left to see

And come, did they, to me
And knocked upon my door
Seeing those boys in green
I collapsed upon the floor

So walk, do I, along
The graveyard's looming path
With soldiers, standing strong
Survivors of the bloodbath

This coffin, it is empty
Tis for the closure of my spirit
The reason it's so heavy
Is because my heart is in it

Old City Bar

Together we are here today
We friends, the fewest few
And drink we, in the deepest way
This strong and bitter brew

Acquired, is the taste of loss
A different kind of joy
A pleasure we have come across
That follows those destroyed

And we, we're but the remnants
Of that which once was youth
And like the smoke of incense
We linger here as proof

Our weapons these days be
The glass and smoky lungs
To each but help us see
These latter days be done

To dim the well lit fog
Of painful memory
And cease the endless slog
That leads us but to grieve

And one by one, each meeting
Is less and less a crowd
Until the hearts here beating
Is one that's not that loud

A toast, with foggy glass
And eyes lit rather dim
A very lonely mass
A very lonely friend

Grouped Alone

In this our last meeting place, we group together

Between the conception
And the creation
Lies the shadow

For this is the way the world ends
Life is the way the world ends

Here we go round the prickly pear at five o'clock in the morning

Having A Smoke

The flame, it flicks, and wraps around
The cigarette's round tip
I drag, the smoke, and keep it down
To fill my lungs a bit

The ember at the end, it glows
And then it fades
As red veins crack the ash, like snow
The wind blows it away

The smoke, so thick, I hold it
To slowly breathe it out
And sit, to gawk, at smoky death
Whose hand is reaching out

And through the smoke, deep in its wisps
There be lonely shapes
Of friends long gone, I see them as I sit
A long smoke do I take

It's like I'm back, straining my eyes
Staring through lonely mist
Waiting, perchance, just to sigh
As fear twould hold my breath

My bated breath would quake, as the enemy closed in
Nearer, nearer and nearer
My hands now start to shake, and I toss back the gin
And shake the fog to clear

The silence, echoes round about, the voices of my friends
Shouts that turn to screams
And I, smoking, try not to ponder how those screams did end
So horrid and obscene

And as the putrid incense, envelopes my empty glass
I think so much the clearer
Perhaps it was not they, who lost their lives in that clash
For they're not sitting here

And I, the lonely one, wash well my memories
With a tonic oh so strong

And then, do I, wring out my grief
In me no tears belong

And as the ash hangs long, devoid of any spark
I flick the butt away
The smoke lingers in the air, I listen to my heart
And not one beat be gay

The Veteran

Sat there, did I, drinking
My mind but hardly thinking
As through the milky malaise
Of the smoky room I gaze
Another who was sinking

And saw, did I, right there
That long and humble stare
Whose vacancy did tell
Of something more than hell
It twas the great despair

Whose glass, I spied, was empty
A thing I found a pity
As ordered, did I, two
And sent them both to you
I then but took my leave

To stagger through the streets
From memories, retreat
As all the more it seems
I'll find them in my dreams
And cry myself to sleep

As off come all the trappings
With all their special meaning
These weighted pins
And ribbons thin
I don't find them relieving

Youth

There's something in that young boy's eyes that takes me back a day
Back to a time I thought of most, in the days I laughed and played
I remember dreaming fondly then, during those brighter days
Of fighting in some war torn trench, seeing through smoke and haze

Those days, oh yes, I do recall I yearned for death and glory
Oh how a young man so deeply feels the need to live his story
Oh yes, the clearness of it all, comes back in many colors
So too the death rattle of many a friend, and fallen bands of brothers

And so I watch these children play at war, like oh so many others
And think, I do, of their undone deeds, and the tears of all their mothers
For young boys, it seems, dream more of war than romance, love or pleasure
So unto them I write this poem, the greatest of love letters

Old Man Death's Beard

Within my eyes lies a void eternal and unending
Of wisdom vast and friendship through war trodden hellish holes
My friends have traveled far from home and never did return
Today though they seem closer than they ever did before

Glory, glory to the wisdom earned through love and hatred
No respect is given unto those who go through all to know
Life, knowledge, and death
Now as time's ticking takes me home
I walk alone through shadow and flame

I walk alone
I walk alone
I walk alone

The Poet's Library

What Is A Poem

What are words but chicken scratch?
Who are we but chunks of flesh?

Why do we fight over who's the best?
Who's wrong who's right and all the rest?

Why do people feel for others, when they themselves are feeling not?
Who told you that love is true?
If that's so, why did they never show their true side to you?
Do we have a destiny, or are we doomed?

What is a poem and all of that?
But aren't our words just chicken scratch?

Jingle

Dingle, Dangle Doongle, Dong
This is the song that no one sung
And so I'll sing it, it's not long
Dingle, Dangle Doongle, Dong

Dingle, Dangle Doongle, Dong
When the monkey saw his tail was gone
He sighed and said "It won't be long"
Dingle, Dangle Doongle, Dong

Dingle, Dangle Doongle, Dong
The cow will chew its cud so long
The longest that its ever done
Dingle, Dangle Doongle, Dong

Dingle, Dangle Doongle, Dong
And so the unknown song is sung
Now don't sing it to anyone
Dingle, Dangle Doongle, Dong

Rhymes

Oh woe is me
Like the mosquito and the flee
I take life from all I see
Oh how hard it is to be me

Kaden Moeller

As a plague I spread through thee
So maybe now you'll see
Why no one can truly fear me

Cinema

An experience of fictitious life
A false biography made true
An imaginary image through the mind's eye

A Bad Film

A plot that exists not
A trivial expenditure
So sad, that it's just bad
A terrible adventure

You laugh at such a gaff
Oh buyer beware
You'll regret all that you get
And pull out all your hair

No recourse for your remorse
You'll not understand
You won't believes it when you leave
Money, gone from your hand

Avatar

Living through another's life
A soul within another
Represented by an imaginary icon

Comic

A bubble of speech
A cloud of thought
A box of narration
A hand drawn picture
A world on paper

Scroll

Symbols scratched upon papyrus
Things that can be read by us

A little bit of illumination
It's just a funny culmination

Books

A life compiled
Thought rehearsed
Can't figure it, you're the worst

Lefty Loosely

I'm writing left handed now
What a wonderful sight to see
So clumsy is my written word
Though no better unfortunately

Much straighter are my letters, and so much larger too
I wonder if I should write, with left as others do

For though my comfort zone is shaken
I do believe I'm not mistaken

That with each pen-stroke upon the sheet
My left hand's writing makes my right's look bleak

Tale Teller

Oh dream I, not asleep
But rather wide awake
So that my mind twill keep
These dreams it loves to make

And so I sleep to black
So when my eyes alight
Those dreams, they do come back
They don't leave with the night

And bring I to the eyes
Of other dreamers minds
Those things my mind devised
As beneath the light they shine

Yes, bleed I out these dreams
Through the black ink of the pen

Each laugh and tortured scream
Are dreams I share with them

Come walk, will you, with me
And dream awhile awake
Oh travel deep and breath
The smoke that dreams do make

And wonder out aloud
Why is it that I bring
My dreams before the crowd
And not while I'm sleeping

So think, do I, perhaps
This world that I'm in
Could be but shattered glass
Upon a dreamer's skin

That I'd be nothing more
Than someone else's thoughts
And that's why I don't soar
In all that sleep I got

So what if I'm a dream,
A toy in someone's head?
For just like life, it seems
All other dreams be dead

I'll never know for sure
These things we call our dreams
The who or what they are
And whatever they mean

A Skill

So you can scale rocky peaks
And touch the endless sky
While I cannot, this horizon greet
I can write poetry, and make you cry

So you can be a warrior
And for my freedom die
While I'm blocked by a barrier
I can write poetry, and make you cry

So you can paint a landscape

But no matter how I try
My paintings aren't that great
So I write poetry, and make you cry

So you can love quite deeply
And with envy, I sigh
Oh such a sight to see
While I, write poetry, and make you cry

So you strive for human rights
And with bravery, you decide
To stand in strength and fight
As I write poetry, and make you cry

I know I come off shallow
While others truly try
But I want my words to travel
Writing poetry, to make you cry

So these tears that you shed
They pour down from your eyes
They drip upon the page you read
Because, I can write poetry, and make you cry

To Define

What is a poet?
He is a singer
Sorrow, he sows it
With his fingers

He brings with him a lullaby
And with the day's new dawning
He slowly wakes the sleeper's eyes
With this song of the mourning

His words
They are like drops of rain
When heard
They magnify your pain

And speak, do they, into your ears
Bringing out what's inside
These parts within that hold your tears

Kaden Moeller

Those parts you try to hide

Tis funny, how
These words without
They bring out now
What's within

For this is what the poet does
He brings out the real you
And that's important, because
He shows you if you grew

Rhyme

A funny little bit of time
Enjoying the dictionary tomb we mine
Thesaurus travel of the most comical kind
We play the game of hide and find

Art

Translating a poem is bad
It makes me feel sad
Like translating a song
It's just so vary wrong

The lyrics, they stop rhyming
And lose all of their timing
We should never digest art
Twill make it but a fart

With all its beauty rendered stench
Eclipsing now what once was meant

Such Sights To Show You

Art reflects life
Great art
It comments and deepens our thoughts
It takes us, further, into our experience and conveys
What life really is

It's dirty
Gritty
Unpleasant at times
There is beauty

But in strange ways
We see it
Reflected back at us
But we, at times, don't like to look

Art, it's uncomfortable
It makes you question preconceptions
Starting points are moved around
Even jettisoned completely
And we're left wondering
'What went wrong?'
We feel unsure of our perceptions and our beliefs

Art, it takes us on a journey
And as we travel
It asks us to relinquish things
Beliefs, people, even our time
And then asks us
Once we have reached the end of the road
To look back
Look back and judge
Were the prices you paid
Those precious things
'Was it worth it?'

Art, good art, never leaves you the same
It changes you, as it itself may change
A powerful mover and shaper
And it move and shapes itself in as much as it moves and shapes you

Art, is beautiful
It is beautiful because it is un-content
It demands more
More dreams
More time
More life
More

We are the artisans of the future
The artist, whether he knows it or not, sets the farer ideals
Sets the heart's pace upon the dance-floor of life
And takes of our dreams and makes them here and now
The artist speaks into the winds to give them form
And so they dance with us

Kaden Moeller

The gale blows us to and fro and we are moved by its passing

Yes, art begets life
Art reflects life
Art is life
And we
Are Art

<u>Death</u>

Life

Death is a doctor
Here to relieve the pressure
Of life from your shoulders
So you can float away from time

The Spade

I'm digging a trench
I'm digging it wide
Moving dead men
And stacking them high

I'm building a grave
I'm building a tomb
Where in all laid
No flowers bloom

I'm killing the land
And salting the earth
So that not a man
Brings it rebirth

To reap the harvest
To take a life
By stealing the breath
In midst of night

I come in a moment
That proper time
And will not relent
Until you're mine

I'll vanish the instant your candle is snuffed
Leaving an ominous gloom
A feeling of dreaded disgust
Wherever my footsteps have moved

The bodies I pile
The lives I will take
Escape for a while
Till I repatriate

For when the abyss spits you out
I'm the one who's dragging you back

Care not I your scream and your shout
You're but a body I stack

If there is a hell or a heaven
I'm the one who's taking you there
Indifferent to which you are in
Whether you're happy or scared

I tune out your tears
They are useless
I care not your fears
Or distress

For when I come calling for you
Your response matters little at all
For it matters not what you will do
Each stock that grows up; it will fall

I do not shed tears of remorse
Nor do I laugh at your plight
Of these things I am divorced
I feel not pain or delight

So run if it makes you feel better
I follow you, steady and slow
Knowing that soon I will get there
No matter the lengths you will go

For you are but one lonely body
Soon to be lost in a mass grave
In the yawning maw of history
All persons are buried the same

Portal

I stand before an open grave
This hole in the ground
A black and soon to be filled cave
A soon to be sacred mound

This open bit of land I see
An eerie open portal
A door once shut, can never be
Opened by us mortals

Oh when will I enter this chasm,
And take the darkened plunge?
For this part of life is hard to fathom
That death comes for everyone

Oh what's behind the curtain?
Can one pierce the veil?
For death, though it is certain
Tis a foggy sea to sail

A cold and lonely place it be
The depths that are the soil
Where darkness is all you'll ever see
A thought that you recoil

Drowning beneath the dirt
Forever sealed away
This thought, though we do flirt
Tis a scary thing to say

For beneath the placid sea of grass
And greenery you see
You fear your hands will pound quite fast
Against your coffin's door, now buried

You fear screaming beneath your tombstone
Amidst the cemetery
And hearing your neighbors round you grown
As rotting reliquaries

So wonder do you, will there be
A boatman or a ferry?
And will you sail upon the sea
Of misty mystery?

Will your spirit survive?
Will your soul live on?
Can your will but strive,
With your body long since gone?

Now comes the chilling answer
The cold wind that doth blow
It's not what you want to hear
The answer, it is *"No!"*

And so I stand before a grave
This hole in the ground
A place from which, you can't be saved
The place where you are bound

Bell

The bell has tolled I say farewell
There's no place like heaven, no place like hell
And while you may wish to repay all of your olden days
Just remember that you're all alone and everyone wants to go home

You're never home until your dead
You're never gone even when you're dead
So sleep now, forevermore
The bell has tolled, I say no more

Get Together

Come, gather family
Both friends by blood and time
To see off one, departing
Leaving us all behind

Before that final journey
Their last trail to blaze
Where we will watch them leave
At that gate they call the grave

And wave them off, will we
The captain, we're disturbed
May have difficulty
But we needn't pity the reaper

And join, do we, together
To pass round memories
And think upon the better
Of one we use to see

For the dead, they need no company
They require no more giving
For they don't care, nor see
Funerals are for the living

Weight

You'll wish you could stay death's hand
To force death to relent
Speak to it with stern tone
"Wait"

When one holds death in one's arms
It carries a weight
A weight of emptiness
Matter bereft of spark
No longer a vibrant life; filled brimming with experience
Just weight
When you hold it, it's just a thing
An object
Nothing behind its surface
Weight

Oh the tragedy of death
It's unending mocking of the living
Perpetually reminding us that, we too
Are but inanimate matter on loan to animacy
And that it is but a brief loan
A second upon the eternal clock
Wait

The beauty of a life
It vanishes quickly
Passes oft without notice
Until it's gone
Leaving a dreaded reminder
The husk of the once loved
Now weight

Remember that horrid despair
That sinking there deep in your stomach
That weight that you feel when you near
What you will discover; regret
Each step you go closer
You'll wish you could
Wait

When Death Comes Home

An empty room is hard to enter
An opened door can be barred

By the vacancy behind it
And you can be hard pressed to try,
In the midst of that still silence,
To stand and feel the quiet
And know that silence will persist

To look at all the objects
Within that empty room
Possessions, pictures, dreams and desires
All there, in that empty room
To breath a familiar scent; grown stale
And know it will fade, fade, fade away
Into the stillness of the empty room

That all and everything, in that room
Is now no longer what it was
Lacking the thing that made them unique
They're empty, like the room

So yes, these sights can cause thee pain
To cry a stream from you
Your inner soul, your spirit
You'll weep and pour it out
Wringing each droplet one by one
Until; like the room, you're empty

Its Quiet Now

They have gone away now
Their eyes have closed evermore
Their light has passed to shadow
And life has closed its door

And though we weep for them
As all who've gone before
Know that the tears we spend
Break not the silent chorus

Of every soul who ever was
And those still yet to be
Those gifted from our loins and love
And those we cannot see

They sing of life and funeral

The joy and pain you'll see
That nothing be eternal
And if you love you'll grieve

That silent chorus, off
Oblivion's precipice
Where life is both begot
And snuffed out of existence

Oh they have gone away
And others have been birthed
I don't know what to say
But *"Welcome to the earth"*

Life Support

The sickbed of the beloved
That bedside of despair
Where pail fingered glove
Conceals loving hand from hair

Where illness takes to hospice
The treasure of the soul
What's sweet, tis turned to ashes
Where embers barely glow

Your lips, now barred from me
Behind that breathing mask
Imprisoned there, so lonely
Behind that plastic glass

Those dark and sunken eyes
They seem so much the less
Oh why, oh wretched why
And yet, I could not guess

Your body seems so small
And fragile, that your breaths
Seem strongly labored calls
For one last warm caress

The longer that you stay
I lose you day by day
And hear your heartbeat fade
Like steps further away

Until that final shallow whisper
Does grace your pail lips
Once luscious, now so withered
Dried from the hand of death

And my heart, once strong, tis cracked
Beneath this blow of loss, so vast
And now, with pain, I'm wracked
Those shards of heart, like glass

Though know I well you'd not survive
If it were my ash for you to scatter
Your brittle heart, oh grief twould drive
Until it crashed and shattered

Your heart, it was too weak
To house the contents of your love
Oh I could hear it creak
And strain to keep its blood

Oh death, he took you from me
He stole you viciously
Taking pieces, oh so slowly
Until you were with he

I miss you more than anything
I know not where to start
But death is not an evil king
He left the strongest heart

Party

Comes down the rain upon
Those shoulders slumped; depressed
Whose heart is less than strong
Though always under stress

These rivulets pour out
Confetti of the spirit
A dreary mournful shout
Be all that come of it

Oh what surprise it be
That it would also rain

What's outward, now it seems
Reflecting inward pain

A lonely soul, surrounded
By people all about
And though the scene be crowded
It's empty, in and out

And as the heart, it beats
So slow and mournful now
A song; harrowed and bleak
Beneath the thundercloud

The lighting-bolts, they but reflect
Upon those tears that fell
And though raindrops show no respect
They wish not bad nor well

The weight of the rain upon
What weighs the shroud of grief
A garb you'll wear, and long
Will you know no relief

Long Time Coming

I don't like this process of death
It seems to make life such a mess
It makes others sad
And then I am mad
That I've caused them such distress

The Sole Survivor

Oh know I what it's like, to lose
The one to whom you cleave
That special soul you'd never choose
To slowly watch them leave

And yet, like two on separate rafts
Who drift upon the sea
And just by luck, happen to pass
And for a moment see

Each sailor stands and stares
Amazed they've found another
Though board, they do not dare

As each can't find a harbor

So try they; each desperately
To linger little longer
Know they well lonely sea
That for it they're no stronger

But each wave tempts the vessels
Out to the open serf
The place where they will wrestle
And test the sailor's worth

And so, the sailors battle
Against the mindless ocean
And try they not to travel
Away from this lone person

But the vastness does ignore
Every single act of will
And they will wander more
Across the empty still

And like the ones we love
As time moves us apart
Though with our arms; we hug
We know death grips their hearts

The horror that does come
As watch, do we, them age
And drift they further from
For, know we, they can't stay

And so before crest they the edge
Of our horizon's end
Endeavor, should we, just to pledge
That know they we love them

Bravery

The doctor's words to me
A strange brutality
The word *"leukemia"*
My daughter, my Carina

Kaden Moeller

This little one I hold
She's but a five year old
Who's barely lived her life
And needs to stand and fight

And so, we go for treatment
These needles, she resents
And as I sit and pray
She says *"Daddy, I'm brave"*

So time, it waxes on
A journey oh so long
My daughter, now at six
Is thin and very sick

And so we try it all
And yes, my spirit falls
With each injection's sting
And all the pain they bring

To watch my daughter's soul
But dwindle down to coal
To watch her labor there
Those breaths of shallow air

She looks at me; with longing
Yet I can do nothing
There's no protection from
A thing that's not someone

To hold her here at home
She's skin but over bone
To clutch her to my chest
To hold her and caress

And as she looks at me
She says to me, sweetly
*"Daddy, when I turn seven
I want to go to heaven"*

I cannot say a word
To these things I have heard
As uttered from a nightmare
But said with greatest care

And I, a hollow man

Who now can barely stand
Do tuck her into bed
And kiss her little head

And when I'm down the hall
My legs, they give to fall
I'm huddled, weeping there
I can't describe how scared

I never would have guessed
That I would wish for death
But just to make her whole
I'd give my very soul

Yet every day's a year
And draws the specter near
To take her little light
And vanish it to night

Oh how it pains me so
To watch my daughter go
And made to hardly speak
Until she's far too weak

Now there on life support
Drowning, with breaths so short
I stay there at her side
Though all I do is cry

And when the blue is called
And no longer forestalled
It's called at twelve-eleven
The day that she turned seven

I stand there in the corner
And silently, I mourn her
I've no more tears to cry
Those wells have long since dried

Last Request

Harkin not unto me O death
Hear not my cries of pain
Listen not to my screams for mercy

Kaden Moeller

Ignore the names I take in vain

Be of a lazy mood death
Apathy makes thee a friend
My end has not quite come yet
The beginning's before the end

Your ignorance is becoming
It flatters your every side
You would look so wonderful
No man would dare to hide

So have I made you reconsider,
This is the talking of my soul?
Don't speak I know the answer
The answer is always *"No"*

Pro-Life

"Hold me" This I say
Unto the one I love
As time, it ticks away
And fear be all I think of

As grope, do you, to me
In the knowledge of my illness
But, it is this you, I see
That fills me now with strangeness

Your hands do cling to mine
Pulling me close thy breast
But something in my mind
Makes this love to stress

And as your arms surround
Enveloping my body
In this embrace I found
That you're not there with me

This thing that's captured I
This shadow of yourself
That causes me to cry
For the good of my health

This monster, I feel it claw
And hook into my flesh

This raging beast I saw
It will not let me rest

I feel its hulking frame
Looming over my weak body
Its strength, it won't restrain
Nor will it choose to leave

This demon's outpouring
Of what is best for I
Its raging angry roaring
That leaves me terrified

Shoving its hands into my neck
Forcing my lungs to breath
These gnarled fingers refuse to let
The one they hold to leave

And though I push with all my might
Against this one that holds
I wonder why I have to fight
When I say *"Let me go!"*

Suicide

Today I have decided
Tis time that I let go
Of these parts of me divided
My body and my soul

This bit of me
My inmost part
This spirit that be
In my heart

To but release thee from thy cage
These prison bars, my ribs
And loose you from this tragic stage
On which life and death doth bid

Taking you out of me, do I
Cupping you in my hands
As tears well up, I start to cry
And morn you as I can

And so I lift my hands above
And let you take you wing
A beautiful ascending dove
My spirit, now, is flying

Gravely

Why run thee towards the open arms
Of the acceptance of the grave?
Be it but for its charms
Or that macabre play?

Oh when and why to die
For such a pretty thing?
A thing that will not cry
For you upon your passing

To pound your chest in love
While diving towards your death
Know I not what you think of
When take thee thy last breath

You wanted thee a lover
To suckle at their breast
Chose you the darkest other
That lover known as death

Though no one more intimate exists
But the one beyond the veil
That shroud that keeps you separate
It keeps that lust; not stale

But why you chose the reaper
I'll never understand
For her love must be deeper
For you to take her hand

Lament Of The Suicide Survivor

Never a one was there
Whose light would shine like thee
And brought beauty to bear
Bringing sweet joy to me

Whose radiance did bring

A happiness; so bright
Twas like the bells that ring
Upon the morning's light

But when your candle dimmed
I left thee all alone
Hoping that oxygen
Would feed thy flame, but no

And now I'm here but saying
Sweet nothings of your life
With others; they are praying
What's dim has gone to night

You were a friend to me
Much more than I could say
"You're like my family"
I should have said, yesterday

Passing Away

Oh be too quick
Thy breath hath slipped
Liked embers in the ash
That fade until their lights doth quit
And gleam, do they, their last

And here I sit
My heart now slit
A soul of shattered glass
That echoes softly in the quiet
Room thy spirit passed

As stay, do I, till morning
And with the mourning's light
As emptiness drawn near
Without my spryly sprite
I quake in humble fear

Too soon was death to bring
This flight upon his wing
And yet, through tears, it's clear
As I now come to sing
"To me, Death, do come here"

The Tenant

When you release life from your chest
That single simple shallow breath
That final sigh before relief
That whisper silenced at release
That vacancy now that is left
An empty room; now home to death.

The Donor

In death

I give to you my heart
May it beat for thee, as it did for me

A gift now be my lungs
Which from my death, shall give you breath

So too are my kidneys
May they purify you, as they should do

Take also my liver
A poison filter, to keep you here

Do not forget my eyes
They grant you sight, under the light

Leave nothing for the rot
What I give away lets me say

"Let there be life"

Dim

You can hear the fading of a loved one when they are near death
It's as if one can almost see the soul waiting just behind the breath

You find yourself in conflict with your love locked deep within
Holding them too tightly to yourself is such a selfish sickly sin

But find yourself, do you indeed, grasping out in vain
The love inside you lurches out to them, and causes you great pain

You sit and watch, and wait and pray, and then one day their gone

Their body, like a melted candle with no flame upon

Your heart now, it is broken, your mind is rather lost
You find yourself thinking now of the price that life must cost

But someday you will be the one who waits lonely at deaths door
Try to be brave, and try to say, *"I wonder what's in store?"*

A Wager

Tomorrow is another day
For someone else to die
Tomorrow comes, and as they say
One needn't give a sigh

Now which do you believe
Will be the ones to go
Don't pick the elderly
Their payout be too low

Will bet you on a child,
Or someone in their prime?
It may not yet take awhile
The question's *"How much time?"*

The prize is very high
To those no others see
Now drawn to suicide
While in their early teens

And on those derivatives
Of high level family sorrow
A bonus will we give
If one of them's to follow

So step up to the edge
Throw a penny in the pool
And look upon the ledge
Where there one stands, a jewel

Ashes To Ashes, Dust To Dust

It's musty in here
I wait for dust to clear

Having not really thought that much
Of what it is that dust makes up

Surprising really when you think
That dust is something quite distinct
They are the shaved off sparks of life
Coals no longer holding light
The smoke of loved ones gone for good
A sight of age, where time has stood

Oh dust, it covers everywhere
And calls, does it, your mind to bear
On the strange truth that where you go
Through dust you'll never leave it, so

When cleaning through dark dingy room
Where dust, all about, is strewn
Wander will you, in your mind
Through memory, now out of time

Which fire did these sparks fly from,
And is that fire dim, or gone?

Shrugging

It seems impossible to think
Grief has a bottom when you sink
That someday, you'll come crawling out
Then look will you all round about
Remember will you what you've lost
And how the darkness took its cost
Though know you not these tears you cry
Though wet now, will someday dry
And tell yourself a lie within
You will not sink, or lose again

Womb

Ashes scattered through the air
The wind carries them everywhere
From streams, to lakes and endless seas
These ashes travel with the breeze

Sprinkled are they across the earth
Nature made fertile for giving birth
Her womb but ripe and ready now

This ash but feeds the seed somehow

A new life born, we shout and cheer
Born from the ash of loved ones dear

Patience

Oh how we fight for life
To breathe another breath
To but delay the scythe
Upon the hand of death

In take, we food and drink
The stuff that makes us merry
And try, we, not to think
How in life we but terry

The shortest while we have
This time beneath the sun
And how it makes us glad
When time feels slow to run

Yes, every day's a lifetime
That dies upon sun's set
As feel we, the grind
Of the clock gears of regret

Oh every day ahead
Leads to a later date
What cryptic words are said
By death, they are, *"I'll wait"*

Walking Round

When death comes
It be not proud
Death has nothing

No matter where you run
Or hide within the crowd
Death will find you

And like the devil's hound
The hunt is not for fun

Kaden Moeller

It's necessary

Tis steady, through and through
And soon enough is done
No matter time nor tarry

And death twill come and go
Never to morn or merry
It walks, it need not run

Your time beneath the sun
No matter hot or cold
Tis only temporary

Each second on the clock
A step towards someone
Now in the momentary

If only but to reap
Another standing stalk
That brings the tears to run

So hard is it to see
The flavor, death, as sweet
When bitter to the tong

And every soul it takes
Tis hid behind the lock
Away from love so deep

It rends all undone
And then it seems to make
Our life a lonely one

And so death undertakes
As more and more it keeps
And with each setting sun
It brings to us this grief

No, death, it doesn't hate
From you down to the leaf
And on the day it comes
But hope it comes in sleep

First Date

Oh the beauty of despair distilled
Tis almost as sweet as revenge chilled

Topped off with a hint of hopelessness
And garnished well with loneliness
But one thing is missing, I must confess
The freezing hand of death's caress

Oh what a fateful gathering
A table for two, how flattering

Under A Tree

Oh weary one, long in the day
You needn't walk further, I say
You can but stop and stay
And wait there by the way

For life, beneath the sun
Tis filled with trial and toil
But tires, everyone
With calloused flesh and boil

With all to fill our cups
Be draughts of weariness
And drink, we, far too much
To vainly quench distress

Beneath the heat, of life
Tis rare for much relief
From drowning in the light
Of which you writhe beneath

To swelter as a slave
But chained by beads of sweat
That hang upon you, to weigh
And drag you to regret

Take shelter in the shade
Here, off the beaten path
And rest, as in the grave
In the shadow that is death

Kaden Moeller

A Goodbye Kiss

Let this goodbye be sweet
This parting from you now
Though never a next we'll meet
To this, friend, I'll avow

I'll keep your memory
Stored closely to my heart
For deep inside of me
Never twill you depart

And I'll carry your name
Ever upon my lips
So that, with me, again
Your presence will persist

And I'll live by your wisdom
That you gifted to me
Such marvels be in them
Those words spoken from thee

And ever a quiet moment
When silence undermines
I'll shed a tear for then
That once upon a time

When last we met in parting
That moment; bitter sweet
I find my heart was starting
To break at your release

For now that you are gone from me
And ever from my eyes
I wish that I could laugh with thee
But those thoughts make me cry

Worry?

Oh, what do dead men worry?
They're blessed above all others
No never need they hurry
Or think upon their lovers

For nothing can they lose

And dream they not of gain
As never need they choose
Between the meat or grain

No, dead men wait for none
Nor ever go they out
For what, from them, would come
No sigh or joy filled shout

For dead men have no longing
They do not crave the touch
Nor need they the subtle fawning
By those they love so much

For dead men do not sleep
And dead men do not cry
Yet best of all it seems
That dead men do not die

In The Long Run

When stand, will you, before
The whole of your own life
To be judged, much the more
Of your works, day and night

And many judges there will be
And be they the witnesses
So many there to see
To testify, you guess

And they will speak your worth
In truth, perhaps, in lie
Some may speak of your birth
Others, the day you died

Each speaking of your impact
Perceived or made as real
The history of that
Which your life has revealed

And there will be some cursing
And some joyful shouts and cheers
As stand, do you, there wondering

Kaden Moeller

The verdict of your peers

And play each part again, will they
Upon deliberation
As final statements, they will say
Before you stand before them

For all you have is guilt
It is the life you've lived
Your history will wilt
Depending on what you did

The Following Friend

Death, oh loyal companion
One, but steps away
Who always opens one's arms to embrace
The most accepting of all who live

Death, purveyor of diversity
One who sees all and desires all
Each is to be had, each, to be held
None is unsightly to you
You are ever the more so a patient lover
Awaiting the proper time and place
So anxious for our meeting

Death, never bashful
Always direct
Slow and steady
Or quick and crass
You come, a suitor, at the last

Grim

I am here for you, my sweet
In this place, in which, we meet
At the sight of me you shiver
Your hands shake and legs do quiver

You see me standing there in stillness
This sight becomes clearer with your illness
My cold and clammy hands upon the scythe
My implement to harvest life

Your eyes well up with tears of fear

Terrified are you that I've come near
You fear the day you'll be unmade
I whisper to you *"Don't be afraid."*

The Angel Of Death

The flower withers at my touch
Its beauty tempted me so much
I cannot hold to pretty things
My hands grasp not to what I cling

So in great loneliness I wander
Through all this loss I am no stronger
Life, like water, through my fingers slips
No matter the tightness of my grip

Beauty surrounds me, I cannot have it
For I shall lose it if I grab it
And so I love you from afar
Bask in your glow like farthest star

So when I see you writhe in pain
I will come close, and call your name
And brush my hand across your cheek
And loose that beauteous life you keep

Epitaph

To every soul we meet
And every life we touch
To every heart that beats
And every hand we'll clutch

May hands ever reach out
In friendship, they extend
May their help be devout
They offer up a friend

For every word that's spoken
May they be words of wisdom
Where knowledge does spring from
Pray others remember them

And let our actions weigh

Kaden Moeller

Heavily upon our shoulders
Let everything we say
Not bring others disorder

Oh let our lives be standards
That bear the human spirit
Aspire to the grander
And better parts of it

Oh for we do decide, the height of human worth
Our minds, they shape, but to derive, the meaning of the end
But when we die remember, seek not our tombs on earth
Rather we find them deep within, the hearts of fellow men

So Long

So sorry
Do not cry
Not everyone's afraid to die
My time is up
Thanks for reading
Smile please
And say goodbye

<u>Author</u>

Kaden Moeller

The Mystery

You glimpse me now but through a keyhole
There is no window to my soul
Just a shimmering glint of what you will see
But nowhere near yet where I will be

Oh look through that hole so small
And see some things, but not them all
But one day I'll slide beneath the door
The key to what you've glimpsed before

And there you'll stand, quite perplexed
I wonder what will happen next?

The One Who Walks Among You

Oh when you look to me
And all you see are smiles
So happy do I seem
Just me and all my wiles

I offer kindness to you
And warm your heart each day
Like watching flowers bloom
You bid my presence stay

And I; I speak so softly
A voice so light and fair
Few words do I entreat thee
Though they hover in the air

Yes so polite am I
My flavor be too sweet
You ask yourself *"But why
Does this one act so strangely?"*

And never you understand
Why be I such a help
Oh such a loyal friend
But why, you cannot tell

Yet, know one thing, should thee
That when I come a' calling
The only angels that you see
Are angels that have fallen

This Is Who I Am

I've lived one thousand lives before
And know not where to stop

Persecuted as a Jew, who lived among you
Crusading as a Christian, who lives to take a stand
And worshiping as a Muslim, reverent and devout

I've conquered land a bone apart
And lost my land as a true American
I killed myself in Berlin, as the walls caved in
And fathered two countries on a Hindu walking stick
I ended separation in the free equal world as an X-King
And fought as a Cong in Vietnam

I've lived one thousand lives before
And know not where to stop

I wonder now who I will be
And what history shall be brought

Wondering

I am a savage feral wolf
Alone am I with mangy coat

So thin and sickly is my skin
My eyes have sunken deep within
My jowls, they curl slowly up
A snarl from my rabid thought

For this is what it feels to be
The lone-wolf deep inside of me

Not Me?!

One night I lay a dreaming, of what is best in life
Thinking through, quite deeply, of both the pleasure and the strife
And dawning on me like the sun, came this one glaring thought
That the best feeling one could ever feel, would be to feel not

To be a cruel heartless beast, with no right or wrong imbedded

No love, no hate, no petty thoughts that leave a man indebted
Just heartless lavish living, and all that would go with it
Imagining power so pure, as to grasp the world in iron gauntlet

To crush ones opponent beneath, under foot, and listen to his lamenting
Or hold his love as hostage, and watch his life's reflecting
To be a brute of sadistic pleasure, and act out in the worst of ways
Such life should be what's sought after, and not looked at as depraved

But I, not I, shall it be who treads this path of the jaded
Such a time has not yet come for me to be that hated
So time will wax, and time will wane, for many a misty night
And I will wait, and bathe in the rays of the pail moonlit night

For though I seem to yearn to be the monster within me
My wretched conscience laughing says *"Son it isn't thee"*

Out Of One, Many

To all of you I see
If you have any sense
Just know, you'll never know me
You are but an acquaintance

It matters not the years
Nor ties of bond or blood
This person you see here
You'll never know truth of

Perhaps you've hear me say
And wax long of love to you
But this holds little sway
Of what I lust to do

The violence I desire
You see not on my face
But crave my lips inspire
A vicious raging hate

Though I speak such words so clearly
The whispers in my mind
You hear them not from me
But speak they all the time

So preach I tolerance
The ideals of democracy

These words I do not mince
And they do come from me

But just beneath my skull
The place you cannot see
There be a million thralls
All slaves to misery

Each be another person
But slightly modified
They be no so different, each of them
Be similar inside

Oh when I play the writer
I do it utmostly
But I'll become another
In an instant, just for thee

For all the worlds' a stage
And wear we many masks
I dare you but to gage
Beneath which do I bask?

Which mask be now before you?
What script do they read from?
Which play do they dance through?
And when will they be done?

Oh look upon me now
And do you faintly see them?
As if but through a cloud
You'll know that *"I am legion"*

Imaginary

My fantasy is fun you see
I get to be the real me
A thing that which I can't describe
The thing that which I try to hide
Made up is it, of my life
And secrets never come to light

A shy one is it to outsiders
Out of sight of all the others

And yet you would not recognize
The me behind these strange new eyes

You'd pass me as if in the dark
You'd never even see my spark
There I could be, dancing before you
To you, this me, would not be true

And even if I came right out
Singing with the greatest shout
You'd shake your head, and say *"Not so!"*
Turn your back, and off you'd go

For it isn't what we are on skin
Rather what is deep within
And sadly you will never know
The one within who dwells and grows

Spirit and soul, the brightest star
The bearer of so many scars
The bit of me I share in parts
The deepest place within my heart

Soft Light

This blackness where I sit alone
This emptiness I call my home
It's cold and without light or hope
This nothingness I hold and grope

Stairs deeply, this void does into me
This hollow space I love to see
My all consuming endless night
Who hurts me not with burning light

Make love to me, my empty skies
Come soft darkness, kiss my eyes

What Doesn't...

I refuse to break, and accept defeat
I will not lie down or beat retreat
No matter what, I will not flee
No one can take what's inside of me

No one can take away my will

What's deep within, they cannot kill
For what makes me up cannot be gone
If I'm not killed, I become strong

I'll make my heart an iron-maiden
A place where all my pain is laden
A place of sealed agony
The place you cannot take from me

My Strength

I have a loathing of myself
This hatred comes out in my health
A treachery from deep within
It hides from me beneath my skin

A burning form of condemnation
An internal mindless mutilation
Cutting at places in my mind
Stripping away my strength with time

Oh this strange self-destructive hate
It turns the clock, early, to late
And tears from my hands, that precious youth
Leaving me disillusioned in truth

It dims, blurs, and blots out the eyes
The limbs will numb and paralyze
And those dreams, once wished upon a star
Will fade as calloused mental scars

At times, will come, the mild sadness
When I realize I've drifted into madness
Those things I can't control inside
Will leave me weak, and then deprived

So I build my hate up, and my rage
And stroke the pen across the page
I'm building something when those dreams die
A stronger me, myself and I

Altruism

I'm not so kindly as you think

Kaden Moeller

No altruist, I just think
When trodding on others down below
You hurt those who elevate you so

Who hold you up above them now
And idolize your life somehow
Beware of their objectifying
You'll find that it's desensitizing

And make yourself to be much more
From those who work their hands all sore
So fair and soft your skin will be
Compared to those calloused hands you see

So never should you make the mistake
And compare yourself to them, and state
*"That we are all the same you see
And, someday, you'll be just like me"*

For this is wrong, and so untrue
Most never get to be like you
And this is why I watch for others
Treating them, do I, like my brothers

Because I wish to be treated so
I do it so I let them know
That I indebt you with my kindness
And when I need you, you best not mind, yes?

I do to you, so you'll do to me
I know I'm being quite greedy
Demand, do I, of what I've given
By reciprocation am I driven

I may not like you in the least
But one day when I need release
I'd better have helped you well before
Or you won't help me open the door

To be alone is to make a prison
Turning yourself into a villain
A neighbor need you be to others
To always treat them as your brothers

Reflection

I stand before a mirror and see
A weak and frail man
One who laughs and cries
One who lives and dies
A soul
I do not know this man

Taking Action

It's amazing what motivates a man
What gives him strength for him to stand
For me it is a bitter heart
A once dim but now raging spark

My anger leads me to the sheet
And with my pen, cut it like meat
A vengeful stabbing of the page
A place to build and put my rage

I slice my pen like knife to flesh
And carve my name into its chest
As I sculpt in sickening surgery
Mutilating the paper now with glee

Though pale from this bloody mess
I read the words, and then I jest
*"My anger is not close to done
I will find myself a new victim"*

And so I continue my vulgar spree
It pleases me, this blasphemy
But know, do I, revenge quite well
It never ends, my privet hell

1ˢᵗ Born

Under the law of primogenitor
I raise my voice for all to hear
*"I will have my double allotment
A higher portion, with new intent"*

"But not just any blessing do I seek

Rather the curse of sweet defeat
Give me more suffering than I can stand
Burn it into me, a brand"

"I challenge you to try to beat me
To try to cast me to the sea
Try to break the soul within
To just put out that ember, dim"

"Just heap upon me endless sorrow
And try to make me hate tomorrow
Oh come and find me in the night
And try to fill me up with fright"

"I may, indeed, cave in and fail
But in this self inflicted jail
No matter the tears that I may cry
No one can say I didn't try"

Side Effects

This throbbing, pounding pain so dull
The napalm burning in my skull
Behind my eyes I feel the singe
With every twitch and tweak and twinge

The side effect coming from the drug
Regret the loss of my health's love
For without taking the counter pill
These side effects will sap my will

So I inject my skin with poison
To kill myself a bit within
Giving myself some scars without
To prevent the calluses inside from coming out

This is not my preferred recreation
It is unwanted self flagellation
Thus forcing me to bend the knee
To the tyrant whose inside of me

I do not want to be a slave or serf
Allowing this disease to dictate my worth
But I don't have a lot of choice
It does not listen to my voice

Inspiration

What is it about my misery,
That makes me write prolifically?
Is that it highlights life?
That as your getting through the strife,
You see the hues that living has,
Their differences both good and bad?

These shades, they speak much clearer than
In loss, rather than happy end
Is it a curse, or just a blessing?
Perhaps it's both, but I'm just guessing
But there is one thing that I know
If I'm happy, my work won't grow

All Alone Together

To my friends and family
My source of love and pain
I have to ask you candidly
"Why do I feel estranged?"

"How do I know you live me?"
I ask you now, my kin
*"How is it that the 'I' you see
Is viewed by the 'you' within?"*

Why is it that I feel strange
When it is you say
"I'll love you no matter how you change."
A promise, come what may?

I feel so separate from you all
A growing isolation
A gap is widening, so I call
Begging your affection

For I'm a single person
No matter who I'm with
This knowledge, like a prison
It makes me beg and wish

That I could be one with another

It doesn't matter who
For if I was in this other
Their heart, I'd say, I knew

Relationship

I want to be comfortable within
Content with the company of myself
To accept me as my deepest kin
My highest form of wealth

To embrace every part of me
Not just to see it, but to receive
Oh how I wish that I could be
My Adam and my Eve

Complete in my totality
So tightly interwoven
A strangely human tapestry
Together, never cloven

I want to feel love
When I'm alone with me
Not wanting away to shove
My inside that I see

Oh to be beautiful
Is one of my desires
So to, to be terrible
To walk amidst the fire

To be a contradiction
And love me as myself
But here there is restriction
It's not right for my health

I search not for self-esteem
Or even happiness
Rather, I but wish to glean
Some peace, from restlessness

But know, do I, this wrestling
There can be no respite
No amount of inner cunniling
Can save me from this plight

So hard is it to merge
That which I keep apart
Tis like an inner scourge
That rends my spirit's heart

My spirit wants this marriage
But, my soul, it makes divorce
Bringing hope great disparage
For life makes their like coarse

Oh to be complete
And wholly be made one
I'm forced to concede defeat
This battle can't be won

But oh, no sorrow comes
No tears do I now shed
For though I am undone
This does not make me dead

For victory is not the answer
But rather the ideal
The beauty of the dancer
That one can't touch or feel

To be knocked down by life
And get back up again
To be consumed by strife
Within the lion's den

Knowing with certainty
Defeat, oh it is coming
And that I'll never be
Triumphant where I'm running

To go towards the finish line
Striving to be better
This is the hero's sign
A fist raised high, unfettered

Against the fates above
And the will of those below
I stand and push and shove
And take their kicks and blows

My voice mocks those who shout
"Why don't you just stay down!?"
Their bruises give me clout
And causes them to frown

And so, I stand there smiling
Soul beaten, spirit bloody
For though my body's dying
The rage against me's lovely

Still, do I, look inward
Wishing to reconcile
My soul and spirit's words
And both of their strange wiles

But no, they won't unite
Even against the world
Though together do they fight
Round like a wind they whirl

And so the outside breaks me
While inside I'm divided
The world, a brutal place to be
Where all of me's collided

So here I am
All alone
Do I now stand
A stone

Ink-Heart

The darkest places in my soul
Spill from my pen in blackened oil
A landscape that I do not dare
Revel to those of whom I care

For I fear they'd find this part of me
A place that they won't want to see
A blackened pit of hate and wrath
A place of sorrow and darkened laugh

The sanctuary for all my sin
A place that I protect within
Oh what is it they would say to me?

How disappointed would they be?

To know that face who smiles kind
Is angry at his life and time
But they can't know, it's too private
And so I walk alone and sit

Contemplating a life lived in shame
'I am so weak, what worth's my name?'

Behind The Door

Do you remember?
The door and keyhole?
Tis time to enter
I'm scared, you know

You've been being teased
Yes, this I've done
But this for me
Has not been fun

This neighbor who lives next to you
With skyscrapers of books
He now waits for what you will do
As nervously he looks

Please think me not a fool
I've worked so hard to learn
I'm using every single tool
For knowledge have I yearned

But I am nervous, that I am
To admit to you this thing
I feel like a lonely lamb
Afraid my words will sting

The greatest fear I am thinking of
Oh, feel now I sweating blood
Is that I will now lose your love
That with my confession, away, you'll shove

I feel that I've betrayed you
For now I can't go back

Kaden Moeller

No matter what I do
This silver has turned black

My kiss, it seems, no longer sweet
And now I stand alone
I stand before the judgment seat
In fear before the throne

You are now my Pilate
And I your Judas Christ
What do you see from where you sit?
I will not stand and fight

You ask me "Do you believe?"
I tell you *"I do not."*
And stare, you do, quite vacantly
At this answer that you got

Believe I now, that those I love
Those ones of special worth
When dead, they lay not up above
Rather, beneath the earth

Well, if you haven't got the gist
And still wonder what I mean
I'll say it *"I'm and atheist!"*
Now, have I become obscene?

So here, before you, do I bow
This deed of mine is done
You have heard my testimony, now
Woman, behold your son

Putting It To Paper

I'm taking out my heart
So as to hold it in my hand
To clench my fist and crush it
And give ink to my pen

I squeeze out all its empathy
And write out others pain
Each stroke, a razor, cutting deeply
To make me feel the same

And so I hurt myself inside

And cry as I rape me
Letting myself reside
Where I don't want to be

Casting myself away
Letting me feel alone
Hating the words I say
As myself, do I, stone

I rip away all love
And dive into despair
Never to look above
For hope that isn't there

Well maybe you don't get it
This thing that I confess
I do, not to my spirit
It's done to one who's soulless

Contrarian

I'm going to argue
Not just with you

But every person I meet
Isn't that neat?

You'll never understand
My arguments so grand

Rather you will be dazzled
And your mind, it will be frazzled

For these thoughts are hard to get
But you'll see it my way yet

The best is yet to come
I'll never yet be done

Passion

Within my heart
A fire is burning bright
Where's the water?

Evil

Every little child knows
Villains cause so many woes
I on the other hand disagree
Letting their actions motivate me

May They Find Out

May a good man find out
That I did right by humanity
Maybe take notice on my passing
And say *"Goodbye, my brother"*

May he proclaim my deeds
Unabashed and with glee
And as an example of living decency
He speaks me with authority

Perhaps, I'll seem a better man
Once my memory has passed from thought
Maybe so idealized, that
What they say I did, I did not

But I hope the good say it
And say I'm good with them
Mayhaps my better words
Linger longest upon the earth

I do not know the future
Nor can I travel back
And so I stand here waiting
For me to be the past

But I hope the good men find out
They discover me as worthy
And with a happy heart
Take me with them

I'd love to travel long
Right here upon the earth
So, I hope they take me with them
I hope they find out

The Architect

You may be kings
But you are poor
And I, a pauper
Have much more

For you've grown rich
But killed your dreams
You let them die
What have you gleaned?

And I, though not a king
Oh I need never cry
I do not pound my dreams to dust
I'll never let them die!

I build them with no motive
But pleasure for my soul
They are gifts that I give
To make the gifted whole

To grant a piece of wisdom
Unto the readers mind
And let those reading, then
Build greater dreams than mine

But you have built for coin
And weigh your worth in gold
You think yourself refined
The more that you can hold

But kings, they pass away
Their riches are forgotten
But gifts from pen can stay
And build new dreams from them

Beneath The Surface

I give them what they want to see
The shallows of my soul
The only depths to wet them, be
That placid surface, though

They know not of the currents
That run beneath the sea
They find that though deterrent
Full of unpleasantry

Care not they for the dark spots
Hidden deep down from the light
They shutter at the thought
And shiver at the sight

For though they think I'm silent
I am a raging sea
So deep and oh so violent
Be I inside of me

Thanks

I am thankful for my time
And what time I may have left

So happy for my pain
For it has taught me peace

I'm thankful that I feel something
Even if I do not show it

I thank God for the people I know
And the friends between them

But most of all I'm thankful for
My family and my pets

My friends who are like brothers
And more than most, my end

<u>Mara</u>

My Angel Released Away

I can't wake up
I want to scream
Please let her go
Be not as it seems
I wish I were asleep
But I don't dream
My love is leaving
To the land of forever sleep

?

My friend
A kind smile
Really shows
A lonely love

Funeral

You were but my shining star
Gone now dim and left a scar
The trickling down of tears of pain
My soul a storm of wind and rain

A heart so crying out in loss
Each teardrop tis but threshed out dross
As memories shimmer through the night
Sparkling forth the lost to life

And as the pain drips from our eyes
See we the beauty of their lives
While in our loss is tragedy
Our pain twill bring forth ecstasy

For if at once we felt unsure
Our sorrow proves our love is pure
I know no other way to say
Our loss has proved our love today

The Horcrux

You were
My strange horcrux
The best part, of my soul

Now gone
All gone

Stolen away from me
Taken by the sleepy death

I clutched you
Gone
What is left
A husk
I walk a shell

Listening for your smile
Watching for your voice
Waiting for your hand
Feeling for your love

Nothing
My strange horcrux
Is gone

Fatherhood

I had a little girl, oh this I can't believe
The doctors wrapped her in a blanket and handed her to me
I took her in my arms, and held her little head
Her eyes were bright and shiny, with an innocence that can't be said

I carried her home with me
So much was there to see
A little life was in my hands
And make, would she, many demands

I watched her grow, watched her learn
Many a time was I quite stern
But how much love did she receive
And how much more would I retrieve

But ten years in, she found drawing breathe a chore
So off we went to the doctor to find out what for
The disease had taken up residence in her lungs
It would consume all until her last breath was done

I waited, I watched, I sat and cried

Kaden Moeller

She is too young, but there is no why
I had a little girl, oh this I can't believe
The doctors wrapped her in a blanket and handed her to me

Her eyes were grey and dim, nothing can be said
I took her in my arms, and held her little head

Gone To Sleep

To the one that I let go
Oh how it is I love you so

For as they slipped the needle into your vein
You looked at me, and through the pain
You spoke to me, right through your eyes
I gripped you tight, starting to cry

"Please let me go now, would you sweet?
Just let me rest and go to sleep"

And with a nod, I let the man
Inject the poison through your hand
And as I clutched you to me, my daughter
Your life slipped through my hands like water

My body trembled as I watch
And felt your body, cold to touch

But joy, slowly washed over me
Looking at you, for now I see
The pain you suffered through is gone
This death you sought, it was not wrong

I look at you, now locked in place
A smile on your frozen face

Rasputin's Lament

They say that up in heaven
There be a throng of angels
Perfection, be each one of them
Made to be beautiful

But, oh what angels could there be
That be more beautiful than she
Whose black hair flowed into the breeze

Whose eyes, they fluttered playfully

A cherub, come from up above
Who wore a charcoal dress
And shot my heart through with her love
As, my life, did she bless

But called away too soon was she
Her heart did god doth quell
As others sadly said to me
"He needed one more angel"

Of all the angels he could call
He took the one in black
Oh beg her, do I, choose to fall
I want my angel back!

A Dream

Oh in the waking hours
Before the frost twas dew
Much to my joy and horror
I felt my arms round you

Those steady breaths of life
So close, each one of them
Their warmth, it felt so nice
To feel them once again

But know I you're not there
You aren't the one I cling
But still, I do not dare
Bring our reunion to its ending

So happy am I now
I hate to say goodbye
On the edge of sleep, somehow
I feel the tears I cry

I curse the light that wakes me
And watch you fade away
Oh you I'd rather see
Than any breaking day

Kaden Moeller

Early Hours

When I wake up in the mourning
I don't know what to do
I look across the covers
Half expecting to see you

When I wake up in the mourning
I think it's all a dream
The reality that you are dead
It can't be as it seems

When I wake up in the morning
I try to remember you
To think of all the things you said
And do what I can do

Thinking On A Friend

Oh my love, I miss you
I cried for you today
Your memory, ran my heart through
I found words hard to say

Reflect, did I, upon
Our lives we lived together
Twas like a happy song
Now sung in rainy weather

I've never known a love
That was as pure as yours
And I fear the finding of
One similar to ours

Oh nothing is as beautiful
As showing love to another
And having it returned in full
By the hand of your kind lover

But, my love, I must confess
It is a hard thing to do
To feel the distress
Of loving without you

Oh it is strange indeed
This loss of our connection

Like a mirror before me
That won't hold my reflection

Though my love for you won't stop
I know that you are gone
Oh such a painful thought
Two lovers now made one

This love, it is a game
One cannot play alone
And yet, one cannot say
That with you, my love's gone

It has not disappeared
Though you certainly have
Oh how I wish you near
I'm lonely and so sad

But this is what it is to love
It never really ends
Rather it hurts to think of
My heart your memory rends

Reunion

If there is a heaven, and I am greeted by someone
Someone I loved, long gone from me
One someone I could not stand; for joy
I'd break upon their sight, as they ran to me, as they leapt into my arms
My tears would stream from me, and I'd hold them; trembling
Their body in my arms, their happiness coming from them in excited cries as
they squirmed
Nuzzling my chest and gripping my body to them; clumsily
They'd yelp and whine in ecstasy; their long lost friend now found
And I, I'd weep and weep; arms wrapped round them; disbelief resounding
within me
Those padded feet; my four foot friend, who loved me purer still
I'd be so weak before them; my love would make me small
No god is greater than; those loved ones who love most
Nothing is worth more to us; than the love of loved ones lost

Over The Rainbow

Somewhere over the rainbow, in the land of all my dreams

Kaden Moeller

Though life flows like a river, I'll bath in my memories amidst a tranquil stream

When I go over the rainbow, I will be a different man
I will stand up as a lion, and lay down with the lambs

When I get over the rainbow, I will see a different land
With a home for every lost soul, and a smile behind every helping hand

Just over that rainbow, somebody is waiting there for me
We'll dance atop its arch, touching the dew atop the trees

I'm waiting over the rainbow, my heart tis torn in two
And somewhere over the rainbow, I'll meet up with you

The 'New' Atheism

Forgetful

You forgot the purpose of the lie,
And how it leads to the question
'Why?'
I do not know the answer yet.
But when I do
I'll think of it.

Truth

"Truth!"
"Truth!"
The prophet shouts
"Is but a passing dream!"
"Proof!"
"Proof!"
The people scream
"We know not what you mean!"

Blindness

I can see the sun on the horizon
I can hear the church bells ringing
I can see the masses gathering
I can hear them all a' praying
I can see their hearts are open
I can hear they're cries of pain
I can see that
I can see them
But why can't they hear me?

Cult

Spread the seeds of doubt all throughout the air
Just let them grow and fester there
To fill this world with animosity
They all end up believing in me

Dogmatists

It's all the same, all of it
The people, the places
The names and the faces
All the same, all of it

It never changes, never
They beg and they plead
They stand on their knees
Never change, never

Their creed is the same, always
They twist and they writhe
As they wish and they cry
But the creed is the same, always

Beauty Defined

What is beautiful?
That which is temporal
The things that come and go with life
Reflecting love and constant strife

For through it all, the muck and grime
The must seductive thing is time
A thing of which there's not enough
No pain or pleasure can be too rough

For time is of a fickle mind
Going forth, a constant grind
Fading the flower, brown and dry
Quenching the breath, to watch them die

Passing gesture, kindly glance
A light in darkness, passing chance
It is the things that do not last long
That makes me love them when they're gone

Innocence?

Why should innocence be defiled?
Because ignorance is oh so vile
When calling it a different name
We play with it a little game
But let it sit for much too long
And we will regret the things it's done

For innocence is another name
For a lack of knowledge made look tame
And if we all perceive it good

Kaden Moeller

We put ourselves in noose and hood
For with innocence comes apathy
Of the suffering we do not see

God With Us

God is with us, said the other side
They're faith was strong, but still they all have died

God is with me, said the fish now fried
With lemon butter golden brown, we flip to other side

God protected us, says the pig who flied
The camera man was there to catch his better side

God save us, says the prisoner condemned and died
He hopes with angels wings to reach the other side

Things

You are different
I want to see
If you can see yourself as me

Compassion

If you look out, and cannot see
Your enemy requires you your pity
I know not what to tell you now
Except that you are worse somehow

Here-After

The afterlife
A page beneath the light
Ink spatters without mystery
For tis the text of history!

Where thoughts and words pour out like rain
Each trickling word tickling my brain
For through these portals I will meet
Those of the names man loves repeat

I'll walk along with them, side by side
And but attempt to keep the stride
For through each page of written word

They live again through being heard

These dry bones, yes, they come alive
The ink, their blood, gives them new lives
Oh certainly they do live on
But in a way where life is gone

Yes

A simple question do I have
One which seems hard to grab

Is it that I misunderstood you,
Caught the wrong word that you came to?

Perhaps this may indeed be the case
I only hope we see next face to face

Depression

Oh, the fear of feeling loss
Our load to bear, out secret cross
The loneliness that spreads within
A shadow making life's light dim

Stealing the joy right out of life
This slimy thief, all slick and lithe
This cloud above, and pit below
The thing inside us that we know

Its loss is not what we elect
But rather, tis what time selects
So how overcome do we our sorrow
By living today, into tomorrow

Partition

There is a line at heaven's gate
Where all the condemned sit and wait
The believers, whey file right on in
And as they do, they shout within

"There's room enough in hell for you
The rest can all be damned

What we sing is more than true
We don't want heaven crammed!"

And so the precession continues on
Until one of the saved looks down upon
One of his fellows, in the pit
And then, at once, he stops and sits

"I will not go into the gate." He says
"How can I leave these people in this state?
Am I not a better man, to suffer with the rest?
Than to go up and sing such a song within that hateful nest!"

The angels hear that someone is holding up the line, and causing quite a mess
They were not expecting to find this strange peaceful protest
They try to pull him up to get him into the gate
For this hour of eternity was getting rather late

But they could not do it, so they had to up and call the boss
He came down, in a cloud of fire, his mind was at a loss
By this time, the man had gathered quite a following
The people now agree, indeed, hell was a disgusting thing

God had never held a vote before
But it could no longer be ignored
Decided he to open up
To all those, down there, in a rut

I imagine those once singing, now quite perplexed
They looked at God, now mad and vexed
"How dare You grace them with our bliss!
Are not we more special than this?"

But God, he shook His head and said
"There is no hell now, so instead
I'll treat you all equally
I know it's tough, but don't you see?"

"If you did this only for the reward
Then you aren't worthy of the Lord
The man who defied Me, did his best
His love of others passed my test."

The Purely Gates

The Atheist dies, and not much later

Meets a God, does he, without a wager
The God then asks, "Don't you regret?
Do you not now feel a fool not having placed a bet?"

He shakes his head, and with a sigh
Says *"No man can know until he dies*
And I refuse to join the toadies and the serfs
Such stooges have tainted, and injured, your poor created earth"

"My mind, I cultivated by learning all I could
And worked I well with all that I understood
I never put a damper on my curiosity
The answer 'God' was much too simple an answer for me"

"The faith argument, I must confess, doesn't make that much sense
It's followed also by the fact that there's a lack of evidence
Exemplified by the prayer, the most hollow of words
Oh god, please would you save us from your followers?!"

"But apparently I'm wrong for thinking, thoughts and doubt
Of questioning and learning just what this worlds about
So all that work I put into filling my mind up well
Means nothing to you, unlike belief, so cast me into hell!"

The God sits back, strokes his beard, and chuckles deep and low
Opens heaven's gate, and points him inward to go
And as the atheist passes the God, who's face is smile filled
The God thinks to himself, 'He's just like me, independent and strong willed'

The believer, behind him in the line, is quite unhappy now
He goes right strait up to the God, and asks him loudly "How!"
The God says, "So you wonder why into heaven he can go?
How can I condemn a man who is just as I made him so?"

Creation

Look at the intricacy of the bad
The glorious beauty of the sad
See the voracity of the cancer cell
A perfect personal little hell

Or of the lion's slender claw
The scarlet round its gaping maw
And what of the supple leech

Kaden Moeller

Its love of the blood beneath the flesh it breached

Or of the wrathful heart within
It moves the hands to paint red the skin
What of the maggot and the fly
Their home sweet home in those who die

The pretty sight that is the corps
With royal purple rigor mortis
Or of the sweet perfume that comes with rot
A generous sent, more than is sought

These things that go bump in the night
These things we fear and try to fight
When people speak of the creation
Forget they these things that I mention

If Only

If God were a living God
He'd care more for our trials
He'd never suffer us the rod
Nor injury of child

If God cared more for justice
He'd meet it out right now
And blot out wickedness
To lift this tearful shroud

If God did love the poor
He'd abolish such a thing
Make poverty no more
With all the tyranny it brings

If God were true compassion
He'd never bring us loss
That which brings love, to have them
And hold them close to us

If God were truly selfless
He would demand nothing
He'd never ask for worship
Oh such a petty thing

If God, he truly loved us
Like parent to a child

Why does he seem so jealous
And not so meek and mild?

Morality

Insanity! Insanity! Insanity!
Madness! Madness! Madness!

Without guidance all is pointless
All is permissible if no one is watching

Those responsible are insane
If no one is there, why should one care?

All is vanity and pointlessness
Without direction, chaos and sadness

No authority must mean free reign
Take no one into account but the self

It would be impossible to fathom
Empathy without dictation

For if no one orders you to kindness
Impossible for you is goodness

Without the boot atop our throat
Knowledge of others is too remote

For if everything falls to the abyss
Forgotten and disappeared

All light gone out
With no hope

Darkness, sadness, and misery
Swallowed up into nothingness

All traces of our spark
Never to be seen or known again

Then is not our greatest gift
Our strongest achievement

The acknowledgment of
And overcoming of this reality

Of this most horrid
Of this most glorious

The nothingness that is coming
The endless expanse of our extinction

Void without consciousness
Thing without recognition

The mirror without spectator
Our greatest fear

Insanity! Insanity! Insanity!
Madness! Madness! Madness!

Words

Why do my actions not speak louder than your words?
This hateful preaching that I've heard
You say I am morally bankrupt
But your morality doesn't keep your mouth shut

Your forked tongue, it flicks out your mouth
As your venom drips and drops right out
Poisoning the minds of men
Saying that, I'm not one of them

Your evil oozes from your pours
Infecting, oh so many more
Making sick even the youngest lad
This disease it drives a good mind mad

You raise up a vary hate filled force
Who from the rest of man, feels quite divorced
And alienated as they are
Drive out their neighbors near and far

And now they sit alone with you
And do what you tell them to
This is a sad thing to see
That you cannot love someone like me

Atheist

What if there was no afterlife?
How would that change our lives?
What would I do differently,
If I saw the world with these eyes?

I think I'd love much deeper
Remind people every day
That you are special to me
In each and every way

I'd campaign harder for justice
It won't be coming later
My indigence toward the vile and violent
Would be that much the greater

I'd appreciate the world more
Protecting nature's beauty
The world's a special little place
Its preservation is our duty

I'd appreciate the art of man
All forms of his expression
And marvel would I at the fact
The past come through their passion

Appreciate things more, would I
If this be all there is
And value things much higher
If I knew that this was it

Eternal Life

The problem with death, it seems
Is not that life, it ends
For the same things happen to our dreams
And this does not offend

The thing we fear is not that, the party will be over
For this wouldn't be hard to believe
Rather we fear the tap upon out shoulder
And that we'll be asked to leave

Kaden Moeller

That we'll be put outside the door
Kicked out black and blue
We do not want to leave, we want more
This party can't go on without you

And so we think that the party's host
Will give us some good news
That he would give us more than most
And not make us feel abused

That he would say *"This party's great!*
So good you cannot leave!"
And though the hour's getting late
It's too good to believe

Oh to be stuck at this celebration
To leave would be a crime
You better like inebriation
For the boss insists on having a good time

What people do not get
Is that others can't come in
Until after your turn, you let
Others come within

For life is very precious
This I can say is true
But without death, it's worthless
Eternity's not for you

For to appreciate the party
You someday must go home
And though our love for life be hearty
We will always be alone

For this is what the true fear is
The awkward solitude
Staggering past the garbage lids
A bit angry and confused

Unhappy that we had to depart
That party, oh so fun
But though the joy, it leaves our hearts
We are content it's done

Without A Hitch

Open up a can of worms and find out what's inside
The answer is as plain as day, so let's not try to hide
For the dialectic soon to come
Should prove to be quite more than fun

So open up the can, do I
And, not so surprised by what I spy
For though I knew what was in store
These aren't the worms I'm looking for

But I will take what I can get
And argue with the one I've met
I speak in sense, while they in tongs
And find this mess to be quite fun

I ski across the razorblade
The king of danger, it's my trade
And with my tongue I thrust and parry
This conflict makes me rather merry

The argument is quite obvious
With answers pieces of our chess
Play we the game of mind division
The questioning of man's religion

For the clearest mud that one can find
Is of the mud of the divine
Of which, some say, there's no debate
That interpreting leads to no mistake

I must confess I find much glee
In watching them contort for me
While I'm subjective, they are sure
While I'm a sinner, they are pure

I speak of randomness and chance
They say that, all of it god grants
I expound on my responsibility
While they, on God's authority

We back and forth on absolutes
I give exceptions; they say "No proof!"

And chuckles a bit within, do I
At the fiery passion in their eyes

And so the battle of wits ensues
I can't complain, I'm quite amused
But the time, it seems, it does not stop
And so the bell tolls on the clock

I feel a hand upon my back
With fingers going tap, tap, tap
Of this debate, I'm asked to leave
Not for a while, but eternity

And so they ask, "What if you're wrong?
It'll be too late to change your song"
I say *"I'll tell God, with good sense*
You didn't give much evidence"

And so I rub my throat, now sore
And quip, as I go out the door
"I may have to leave now, it's true
But someday, so will all of you"

Close Your Eyes, And Pray

"Never ever, ever stop praying
This is the great and famous saying
For what they say of prayer is the truth
It's all you need, and faith's the proof"

"But what of the family down the street?
I heard that they are starving
That they don't even have a sheet
Or but one single farthing"

"Worry not for them my friend
For their suffering shall one day end
Just keep them in you prayers, you see
Your prayers will make them strong and free"

"But should I not invite them in?
Give them a place to stay?
I feel their hearts breaking within
As despair comes down their way"

"My friend, this proves to me all the more

Your prayers are what their waiting for
Just put your faith into your words
And know the heavens high have heard"

"But I see the tax collector outside
Knocking at the door
I know they're in there trying to hide
Or crying on the floor"

"Worry not, if you believe
Your prayers are blessings they'll receive
Make sure your faith is strong indeed
Weak faith won't give them what they need"

"The authorities are at the house
They're throwing them out on the street
The little girl in the worn white dress
Has no shoes on her feet"

"Your faith, it seems, was token
Those words, if you have spoken
You did not believe them deep within
So now they suffer for your sin"

"But did I not do everything
That you, my friend, have said?
I thought my faith would surely bring
Salvation upon their heads"

Televangelist

Out comes the Pharisee to say
"The poor must go from the rich man's way"
Their words, they are like sharpened glass
They cut the poor man's flesh, they ask

For these preachers are not for the weak
The helpless or the vary meek
They stand to keep the status quo
To hold them back so they don't go

And speak of treasure, up in heaven
As break they the bread of the unleavened
Saying *"Revel in your poverty*

Kaden Moeller

A poor spirit grows more you see"

These brood of vipers in their nest
They say they love the poor
But why are they the ones who say
"Work hard to earn your bread today!"

They seem to think that circumstance
Is not influenced by random chance
Oh why are always they the ones
To push back the help under the sun

Tears Of Evil

No matter the sincerity
Or tears behind the eyes you see
A person may believe quite strong
And still be much more than wrong
They may indeed be sinister
No matter what they minister

But you will be moved to pity them
As nothing but ignorant children
And yet this does not absolve their deeds
As fulfill them what they do believe

What compassion should you give,
When they threaten those who live?
Proclaiming their intolerance
And reinforcing their ignorance
For they'll reject reality
For their beliefs that they can't see

For this life is just a veil
To be pulled away as you travail
And when you finally reach your triumph
Your suffering will then seem defiant

Believing evil of their brothers
They're not with us they're the *"other"*
But in heaven we'll all get along
Unless you're not there, then you don't belong

Moral Question

If things do be eternal

590

And they be never ending
Would this not be infernal?
A watered down moral blending?

For if there is no finality
No tragedy to fear
Why heed we to reality?
Why call the living dear?

What concern should we show to others?
It's not like they'll be gone
To our immortal brothers
What hurt can do them wrong

For if you lose today
You still do have tomorrow
Do not complain, just up and say
"No reason now to sorrow."

Why hold we to the present?
Another day will come
So put off, don't resent
The success of others fun

Again, why should we care?
About today, the now
Do we live forever, or do we dare
Believe that we don't now?

Anagram

Atheism is a sin
This non-belief one holds within
However this I must protest
Every belief is not like the rest
I now truly do believe
Someday all things will we receive
Moreover, we'll out grow them

Earth

I am unweaving the rainbow
Through the dewdrops and mist so plain
I am unweaving the rainbow

Kaden Moeller

Sunbeams reflecting through the rain

I'm taking away the mystery
No miracle has made it so
I'm taking away the mystery
Its true beauty comes when you know

We ourselves are the lucky ones
To see such a beautiful sight
We ourselves are the lucky ones
Knowing how water refracts the light

So many others could have
Been born into this world
So many others could have
Painted this beauty on a mural

How dare we complain
When we return unto the grave
How dare we complain
When nothing is remade

To die means you have lived
With luck against all odds
To die means you have lived
With no help from the gods

I am unweaving the rainbow
Oh such a limited time
I am unweaving the rainbow
To describe in verse and rhyme

Religion

What happens
When the believed good is analyzed?
When light is shown upon the pages
And the words understood

The pages
They curl up and turn to dust
The winds scatter away the past goods
Making them as madness

No good
If not looked upon and judged

For all beauty wanes away with time
Going back to nothing

This fear
We have, of doubting our past
Of telling our parents that they're wrong
Chills our souls black

We cannot
Grow or move beyond our predecessors
If we keep their sins with us
The sin of affiliation

We are
Not to be bound to them
But move beyond the epoch behind us
Breaking good as evil

Imagine

No hell
No burning smell
No pain
No blame
No justice
None of this

No paradise
No vice
No judgment
No intent
No design
Just our time

Imagine nothing
That is what there is

God Of The Gaps

There was a time when God, so proud
Sat high atop his mighty cloud
And made this world, which once was flat
The center was where this world was at

Kaden Moeller

When the sun revolved around the earth
We thought ourselves quite high in worth
And when we found that we evolved
Around the sun the earth revolved

This globe of ours, no longer flat
Seemed less designed when we knew that
As hubris shrinks we start to fear
That life no longer is its center

But rather just a random chance
A lot of luck and happenstance
That rather what we thought was God
Is everything we're learning of

And now we think we feel alone
Abandoned we feel in our home
That God forsook us way down here
And left us feeling rather queer

This emptiness that prickles our hair
The thought that God was never there
And so we cry out blasphemy
Convict ourselves of heresy

Angry that far from He we've wandered
Against ourselves defend we His honor
And curse the day we lost the smell
Of the sulfurous stench of burning hell

But what we fear cannot be God
His punishment or loving nod
What really stops us in our tracks
Is our mind at night, who asks

"Could we really be so bold?
To stand here in this world so cold
And make decisions for ourselves
Without the threat of burning hell'

'Without God, can we be good or love?'
I submit to you, this always was

Stability

What is it about religion

594

That causes strife and great division
The truth is in its vampirism
It's leeching off new knowledge risen

Religion fights truth with tooth and nail
And accept it when they can't prevail
It then becomes part of their God's store
Making Him seem cleverer than before

Of course these things were all decreed
For these are things that we all need
So of course their God claims the design
How convenient is the divine?

The religious defend their deity
Theirs is the only one you see
Their atheists against the rest
Except for theirs, for He's the best

The apologists, a special group
Of crusaders do they constitute
They speak of all their absolutes
But forget how things have changed with proof

And so they point to our knowledge gaps
Says it's their God, and that's a fact
Until, of course, we find out why
And then they'll kick and scream and cry

The only thing that they have left
Is the morality they try to heft
Forget they all the evil deeds
That they once thought good and well indeed

And so they now have nothing left
They curl, with legs against their chest
Whispering their mantras and their prayers
Hoping within, as without they glare

The fear of their fellows and themselves
Leaves them yearning for a hell
A place where you can be punished for your deeds, but you'll
Notice that hell's for other people

The religion of the ever receding God
Those who know this smile and nod
This is the truth, or so I'm told
That hell is really other people

Conversion

Why aren't the religious happy through and through?
Because you must believe it too
You'd think they'd be content within
Instead, obsess they with your sin

They speak their words so to compel
Frightening words like pain and hell
But worry not, their God above
He is a God of endless love

They speak of your sin, which is ascribed
And this salvation they prescribe
Interesting, that you're born in sin
But salvation is a choice within

So sad that you are born so flawed
And must work so hard to find this God
Sadder is that God just can't forgive
You have to ask him while you live

Harder still is that great mess
Finding His religion is quite the test
You better find the correct one
Or your afterlife won't be so fun

Percent

Why is it, that knowledge changes your mind
And turns you different over time?
Why is it that faith, it shakes
It cracks, it chips, and then it breaks?

Those certainties that once were thought
Disappear when knowledge is sought
The world then looks ruled by exception
A guiding hand evades detection

The realization that choice and circumstance
Are ruled by chance and happenstance

And that our ethics or morality
Are relative to what our minds perceive

To see the shifting human landscape
This reality can't be escaped
It drives the absolutists mad
They see the change and call it bad

Find that a land with information
Shall build thee up a greater nation
But when they use faith to build them up
They find themselves stuck in a rut

Five People You Won't Meet In Heaven

You won't be seeing Hitler
He was a mustache stickler

Nor will you be meeting Stalin
His eyebrows were appalling

No one's seeing Nietzsche
Oh, but I heard he was so peachy

Nor Mr. Stephen Hawking
He'd rather just go a' walking

You won't even see Gandhi
Sounds strange don't it? Gee...

No holocaust victims or Nazis
No atheists or Commies

No freethinkers or philosophers
No diversity to what we've heard

No tolerance teachers or scientists
Man, heaven's really the pits

If all that gets you in is belief
And without that ticket you go to grief

It seems then that everything you do
Is really worthless, through and through

Kaden Moeller

For if all you must say is *"I do"*
Than what is there that's left for you?

Gospel Truth

Remember, please, to preach the gospel
Of compulsory love
Be strong, and vary forceful
For the kingdom up above

Remember your Father's name
The one that you should fear
Who heaps upon you words of blame
This sweet venom that you hear

Remember to degrade the self
Forgetting all uniqueness
For within a man, no worth or wealth
Comes forth to bear a witness

Remember that it's healthy
To deeply be afraid
Of the one you love so sweetly
The one from whom you're made

Salvation

How is it, to commune with God?
And get to know Him better
For like a child, who needs the rod
We need to speak unfettered

Go forth, and find thyself a lamb
One without spot or blemish
And slit his throat with thine own hand
His blood, oh will you relish

For the only way to speak, with a God so just
Is to slay the innocent
For perfections, it is a must
Such logic is inerrant

For the guilty and the sinful
Cannot stand before the holy
Disguised in righteous blood, your soul
It stands in victory

But such a covering cannot last
And so, in fear and trembling
They kills and slaughter as they fast
So God can hear their murmuring

But God, in His great wisdom
Gave a sacrifice to us
Providing up His only Son
And killed Him, as He must

For why should we not kill a man
So to commune with God
If such a one can play the lamb
And then redeem us dogs

Oh what is wrong with killing the good
So to redeem the evil
You'd take forgiveness if you could
Such a relief, so real

But forgiveness is not for the forgiven
Rather for the forgiver
It eases the wronged man's heart within
It doesn't save the sinner

Oh the heart of justice bays not for any blood
Guilty or innocent
For it's a heart, it's meant to love
To pump it with intent

So please don't hide yourself away
And drown yourself in blood
For it is wrong for you to slay
Even for God above

Supervision

He sees you when you're sleeping
He knows when you're awake
He knows if you've been bad or good
So be good for goodness sake

For it is just, and right, you see

Kaden Moeller

This divine supervision
An eye on you, whom doth command
A holy circumcision

It matters not where you may go
Forever are you watched
Not even your mind within is safe
He even knows your thoughts

So grovel now, upon the ground
And beg Him for His mercy
To swear allegiance to the crown
To praise and never curse He

So love Him for knowing the you within
And then hating you for it
So come before Him as you are
Your self, learn to deny it

Bris

Oh what a treasure, what a gift
Now breakout the sharp stone
This baby, up to God we lift
Do this before he's grown

Now comes this wrong incision
Welcome to the world
This painful circumcision
God's angry referral

For children aren't born beautiful
They must be sawn a bit
For to God are we now beautiful
For His handiwork is shit

Who would say this but the godly?
The dictators of the spirit
The superstitious and the haughty
Who use the mind to kill it

Washing the brain of sense
So as to harm a child
Scarring their innocence
Done with a loving smile

For without this sign of divinity
You never truly can be free
Cut off this fleshly slavery
Rip from the *'you'* the *'me'*

Give your baby the gift of pain
This bloody baptism
And before he even knows his name
You cover him in sin

Oh how the minds of parents
They harm their children first
Thinking themselves inerrant
This blindness is the worst

Parenthood

If God came up to me today
Telling me to prove
My love for He, come what may
For Him now should I move

To gut my child just for He
Oh this I'd never do
If should say He "Do this for me."
To that I'd say *"Fuck you!"*

Yes I love my child more that Ye
This person in my care
A soul who comes from deep in me
Body, naked and bare

"Now burn me all you want to God!
And torment me in hell!"
Though Ye may beat me with the rod
In defiance will I yell

For this child, am I, to be held responsible
Protecting it with care
"Do don't come near God, turn and go
Don't you even dare!"

Kaden Moeller

Sovereignty

I am responsible for all
Everything that is, is mine
My voice is the deciding call
In every place and time

I raise up the just and unjust kings
Approving everything they do
And no matter what plan they may bring
I make their words come true

If they give unto the poor
That is a very good thing
And if they kill and stab and gore
It's fine, for their My king

But the kings are not the only ones
I hold within my hand
Both pleasure, pain and suffering do I run
My will is oh so grand

I flood the earth, and drown the nations
Killing so many souls
But to some, I give them salvation
Though, why, you'll never know

I am mysterious, or so they say
This covers up the fact
That all those people I doth slay
Violates the social contract

Some say that I'm negligent
That no excuse exists
To cause suffering with intent
Or bring down My heavy fist

That if one can stop evil
Or has the power to do so
Is required now to kneel
To the good deeds that are known

They say all blame falls on the one
Who is all powerful
Saying that all things that are done
Are not My *"perfect"* will

I find it unfair, do I, now
That all these sinful people
Hold me to My standards, wow!
So presumptuous and feeble

But not just My will do they hold to Me to
But even to their own
They say they know more than I do
They say, that they are grown

That the high ideal they put forth
Are closing the division
Of the things set up by My cohorts
This powerful religion

Calling belief in Me a superstition
And bad mouthing the faith
It seems to Me that our collision
Is meant to be, its fate

For you are only little men
Who cares what you doth think
Your mind, it seems to sway and bend
And never stay in sync

So what if you are learning
And follow evidence
To me should you be returning
I mean, it just makes sense

Don't say I'm not in charge!
Or that I don't exist!
For into you I'll barge
And make you regret it

Oh I swear I'll do it
Just you wait and see
When I end the world, idiot
These are the latter days indeed

Test?

So Satan saunters up to God

And looks Him in the eye
And God looking down at him nods
As Satan says to Him *"Hi!"*

"Oh King of heaven, way up high
The universe's creator
I say this with a heavy sigh
To He who is the greater"

"I'm tired of running the world
Being prince upon the earth
I'd rather hand the deed, this referral
Over to you, good sir"

"I know. I know, you say to me
'What do you want for this?'
For nothing ever comes for free
Not love, nor even bliss"

"Oh tis a simple thing I want
Just but one small token
This thing, oh it should not daunt
This thing that will be spoken"

"No one else need know
No other needs to look
No need to make a show
Or write it in a book"

"Oh humble King on high
Look at the earth, a mural
If you do this, then twill I
Give You all the kingdoms of the world!"

"Now comes the request
The thing I want comes now
The people you can bless
If all you'll do is bow"

"Just once, but once, is all I ask
And no one needs to know
Allow me, in my pride, to bask
Amidst this pretend glow!"

The King, God, rose up to his feet
Rebuked him, and off he went

Banishing him back to hell's strong heat
For He knew not what Satan meant

And Satan shook his head in sorrow
His heart, oh it was troubled
He said inside *'I'll try tomorrow.'*
And hoped God would be humble

In The Now

Open your eyes!
Look! Just Look!
Do you see!?
Look!

The trees!
The Grass!
The breeze!
Avast!

Did you see it!?
The beautiful thing!?
Here, just sit
Again, it's coming!

The rain!
The wind!
Your pain!
Your kin!

This sight!
It's beautiful!
Right!?
No!?

Hold on
Let's try again
No, don't yawn!
You'll see, my friend

Those buildings!
The cars!
Your things!
Your scars!

Ha! There it was!
And there it is!
I'm happy, because
It's when we live!

That's it you know!
That's what is pretty!
That we are so
Blessed with reality!

The present, this gift I unwrapped
A thing only that I received
A special beauty, that
I almost can't believe

Just look at everything!
All that we see around!
This is our song we sing
A special little sound

Oh I'm so happy, that I am
For no one else can experience
This time that flickers on, and
Then goes out, in an instant

Fear Of Dying

The old man's eyes, so dark and dim
Fogged over from the thoughts within
Remembering, with fearful heart
The lives that never got their start

And so he curses at his pride
For fearing the day when he'll have died
For what a lucky life for him
For even to have ever been

Coming To The End

When you are about to die
You tell yourself a little lie
And then you lay you down to sleep
While others cry and prey and weep

Meaningless?

Living in all my certainty
I care not of life's short misery
For what's life, but a veil,
A shed skin, oh so pale?

And natures fading beauty
To it, I feel no duty
For what value are these things,
To which I cannot cling?

For all these things were made
And meant but for the grave
None of them are better then
My treasures up in heaven

For these things are but the chaff
Those shed bits of the grass
Oh of these fleeting treasures,
What worth do they now measure?

What, beneath eternity
Holds any worth for me
The temporal, it reeks!
A stench unto the meek

Oh watch the proud flower wither
Its life, tis but a sliver
Like fire beneath the rain
Such light, by darkness, slain

This world is oh so haughty
Like a harlot's tempting body
Who with time will fade away
And turn soon old and grey

Oh what a contemptible world
It causes the brow to furrow
So bound is it by limits
By what we can find in it

Such a sickly thing is time
It seems but to refine

Kaden Moeller

The burden of this life
This ever constant strife

Oh, but to be in paradise
A world without such vice
To have everything I want
And no old world to haunt

But for now I must persist
And eagerly insist
That the day is soon to come
When this world will be done

Valuation

Thou shall not...
What's to be got?

What of what one should?
Is it not true, that what is good
Is not what love is for
The opening of doors

When you shut one in the face
You may have left a special place
But some doors should not have been opened
They lead to falsity, and what is token

Absolutes

A world made of blacks and whites
Is much too dark or far too bright
It leaves no room for subtlety
Or complex ambiguity

It puts men in two separate camps
Those who do good or who supplant
And that makes it ok to flog
The wrongdoers, those less than dogs

The good are men, while bad are beasts
Reward the righteous, the rest mistreat

For it would be quite strange to see
The good give the bad empathy
But that might lead to understanding

And cause us then to cease our branding

See we no longer right and wrong
Rather the weak amidst the strong

Those who have stumbled and can't get up
Need not the strong so proudly strut
But rather lend a helping hand
And elevate his fellow man

The world needs not a righteous judge
A petty good who holds a grudge
Lay siege to black and white's last bastion
In grey lies love and man's compassion

The Good

What's wrong with divine morality?

Well
It's shallow

Doing good deeds
For a reward

Sucking up
For fear of punishment

Good done
Not for its own sake
But on command

So
Superficial

Is God that petty?
That immature?

He'd rather love His moral porn
Then hold the truly moral in his arms?

He'd marry the surface
Rather then what's within?

Kaden Moeller

Judging
Based not on circumstance or compassion

But rather
Fear and trembling

Should a lover fear?
Should she wince at Your touch?

What love is this?
Does God beat His wife?

This is nothing moral
Its abuse
It isn't right

The Bible

These words upon the parchment
Each set of symbols here
They speak of human intent
And actions that I fear

Of silencing my sisters
And killing off my brothers
To watch the earth to wither
And scorn it like no other

To my mother, be a servant
My father, a slave holder
Oh this morality is bent
And fosters hearts much colder

These words your mind drinks in
Slide lithely from your lips
They speak of souls and sin
And promote guilt and regret

Build they a cage for children
Their minds now do they cull
As slowly they build in them
This mind forged maniacal

Oh keep these words within you
That's what you're told is best
And store them up you do

Consume this thing so blessed

Oh of this holy scroll you eat
Why bother you with it?
No matter if it goes down sweet
It always comes out shit

Praise

What is more beautiful
Then a lover singing a love song
To the one who makes their heart full
To whom after they long

Hearing a voice lifted high
In joy and ecstasy
Oh of these happy tears one cries
They drop down gleefully

And echo round now does the voice
Proclaiming to the world
A love of seeming compelled choice
As round the mind does swirl

It speaks of seas and boundless skies
Describing and comparing
But no words come close, though they try
To how much the heart is yearning

Lifting ones hands up to the heavens
Standing upon ones knees
This song, one hopes it never ends
These words, the loved one needs

These songs of joy and beauty
The best love songs ever made
But where could the other lover be?
This God to whom they're gave

Oh tis a sad thing indeed
The singings still not done
This question, they seem not to heed
"Why do you sing to no one?"

Bible Camp

To those who self indoctrinate
Or, brainwash their own mind
I find you really hard to hate
Until it come the time

When that fine dogma ferments long
And perforates you mind
A drunken man, with reason gone
And vision, all but blind

But stop you not to think
On whether you've done right
Instead you make a stink
And stir up quite a sight

As round the bole you whirl
But you just won't go down
Oh such a stubborn turd
Who never seems to drown

So eat you more, this crap
And do it with a smile
Desire you this scat
You think it's worth your while

So hard to take you serious
You and your beliefs
And yet, you are a threat to us
Grinning with shit between your teeth

Side Show

"God hates fags!"
Says the fundamentalist
Yelling in his rags
As the bible, up he lifts

Proclaiming the good news
Of those condemned to hell
His antics do amuse
But don't eclipse the smell

The people watch him rant
Curse and make a fuss

Stopping to eat an ant
Or maybe wild locust

Oh some times he's quite a show
So scantly is he dressed
As up the tree he'll go
To raid honey from bees nests

Watching him skulk around
Pounding on his chest
Hurling insults abound
Oh such a filthy mess

There jumping up and down
Howling at passers by
Oh such unpleasant sounds
It causes some to sigh

"Evolution is a lie!
Strait from the pits of hell!"
Says he in his high pitched cry
As round the crowd does swell

Flailing his arms about
Giving quite the show
Standing there, all stout
As attention swells his ego

Many there are shocked
At the thought that this is free
Some think, "Maybe he's lost?"
While others do agree

And to those who join his chorus
Of screaming angrily
To you I must confess
That you are bat shit crazy

Instructions Within

Herein, listen, herein lies the truth
What you must do
What is necessary for the future
And what we must fight for

Kaden Moeller

Death to irrationality!
We must declare a war on delusion
At every corner need we be
To quash we all religion

Why, to what do we declare this war?
Are we seeking the death of fantasy?
The death of creative expression?
The genocide of the fantastic?

No, but an extermination of the fool's food
We wish to clean out the cellars of our fellows
Take and throw the moldy things; consumed
And dump the brew gone foul

We must do this, look at what it has done to us!
A law has been handed down
*"If ye not suspend your disbelief to the margins
Ye shall be executed!"*

Oh weep! Cry out for our brothers!
He who sits in solitary
He who waits for the kiss of the blade
And twill lose his life for truth

How many lives need wax?!
What requires such barbarism?!
No apology can but retract
The life that they have stolen

A candle snuffed can burn again
But a life cut up, it cannot mend
What edict strewn from toxic mind
Could hold our fellows; tightly bind!

Defy! Say I, defy!
Dump the rancid sustenance!
Pour it out in the streets!
A belief you cannot leave is not worth its belief!

Take yourself from faith and search
Take nothing within lest you learn
Lest you be wise enough to discern
Can you understand its worth?

Look! Taste and see the truth!
It seems first bitter
Yet turns to sweet
Life is now!

How many more blood libations are required?
To slit the throat of our fellows
And pour it out; a wretched offering indeed
For a mad blood God to quaff

Reject it! Dismiss it! Despise it! Leave it!
Lest you desire a house of bones and the scent of corpses
A horror that makes the mind sick
And causes the senses distress

Oh brother over a distant sea
Guilty of invisible crimes
Who though, farthest from me
Is human, me and mine

Disbelief! A crime!
Than I am a criminal!
I am guilty of sedition!
A Fatwa be placed upon me!

No man, no god, no being controls this world!
And if ever so, such a soul has no right over me
No privilege do I bestow! I am not property!
No knee shall I bow to such a beast!

And so I say, I speak plainly now
Disavow such loyalties
Never a knee to bow
And never a tong speak creed

These are your orders
Thy commandment
Confront falsity
Stand brave against any strong assertion without evidence!

It is your duty
It is our privilege
Both you and me
Stand for our friend

Kaden Moeller

Each martyr of intellect
Each artist damned to death
Who catches blades: direct
From those who are *"the blessed"*

Stand tall and fight!
If truth is to win out
We must allot ourselves resistance
For this our glorious culture

The culture of reality
The culture of unbridled truth
The culture of joy
And the culture of pain

If we want to win this war
If we believe in fact and treasure fiction
If we hold to beauty and truth
Than we are conscripts all

Let them complain!
Let them cry victim!
For we see the victims plain
And they are certainly no victim here

Challenge all of them!
Every unjust Godhood!
Whatever screed they spread
It has no divine origin

We are best without them
Best human
Best when we are filled with empathy
And worst when we are empty

So, I say we march
March on those holy gates
March on those citadel walls and proclaim
"We are the once and truly free!"

Oh friend across the sea
Brother distant from me
One who waits for death
Whose breathing his last breaths

To all who hear our cry
Declare I war
A battle cry
For when we die, we are no more.

Tree Of Knowledge

While slithering through the garden
The serpent, he did stop
He spotted there two humans
Who were talking quite a lot

Not to one another
Rather to someone else
A sister, or a brother?
The snake, he couldn't tell

So look, did he, around
And spotted nobody
He listened for a sound
But no voice came in reply

And so the snake did ask
"Who are you talking to?"
The people stood lambast
"The God of we and you!"

Confused was he by this
So he asked *"Where is he?"*
The people said, perplexed
"He lives in you and me"

The serpent shook his head
These people did not know much
Slithering away, he said
"They must be out of touch"

He then cut down a tree
And printed off some books
He gave them out, so they could see
How silly they must look

*"You should not talk to no one
It really creeps me out"*

He gave the books out to them
So as to bring them doubt

But rejected they this fruit
From these fallen tree of printed knowledge
Crushed they the snake with boot
And built round themselves a hedge

A story so absurd
One no one can believe
The sad thing is, this turd
Is real to so many

Sparring Partner

Oh how I love my punching bag
It helps relieve my stress
And never does it sag
This bag my blows caress

It takes them without feeling
It doesn't cry or beg
This bag, it sits their reeling
It won't crack like an egg

I pound and bash it hard
Releasing my pain and fear
It helps my heart, now scarred
These blows I'm landing here

Oh of the joy it brings
To hit, but not cause pain
My punches do not sting
Another body's frame

So yes, I love to hit
This bag that's in my mind
It's where I get my kicks
Where I hold religion bind

The Christ

I found myself a friend
He lives here, in my heart
And to him, do I send
The bits, I will depart

Every cut upon me
He takes onto his skin
I trace them to his body
And put the blade within

Does he take them willingly?
Or do I force them on him?
I find the answer hard to see
As, in me, he's imprisoned

So give to him, do I
My worries and my fears
My pain, I do not hide
I let him feel its sear

Oh giving to him, everything
It brings me so much comfort
He takes away life's sting
So that I do not hurt

Some say that it is cruel
Passing my pain to someone else
To say *"I'm not responsible"*
For the pain of my own hell

A True Statement

The burden of untruth, be a heavy cross to bear
But for both ourselves and others, it is made for us to share

These beams we hang upon, made up are they of lies
Crucifying ourselves for our brothers, so that, in us their pain resides

But how much can one hide, of the pain that comes with truth
How much can one body cover, until the lie's weight crushes you?

How can we hang and hold, upon and up, this weight?
Two things so different from another, but their pain in us is great

These lies, as white as snow, be a scourge upon our skin
And our bodies seize and shutter, as we're lashed by our secret sin

Though we wish our pain diminished

And would truly love to utter, the words *"It is finished!"*

But know, do we the truth, and how it would hurt our friends
And with all the strength that we can muster, we don't let these lies end

An Empty Space

I feel empty, deep inside
A hole in my soul
And so, with every vibrant stride
I work to make me whole

I put therein, possessions
Of every shape and size
Along with my profession
And every other prize

I pour, into it, love
And every person in it
This sea, the riders of
They flow into the pit

With more and more each day
This hole doesn't fill
And hear I others say
Such emptiness can kill

But this hole isn't empty
In fact, there's much inside
There's room for all to breath
So come and stop on by

Some Wisdom

My son, I give you a secret
A gift from me to thee
It's special, so don't miss it
Twill save you so much worry

The gift, tis immortality
Oh yes, quite a surprise
Oh wait, hold on, you'll see
Just hear me and be wise

The answer to the question, death
It lies before your birth

In the beginning of your life, yes
Before you knew the earth

Oh, do you see the past?
Are you now comprehending?
For time, it is so vast
And yet, it seems its ending

So do you understand, my son
Oh please, don't sadly sigh
For though we may be soon undone
We never really die

Sight

Religion makes a mockery
Altering everything you see
People as a wretched lot
Everyone is wrong, but you are not

Forgive Them

When you know not what you do
Your actions, fear do I
When you say a thing is true
But don't know it's a lie

What horrors are committed,
When veiled by ignorance?
A gown so surly fitted
Measured by arrogance

When smugly do you discount
The experts at their trade
And spring up, like a fount
The worst man has to say

Not knowing is an evil
But wanting not to know
It promises a meal
From a crop that's not to grow

You'll lash your lover horridly
And tell them it's alright

Kaden Moeller

They'll beg and plead thee mercy
As you beat them day and night

And in your mind, you've saved them
As they lie there broken, bleeding
But your thoughts will not defend
Against the hearts now grieving

A strong belief is evil
If the belief is in a lie
Of course you would not know
Because you do not try

Never In Their Own Town

"We Preach Christ, crucified!
He, who fought the pharoses,
Whose loving sacrifice
Was given unto we"

"We; now not under law
Who fall at the feet of grace
To stand in reverent aw
Beneath his loving face"

And on and on he preached
Until an atheist
Walked up to ask the pastor
What all he meant by this

"Oh father, sir, good sir
A question have I say
I mean not cause a stir
But, what about the gays?"

"They are abomination
As written in the law
Twas God's strong proclamation
We will obey his call"

The atheist; he nodded
Though he was quite confused
And slightly more, he prodded
To find he the "good" news

"But if we're not under law

Why care what law was written?
If grace be all and all
The strongest proclamation?"

"The law was not abolished!"
The preacher firmly said
"It was given unto us
To follow and be read"

"Be not you hypocrites?"
The atheist queried
"The pharoses did this
They followed the law sternly"

"We are the flock anointed!
The chosen ones of God!
Who wait, humble, appointed
Until this world dissolves"

"Ye best learn some humility"
The priest said, with pointed finger
"Humble yourself before he
And learn to love his word"

"But what of, love thy neighbor?"
The atheist pressed on
"If God is love, therefore
He'll love us right or wrong?"

"Of what offends you, cast it off
For tis what God will do
To all who dare to doubt and scoff
And mock he the good news"

"What could cause God offence?"
The atheist was puzzled
"If he made all that is
Did he offend himself?"

"Ye blaspheme the Lord of hosts!
How dare say such a thing
God deals with those who boast
Who doubt His power, pristine"

"What boasting have I clamed,
And why are you offended?
Aren't ye who boasts of shame,
The most humble of it?"

The crowd was not appreciative
They shouted and they jeered
Angrily they said to him
"Get out you fucking queer!"

The atheist did leave
As some did chase him out
Though his heart was grieved
They won't receive his doubt

And so he left his hometown
Where none would hear his voice
A curse that's common found
But one not made by choice

And so he went to change the world
When from they asked him "Where?"
He tells them "Someplace small"
"What good can come from there?"

White

In the white of night
There is no light
Within this blackness is a sight

Trees against the moon, made white against the gloom
A rooftop, made into a work of art from icicles atop
They flow like rivers wide, but small as creeks below
Yet within this silence and the dark, there is a smile on every face

For Christmas is tomorrow
You'll see it every place

A Religious War

In America, there is a war on Christmas
And what a brutal war it is
The store clerks don't say *"Marry Christmas"* anymore
And we don't put Christmas trees and manger scenes
On the loans of our state buildings

Such a tragedy it is
Christmas is so commercialized; people buying and buying
And though they say they hate it, they buy all the same
Televisions, computers, toys of all sorts
And they pass the homeless man on the street
As they bustle to the next sale

Grousing all the way *"The clerk said, happy holidays"*
And they'll rant and they'll rail at the casher
Who hasn't had a full meal all week, and gave most of her
Food to her children, who certainly don't eat well
After all, she should have known the price was lower
And they'll pass by that same homeless man again
Complaining as they do, as he is taken to jail for
Loitering on private property, where he will spend
The holidays wondering where his family is

And those consumers, as they angrily complain,
Will pass the trailer homes of their fellow man
Where you can see a family piling into the car
To go look at the Christmas lights in the *"nice"* part
Of town, though the heater is broken and their clothes
Aren't so warm, the young ones shivering in the
Back, only to be warmed by the wonderment and joy at
The sight of the red and green spectacle

Put the *"Christ"* back in Christmas, that's what they say
As they donate their tax deductable gifts, and think on the return
He's the reason for the season; put the Christ back in Christmas
Over and over they'll chant, as they light their Norse holiday tree
And partake of the winter solstice message of death and rebirth

Put the Christ back in Christmas
The spirit of giving, of empathy, and joy
That peace on earth and good will to all
To feed those who are hungry, cloth those naked, shelter the homeless,
Visit the imprisoned, cure the sick, love thy neighbor and
Give of thyself, sell all you have and give it to the poor,
For what you do unto the least of these so to you have done
Unto me, put the Christ back in Christmas they say

Yet no one is stopping their charity? No chains are around
Them bound, they merely want the pageantry and nothing
More profound, put the Christ back in Christmas they say

As they decorate their houses; to stand out
To display their excess before the world, and show
That they'd rather spend their money on decorations; than the poor
To showcase themselves as having the nicest house
The prettiest house, the one who has the highest electric bill
After all, they can afford it

Put the Christ back in Christmas?
No edict has removed him, behave as Christ would have
And he'll be in Christmas, your actions will showcase your savior
By being a savior to others, the only people removing Christ
Are you Christians who speak but don't act
Do unto the least of these as you would have done unto me
Put the Christ back in Christmas
Merry Christmas, America

Saviors

"God saved my dad"
These words
I heard them said
"He was having a heart attack
But the ambulance came
The doctor helped him
And now
He's fine"

God saved?
God saved him?
Thank God?

I'd rather thank the doctor
He spent years
Learning how to save lives
Learning from books
From those before them
From the first surgeons
The first healers
The first witchdoctors

That first soul
Who
While looking at a corps
Did
With shaking hands and sweaty brow
Cut open

Cut and see
What strange things were kept away
Hidden deep inside

Yes
I thank those countless generations
Whose morbid curiosity
Stirred forth great philanthropy

Yes
I thank every individual
Who builds upon the structure, started
By the curious flesh-carver

Yes
I thank them

The MorTal Case

Good; for goodness sake
Kind, a soft smile
Like a brook flowing over rough stones
Wearing down the jagged edges of fear
Caressing over the places of shame
And speaking words like rain
Which sprinkles down upon all who hear
"Look at all the beauty"

Gift, what gift?
The gift of life, or of this world?
The gift of sorrow, or of pain?
The gift of pleasure, or of joy?
No, no gift
No giver
We are a painting looking back at itself
Seeing the swirling colors and thinking
'Who painted that?'

But no painter is found
At least, no conscious painter
No cosmic mind; brush in hand
No, just spilt watercolors
Running into one another
A beautiful mess obeying simple laws

627

Kaden Moeller

And no law giver to thank

Of death, what death?
Are we not compounds combine together?
Would not these pieces still exist,
Even if the puzzle were not solved?
Can the puzzle be solved,
Is there a puzzle at all,
And is each peace, separate, not a wonder in itself?

Are we a puddle?
The water or the hole?
De we look at the hole we're in and think
'This was made for me, as it suits me perfectly'
Or do we look up at the water, saying
"You were gifted to me, a present from another"
Yet neither are true, and both are strange

One does not worship at the altar of knowledge
Nor sing praise or give alms
Knowledge is itself a product of the learners
And thereby inseparable from the knower
Once gained and absorbed
Knowledge is one with the knower

And beauty; perception
All is beautiful in one light or another
But look and you shall find
The glorious intricacies
And see the strange interwoven tapestry
A glorious chain of life

So yes, I see no purpose
"Devine" of this world
No moral/supernatural lawgiver from beyond
And cannot see why we should assume

We are wonderful
We are watching
We are listening
We are alive

The Scales Of Truth

Truth becomes heavier
The longer you ignore it

As the weight of evidence
Increases by increment

And soon that burden's placed
Upon the denier's back
And sits there; but to wait
Until their mind retracts

You can't deny the truth
It affects you all the same
It's all it needs for proof
It won't relent or wane

It cares not your beliefs
Nor rules of your God
And cares less if you weep
As beg and plead and sob

For truth, it is no mystery
Nor be it far beyond
It stands before both you and me
And never will be gone

So don't deny the facts
And never scorn the truth
Do not think even that
Your wishes matter, too

For never does reality
Give malice unto life
But twill provide a bane
Should you deny it's right

Querying

"What is divinity?" one can ask
"What is deity?" a proper question
Can we be these things?
Is God me? Am I divine?
And, in concert, are not all others?

A patron saint of joy, love, wrath, hate or friendship?
A savior to another soul; in wanting
The one whom makes all things new

By virtue of being there
Of lending a listening ear, a kindly touch
Perhaps granting a word of wisdom

Are you not unique in that way?
The way in which stirs the inmost paces of
Your fellows, gripping their hearts in strong fashion
Perhaps an embrace, perhaps in violent rebuke?

Have we not spoken things others take to heart?
As such, are these things not a sermon?
Unto others whom we disciple along the way?
Are we not disciples of others, those countless
Souls whom have shaped our minds and
Sculpted our virtues from their words
And actions; living examples of the good life?

Do we not all live as proof of our
Potential? Capable of all things beautiful
All things terrible
And should we not relent all worship?
Cease the praise of others by virtue of their status?
Can we all not be wonderful persons?
Boundless in our singular person
No one like the one self we posses
And knowing the same of others

Oh but to revel in our humanity
Remembering our animal heritage, our beautiful
Lineage by which we sprung
To look at nature and know that we all
Share ancestry together
The tree is related to me, as is the dog and
All living creation shares my genes
And, even more glorious, the stars
The endless vast expanse beyond our pale blue
Hails the very elements which make up
Our DNA, our genetic structures
And to know that I share heritage with even
All inanimate matter, glorious!

I, we, are a part of everything
Birthed from the cosmic void and shaped by it
And now, we look at ourselves and ask
"What is the good life?" and we answer
"Let us discover!" and so we do

For what is more divine than this?
To be one with all things
To know that we all are the same
Come from the same beauty surrounding us
And yet
There is no one like you

To Mourn: Without A Dawn

I'll show you a grief without God
What happens here; deep in the mind
Of someone who does not believe of
A deity; high and divine

You feel the weight of an absence
A burden; some call it despair
And wish, will you, you'd remained ignorant
Of this heaviness that you now bear

And you will reflect on its features
The good and the bad you'll address
The elements of what remains here
Those fragments of heart's brokenness

And when you have carried that weight
Each day, from the loss, you've walked forward
You've gained a strength no one can take
The last gift those lost had to offer

They've made, now, this feeling familiar
This most horrid and dreaded of weight's
And now that they're no longer here
It tasks every ounce of your strength

A loss no one can prepare for
The kind that can never be found
And yet, do we know, we will feel more
With everyday forward from now

So when there is no life beyond
For those that you love and you miss
It takes a great strength to move on
To carry those days with the rest

Kaden Moeller

To Cull The Living Flower

I've made a necklace for you
From the flowers of life's garden
Twas to consol your heart, so blue
And lift your spirit, fallen

Oh you did love this gift
But before your shoulders settled
Life's fingers, they did lift
And pluck away the petals

Oh this twas to your horror
This gift, so beautiful
You scream *"Please take no more!"*
As time rips them in handfuls

Each petal, for you, lost
It rends and breaks your heart
It seems too high a cost
To watch beauty depart

So now you stand there helpless
Chain round your neck, now bare
You think that life is callus
And only wants despair

But life, it isn't cruel
Nor is it full of dread
For the necklace, though twas beautiful
The flowers, they were dead

Let not this loss of consolation
Cause now your heart to harden
Come, break the chain in celebration
And join me in the garden

The Janetor

Kaden Moeller

Well, just was sweeping up after the whole affair, I know it was a mess. A lot of work went into this, like over seven years, but I think it went well, don't you? I'm really surprised, it was much larger than I had initially started out, never really had planned the thing, it just kind of, well, happened, product of its time and all. Thanks for taking it in, poetry is like jazz, extremely pretentious.

ABOUT THE AUTHOR

Kaden Moeller - Citizen of the world, intellectual and social malcontent, awkward conversation monopolist, indentured indigent, political sycophant, mental midget, insatiable apathist, curmudgeonly communist, incontinently consternated, antisocial socialist, flabbergasted spastic, masticating Marxist, and all around mostly ok kind of guy, sometimes, but usually not, mostly on Tuesdays but not on Wednesdays, call back tomorrow, don't ask me later, leave a message after the beep.

I'm not lost, I just don't know where I'm going, thanks for following... see you again, soon... maybe... bye, bye.

Made in the USA
Columbia, SC
09 February 2018